W9-BSF-832

ONE FOOT ON THE GROUND
LUGUS PUBLICATIONS

To James and
Genevieve Wallbrook.

Presented May 29, 1994

In Ottawa, celebrating

Courage and support

Bomber Command

support.

Murray & Dawn
Dobson

Ottawa, / 1949

One Foot on the Ground

by

Norman Emmott

Lugus

Published by
Lugus Publications
48 Falcon Street
Toronto
Ontario
M4S 2P5

Canadian Cataloguing in Publication Data
 Emmott, Norman
    One Foot on the Ground

ISBN 0-921633-01-7

1. Emmott, Norman.
2. World War, 1939-1945   Personal narratives, Canadian.
3. World War 1939-1945 - Aerial operations, Cnadian.
4. Canada. Royal Canadian Airforce - Biography.
5. Flight navigators, Military - Canada - Biography.   I. Title.

D811.E55 1992   940.54'4971'092   C91-095648-0

© Norman Emmott, 1992

No part of this book may be reproduced in any form whatsoever
without the permission of the publisher (excepting short exerpts
for review purposes).

The support of the Ontario Arts Council is acknowledged.

Contents

List of Illustrations

CHAPTER ONE

The Royal Canadian Air Force, for a happy quarter of a century beginning in the early 1940s, was the best small air force in the world. The RCAF lasted for forty-two years, from 1924 until 1966, when it vanished into an unified Canadian Armed Forces. What was once the Royal Canadian Air Force is now one arm of the single service which has swallowed up the army, the navy, and the air force. The Royal Canadian Air Force had a short life but a glorious one.

Between the wars, the RCAF was only the shadow of an air force. Its existence was hardly recognized, its resources made poor relations look rich, and from time to time its very right to exist was challenged. Its record during the Second World War made it famous, and for a decade after the war it was the mainstay of the NATO air forces in Europe.

The Royal Canadian Air Force was a daughter service to the Royal Air Force, which in turn was an amalgamation of two British services which fought the First World War, the Royal Flying Corps and the Royal Naval Air Service, which were merged to form the Royal Air Force in 1918. Canada had its own army and navy during the First World War, but not its own air force. Canadians who flew were seconded to the British forces, and they served in British squadrons.

Many of them had distinguished records. The highest-ranking ace to survive the war was Colonel W.A. Bishop, with 72 victories; the great Red Baron had only 80. Twelve Canadians had higher scores than the United States' ace of aces, Eddie Rickenbacker. With this incentive, the Canadian government made a stab at creating its own air service, which was called the Canadian Air Force (the prefix "royal" needed the approval of the King.) Two squadrons staffed with Canadians who had served in the RAF were formed in England. The Canadian Air Force died when the war ended, however—the miniscule air force was disbanded before it could be returned to Canada.

After its demise, a weird organization called the Air Board replaced it. It had a military wing and a civil wing, and was responsible for all aviation in Canada. The military part of it had a fair amount of equipment, since the RAF had made a gift of war-surplus planes, tools, spares and even some airships. The commander of the force was an Englishman with the magnificent name of Sir Willoughly Gwatkin.

The government decided to create a formal air force in 1923, and got assent from the King to dub it "Royal." The Royal Canadian Air Force came into existence on April Fool's Day 1924. This was in keeping with bureaucratic tradition, since April First marks the beginning of the government's fiscal year. A precedent existed. The Royal Air Force itself had been created on April Fool's Day, 1918. The infant service was not very big. It had a strength of 62 officers, 43 of whom were pilots, and 262 men. The whole force was scarcely big enough to make up an infantry company, and was smaller than a single squadron of the wartime days.

Its officers made sure that it was as much like the Royal Air Force as possible. Uniforms were identical except for the buttons, which bore the letters "RCAF" underneath the crown and the albatross on them (nobody has ever settled the argument as to whether the bird is an eagle or an albatross.) The ensign with the Union Jack in the corner and the red, white and blue roundel on a light blue field was the same. The confusing RAF names for officers' ranks were adopted. The ground crew trades were given RAF names; an engine mechanic was a "fitter," and the man who looked after the rest of the aircraft was a "rigger." Items were referred to by English names, so that a wrench was a "spanner," a cotter pin was a "split pin," and a battery was an "accumulator." Propellers were "airscrews," an aircraft was never referred to as an "airplane," and a radio was a "wireless set."

This was natural enough. All the officers had served in the RAF, which they regarded as the best air force in the world (which it was), and they put into practice on Canadian soil what they had learned in England and France. It was taken for granted that the RCAF would operate in war alongside the RAF and under British command, and to speak the same technical language made sense.

The RCAF was officially a military force, but for the first three years of its existence it did civil work almost exclusively. It began photographing Canada from the air, it flew Mounties and civil servants around to pay treaty money to the Indians, it patrolled against forest fires, and it flew sick and injured Indians, Eskimos and trappers to hospitals. It did this work so well that in 1927 the government decided that a military service should not do so much civil work, and formed the Directorate of Civil Government Air Operations (DCGAO) to control all civil flying. All the operational squadrons of the RCAF were transferred to this organization, and the RCAF was left with little to do but training. However, there was nobody available to man the DCGAO, and RCAF personnel were seconded or transferred to the new directorate. This anomalous situation lasted until 1932.

Things were not entirely black in 1928, however, even if all the 'operational' flying was done by the civil department. The Air Force received the first of nine Siskin fighter biplanes which had been ordered from Britain, and also six Atlas two-seater biplanes, which at the time were modern—they had been designed in 1924. Training continued with eight Provisional Pilot Officers learning to fly in 1928. The new training base at Trenton on Lake Ontario was commenced, although some fierce politicians complained that it was located entirely too close to the potentially hostile United States. Actually the location made sense. Most operational flying was done by seaplane, since there were few airports in the hinterland, but plenty of rivers and lakes. Training had been done at Camp Borden where there was no water, although there was enough sand there for any number of beaches.

The RCAF, doing its own training and flying its handful of fighters and Atlas aircraft which carried two machine-guns, one facing forward for the pilot to shoot and the other mounted on a Scarfe ring in the rear cockpit, and also doing all the flying for the DCGAO, soldiered on during 1929 and 1930. Then in 1931 the depression began to bite. Air appropriations were cut from $7.5 million to $5 million, and the RCAF had to cut its strength by eight officers and 23 airmen and stopped training pilots.

The next year the RCAF nearly died. Funds were cut so much that 78 officers and 100 airmen were let go without notice. The 'Big Cut' scarred the minds of those who remained, all of whom expected their careers to end abruptly. Ironically, the ridiculous DCGAO was abolished and its personnel and duties were folded back into the RCAF. The tasks it had done were mostly abandoned. Photography ceased, and flying was cut by two thirds. To keep the men at Camp Borden busy, they were taught to swim.

The RCAF barely survived until 1934, when the Conservative government of R.B. Bennett thought better of previous parsimony. Their attitude had not been unusual; a great many in Canada at the time, and later, considered that military spending was not merely wasteful but wrong. Agnes MacPhail, Canada's first woman Member of Parliament, proposed to cut the total appropriations of all three services to one dollar a year.

In 1934 some second-hand Wapiti biplanes, which had served on India's Northwest Frontier, were bought largely because they were cheap. Four Blackburn Shark torpedo bombers were also purchased. Placed in British Fleet Air Arm service in 1935, they were declared obsolete by 1938, proving once again the expertise of the Canadian government in putting its money on the wrong horse. Recruiting was resumed, putting the force over the thousand mark for the first time in its history.

In 1935 the RCAF installed radios in some of their aircraft; they didn't work. To maintain them, it created its own radio trade, instead of borrowing men from the Royal Canadian Corps of Signals. The force resumed training pilots, and 24 were graduated a year later.

In 1937 vigorous recruiting of ground crew was begun, with engine and airframe mechanics being trained at Camp Borden and radiomen, storekeepers, photographers and armament men at Trenton. The idea was to give ground crew a solid theoretical and practical training before they were let loose on aircraft. This was seriously compromised the next year, when 'skilled' men were recruited for immediate service in the operational squadrons, the men being garage mechanics, carpenters, seamen and others whose experience had been anything but aeronautical. Most of the, however, did quite well. Recruiting advertisements stressed the fact that the men would not be called on to fly or fight. Realistic though this may have been, it was hardly the way to attract adventurous youth.

In 1937 the Royal Air Force made approaches for the training of RAF aircrew in Canada. Prime MInister MacKenzie King turned the idea down. His ostensible reason was that Canada was a sovereign nation, and should not allow 'foreign' armed forces to operate on its territory; the real reason was that the Liberal government's majority in Parliament depended on French Canadian MPs, who were still fighting the Seven Years' War and did not want to offer any aid or comfort to the British. When the matter came up in the House of Parliament in 1939, King lied about it. However, the pressures of war led to the reopening of the matter in 1939, and then to the formation of the British Commonwealth Air Training Plan, which produced more than 130,000 aircrew graduates.

In 1939 the RCAF got its first modern aircraft, ten Hurricanes which came to Vancouver by way of the Panama Canal. The RCAF had Sharks and Stranraers as well, both seaplanes, and both hopelessly behind the times. Stranraers had flown for the first time in 1935, and aircraft became obsolete frightfully fast in those days. As it was, the RCAF went into the war in 1939 with exactly nineteen combat monoplanes, all Hurricanes. The only other monoplanes it had were civilian type transports, such as the Northrop Delta.

By the end of March 1939 the Permanent Force was up to 1693 all ranks, and when war broke out the addition of the Auxiliary Air Force brought the total to about 4000. By January 1944 the strength was more than 215,000—a growth of more than fifty-fold.

Between 1935 and 1939 recruiting standards were high. Pilot trainees had to have engineering degrees, while trainees for skilled trades required a complete high school education. Even to sweep the floor a Grade Eight education was needed. As a result men enlisted during these years were almost all well-educated and capable, and during the war a high proportion of them were promoted to officers. Meanwhile, men without college educations had a habit of crossing the Atlantic to join the RAF as aircrew, and when the war broke out there were more Canadians serving as officer aircrew with the RAF than there were officers in the whole RCAF, including the Auxiliary RCAF. More than half of these men were killed.

The men who joined the RAF were warriors, since the Royal Air Force was always at war in some corner of the Empire. In Canada warlike operations were far from anyone's thoughts, with warlike flying confined to maneuvers with the army, firing blanks. For the officers the RCAf was much like an exclusive flying club, with such advantages as batmen servants, a well-furnished officers' mess, mildly adventurous aerial forays into the hinterland during the summer, and fairly infrequent parades.

Life for the airmen was quite unmilitary after they had completed the conventionally harsh period of training. Most of them worked at very civilian-like jobs in offices, hangars, the motor transport section, or in the other sections that keep any organization going. Many of them did not even live in barracks, but led normal after-hour lives, remote from the harassments of corporals and sergeants. By the standards of the day they were well paid, a recruit getting $1.70 a day and everything found. In barracks they had to mount guard on weekends, clean up their barracks, or do kitchen duty, but their work was not onerous and was often interesting. There were practically no route-marches, physical training sessions, or extended drill sessions. There was not much stress on organized sports. Each day started with a parade, with emphasis on shining buttons and boots, but most of the working day was spent in overalls.

Not many of the airmen flew. Some of them, mostly fitters or riggers, were selected as crewmen for multi-place aircraft which went on extended missions, or flying boats in which a man was needed to start the engines and moor the plane when it landed. A very few were trained as air gunners for the Atlases and Wapitis, and later for the Sharks. Every year about five airmen were trained as pilots. There was intense competition for these posts, and a sergeant-pilot enjoyed immense prestige.

Altogether it was a good life. And then in 1939 the war came and spoiled everything. Instead of a flying club the RCAF became a scene of frantic activity, desperately trying to oversee an enormous expansion. Instead of a collection of obsolete aircraft, the RCAF was to procure the best aircraft the world had to offer. It was to become the most experienced air training force in the world. It was to send forty-four squadrons overseas, operate thirty-seven squadrons along Canada's coasts, run ninety-seven flying schools, and train most of the aircrew who fought during the last three years of the war in Commonwealth uniforms. Its losses, over 16, 000. were more than four times as great as the total strength of the RCAF when the war started. When the war was over, the RCAF enjoyed immense prestige.

At the end of the war it was the fourth largest Allied air force; only the RAF, the US Army Air Force, and the Russian Air Force were bigger. Besides the RCAF squadrons overseas, a quarter of the aircrew flying with the Royal Air Force were Canadian. There were 3.9 times as many Britons as Canadians killed in bomber Command; Britain had rather more than four times the population of Canada, and some 60% of the RCAF dead died in bombers.

It had trained some thousands of Americans who had crossed the border before the USA entered the war, and they prized their RCAF wings, and told their American comrades even after most of them transferred to the USAAF that their Canadian training was far superior (which it was).

With the war won, the RCAF was reduced to 12,000 all ranks, which was still six times the pre-war strength of the regular force. There was a mighty retrenchment, with only a few air stations left open, although there were all sorts of modern aircraft to fly. In 1950, however, the Korean war broke out to herald the Cold War, and Canada was called upon to reinforce the western world's NATO defences in Germany. The service was boosted to 45,000 people, and an Air Division was sent to Germany. The RCAF in Canada specialized in training, teaching airborne skills to Italians, Frenchmen, Norwegians, Belgians, Danes, Netherlanders and even Germans. Additionally, the expertise gained during the war in anti-submarine operations was maintained, with Argus aircraft built specially for the job and cluster of highly-efficient ASW squadrons practicing their trade. Much of the original thinking in the anti-submarine business for twenty years after the war was done by Canadian airmen.

The Air Division, flying Canadian-built Sabre single-seater and CF-100 all-weather fighters, was probably the best air component in NATO. All the men were long-service regulars, as opposed to the draftees that staffed many of their companion services.

The Royal Canadian Air Force remained at the top of the air force totem pole until 1966. Then the Canadian army, navy and air force were amalgamated into one all-inclusive body, which began as the Canadian Armed Forces. Later, the word "Armed" was dropped in keeping with the generally pacifistic nature of the Canadian government, although it eventually crawled back in again. The Air Force lost its blue-gray uniforms—"the colour of heroes" as an American author phrased it in 1940, and its distinctive (and stupid and confusing) air force ranks like flying officer and squadron leader in favour of Army ranks like lieutenant and major. Instead of reporting directly to the Minister of National Defence, the top airman (formerly the Chief of the Air Staff) reported to the Armed Forces Chief of Staff, who could be a soldier or a sailor. Enlisted men were not airmen any more; they were privates, as the soldiers were. From the standpoint of military

7

efficiency there is a lot to be said for integration and one single service; sentimentally it broke a lot of hearts.

As a component of the single service, the air force could have gone on to maintain the same heights it reached as the RCAF, but the anti-military Trudeau administration slashed the Canadian forces. The force was starved for new equipment until the aircraft were older than the men who flew them. It became obvious that the government did not take the services seriously, and soon the rest of the world did not take them seriously either. Those who sang, "O Canada, we stand on guard for thee," could add the words "At a lower percentage of the gross national product than any other NATO country except Luxembourg."

Nevertheless they soldier on, and continue to do so. They live up to their proud traditions as well as they can, and they still win the air-firing competitions in Europe.

The "Canadian Forces Reorganization Act" became law on February 1, 1968, and the identity of the Royal Canadian Air Force passed into history. At least its successor service did not begin its career on April Fool's Day.

The RCAF lasted not quite 44 years. This is the working life of an average man, time to reach his prime, take great responsibilities, and prove himself. It is also long enough to achieve greatness. The Royal Canadian Air Force did. For a quarter of a century, from about 1952 to 1968 it was the best small air force in the world.

The author of this book joined the RCAF in 1937, and served a little less than 27 years. He was proud of his uniform, proud of his wings, proud of his air force. He still is.

CHAPTER TWO

In 1936 I was seventeen years old, living in my home in Nelson B.C. I had long been fascinated by aviation, and at the end of my school year I wrote to the RCAF Station at Jericho Beach in Vancouver, applying to join the Air Force. An answer returned, telling me that there were no openings, but that my name was being held on file. I went back to school to complete my senior matriculation.

In late May 1937 the RCAF told me to report to Vancouver, to sign up as a storekeeper. I asked if I could wait a month, to finish my school year. The officer at the Vancouver air station made difficulties, but agreed.

My father was fully in agreement with my decision. His rationale was simple. "It's a job." Since my mother's father had been a career soldier, progressing from drummer-boy to major in the Royal Irish Rifles, she could scarcely object. My father arranged a trip to Vancouver as a passenger in an auto driven by a friend of his. During the journey I had my first beer (I thought it tasted terrible), marvelled at the fine state of the American roads after the rough Canadian ones, and ended up after two days by registering at a hotel in Vancouver operated by friends of the family.

I made my way to the Jericho beach air station by street car and bus, marvelling at the great city as I did so. At the gate of the air station I was referred to the orderly room, where a corporal in a neat blue uniform welcomed me. He sat me down beside him while he plied me with questions as he typed out my "Attestation Form."

The word "enlistment" was more current, but the other word agreed with the English parlance as of 1790, and therefore sounded better in official ears.

With my papers in his hand, he took me in to see an officer, who asked me why I wanted to join the Air Force. Feeling that the words, "It's a job," were inadequate, I answered, "It's what I've always wanted to do." He nodded, signed a paper, and told the corporal to arrange for my medical examination.

At the waiting room at Shaughnessy Military Hospital I met another would-be recruit, a husky, deeply-tanned man a few years older than I was, who among other accomplishments played a mouth-organ he took out of his pocket. He told me of his exciting life on the farm and in lumber camps, and spoke of the bright future he expected in the Air Force. We were both given X-rays, and told to return the next day.

When I returned I found the man, who looked as if he could have broken me in his hands, in tears. He had just been told he had tuberculosis.

I took my clean bill of health back to Jericho Beach, where the officer produced a Bible and signed me on. He told me the regimental number I would bear during my service, and told me to remember it. It was 371. In 1924 British Columbia had been allotted a block of 200 numbers, from 200 to 400, and I was the 171st man to join in 13 years. About a dozen men a year from all B.C. had thrown their lot in with the Air Force. Then he said, "You'll be sent across Canada to Trenton in Ontario by train. Have you enough money to live on until you get there?"

I had about $30—a good sum in those days. He looked relieved when I told him so. "We've had men trying to get there on fifty cents." It was a good omen; he was an officer who was concerned about his men.

The corporal gave me a train ticket, after looking embarrassed when I called him "sir," and telling me just to call him "corporal." I thought anybody with stripes on deserved to be called "sir," but later learned that anyone embarrassed to be called by a title he did not deserve was a finer person than one who assumed rank he did not hold.

The Canadian Pacific Railway took me across Canada. I had wanted to take the Kettle Valley route across southern British Columbia so that I could see my family before I reported. The officer, however, had decided that I would take the faster route via the main line, because I was already some three weeks late in entering the course I was to take to become a military storekeeper. I climbed aboard my tourist sleeper, where I was allotted an upper berth, and set out through the Rockies. On the way there I fell into a conversation with a trainman, who informed me that the Red Army was far more formidable than it appeared. If Hitler had listened to him he would never have invaded Russia.

10

The journey was the first long trip that I had made by myself in my eighteen years, and I felt myself very grown-up and a member of a privileged minority. Within a few years several million seventeen-year-olds would make much longer journeys under much more arduous conditions, but I didn't know that then, and I was proud of myself.

When I changed trains at Toronto I met two other men headed for the Air Force at Trenton. One of them was a teacher from the poverty-stricken prairies, who had tired of accepting half his pay in wheat, and preferred $1.70 a day as an aircraftsman second class in the RCAF.

We were met at the railway station in Trenton by a stake truck with the letters "RCAF" on it. I did not expect a limousine, so my feelings were not hurt. The truck deposited us inside the air station, after driving past the parade ground with its Air Force flag flapping in the breeze. A clerk filled in more papers, and then we were taken to our barracks. The student storekeepers were supposed do sleep five to a room, but we arrived late, and were put in wherever we could fit. I ended up in a dormitory with five old sweats. Two of them were actually corporals, who had reached the great age of thirty or so. That lasted for a few weeks, until the authorities solved their problem by putting an extra bed in several five-bed rooms. That meant everybody had a locker but me. A kindly fellow AC2, however, allowed me to share his locker. The clothes we had in those poverty-stricken days did not fill it.

The next day I was issued with my kit. It was summer, so we were issued khaki drill uniforms which fitted like tents, and wrinkled in a tenth of a second. The Air Force cannily did not issue us blue-gray uniforms until we had been around three months; it did not intend to waste clothes on recruits who might not stay the course. The uniform included khaki shorts, inherited from the British Army in India. They were very practical in the Ontario summer, but the Air Force, to save money, did not issue the oxfords, the stockings and the belt which it was regulation to wear with them. We had to pay for them ourselves.

The RCAF was largely officered by men who had seen service in the shell-torn skies over France, but the men who controlled the lives of the enlisted men were ex-infantrymen who believed that their troops should be able to march into the trenches and take their places on the firing line. Thus we were issued with great knives, with one enormous blade and a spike which turned out to be designed to take the stones out of horses' hoofs. We were given large tins of dubbin, to protect Army boots against the Flanders mud, but we were given Navy boots instead. (They turned out to be marvellously comfortable, practical and long-wearing, and were adopted three decades later as aircrew boots, after experiments with paratroop boots, knee-high flying boots, and mukluks.) Our uniforms had pockets inside to hold field dressings, although we were never told what they were for, or given any field dressings. We were given Short Magazine Lee Enfield rifles, complete with bayonets and bayonet belts, although we were never taught to fire them during our recruit training, or do anything as undignified as bayonet fighting. We were supposed to get a complete set of infantry web equipment, of packsack, rucksack, haversack, water bottle, and ammunition pouches, but the RCAF, chronically short of money, found there were not enough of them to go round, and spared us the ecstasy of parading in full kit. We were given razors, button sticks (slices of brass with a slot down the middle, through which brass buttons could be threaded to be polished while the rest of the uniform was protected) and suits of heavy underwear which none of us ever deigned to wear.

It was accepted that all this equipment, most of it inherited from the First World War, was not to be used, but was to be preserved for display during kit inspections. Our tin of dubbin, our issue razors, our tin of boot polish, were kept secure, to be produced when an officer inspected us to make sure that we had all the equipment necessary to send us into the mud of Passchendale.

Our uniforms were strictly Royal Air Force, with the usual British greatcoats; it took a war or two to persuade the brass that Canada in the winter is a cold country, and give us parkas. We wore close-necked jackets, buttoned to the throat, although open-neck jackets to be worn with collar and tie were to be issued in the future when the supply of the dog-collar type ran out. These had their advantages, however; they did not require a tie, and were quicker to get into in the morning. Our peaked caps had shiny plastic brims, which we told never to handle, for fear of leaving finger-prints there. The approved method of taking the hat off was to grasp it by the crown.

For the first three months of our service we were forbidden to appear on or off base in civilian clothes. This drew pointed comparisons with the Mounted Police, whose recruits were forbidden to appear off base in their uniforms until they had several months' training and were deemed worthy of wearing it properly. It was considered 'infra dig' to appear off station in uniform if it could be avoided, however, and recruits would risk punishment to steal out of barracks in civilian clothes.

We were taught drill. The Air Force was big on drill, since it was considered essential to make a good appearance on parade. A big easy-going corporal named Hunt taught us infantry foot-drill and rifle-drill. All the recruits moaned about it, but only because this was expected of us; actually we rather enjoyed it. It got us out in the open early in the morning, all properly dressed, with boots and buttons shining, to stamp around in disciplined formations, throw rifles up and down, and learn to act immediately on a word of command. The amount we learned by army standards, as we found when we compared notes with our opposite numbers in army regiments, was minimal. We did not have our drill instructor pace off exactly thirty inches by means of a pace-stick as we took every step, nor were we taught such tricks as having the end man of a flight (i.e. a squad) fix his eyes on a landmark so that the formation did not wander off to the left or the right. The service departed from its military traditions in one respect. We were given no physical training whatever, no calisthenics, no route marches, no combat training. We were taught to do arms drill with our rifles and bayonets, but not how to load, aim or fire the rifles or stab people with the bayonets. This was explained by stating that the Air Force was a technical arm. It probably made sense. None of the men on my course ever came to 'push of pike' with the enemy.

The storekeeper recruits (we were called apprentices) were all high quality. Regulations called for them to have completed high school, and most of them were perfectly capable of having gone on to college if they had been able to afford it. Many of them gained officer rank during the war, some of them retiring as wing commanders.

More than half my fellow recruits on my stores course came from Ottawa. Ottawa, being a government town, was populated by people who knew of government jobs, and knew how to apply for them. The Air Force was as visible in Ottawa as it was invisible in the rest of Canada; there were three permanent establishments there, the air station at Rockcliffe, the Aircraft Depot in the middle of the Ottawa River on Victoria Island midway between Ontario and Quebec, and Air Force Headquarters. Airmen got higher pay than civil servants, and the service looked like a good job. The residents of Ottawa were first in line.

The Air Force may have had prestige in Ottawa, but this was not the case in Trenton. The citizens of this little Ontario town looked on us with profound suspicion, has as little to do with us as they could, and feared for the chastity of their daughters. Knowing the recruits were often young and naive, they offered us shady entertainments and raised prices.

Trenton was close enough to walk to, but for a big night on the town the recruits would go to the great city of Belleville, about twelve miles the other way from Trenton. Belleville operated on Standard Time rather than Daylight Saving Time, with the result that airmen who had to go on duty watch parade to do fatigues, which lasted until eight o'clock, found it was only seven o'clock entertainment time. Of course, when they staggered in that night they found that morning came sickeningly early. One recruit made himself famous by getting in every night for a month after four in the morning, through a hole in the fence that only he knew about. When he was sent to hospital for some ailment he slept for twenty-four hours. He never made it to the end of the course.

The average age of the recruits was about twenty-two, four years older than myself. Many of them, especially those who had done things like driving taxis in Ottawa over to the flesh-pots of Hull, were definitely men of the world. I was not.

I fell afoul of military law only once. Standing on parade one autumn morning, with the low rays of the early sun shining on me, I was inspected by Flying Officer William MacBrien, who later aspired to the nickname "Iron Bill." (His associates, behind his back, called him "Tin Willie.") He put me on charge for the offence of having appeared on parade unshaven. When I was marched in before the chief of the Stores School, he asked me what excuse I had for my horrible crime.

"I always shave on Friday, sir," I answered, "and today is only Thursday."

Never have I seen an officer going through such tortures as he as he tried not to laugh. Finally he recovered his composure, found me guilty as charged, and sentenced me to admonition. All concerned felt that the punishment fitted the crime.

14

During this time I was learning how to become an Air Force storekeeper, at Stores School. Storekeeping was an academic business, with the emphasis on filling out forms properly in many copies. The right way to teach the skill should have been to use normal school-teaching methods. Our Stores School was not run on these principles.

The officer in charge was a flight lieutenant who left such mundane details as teaching to subordinates. Our two instructors were a warrant officer and a flight sergeant, who knew as much about teaching as a pig knows about Chaucer. Most of the classes were taught by a flight sergeant, who might have made a passable drill instructor, being full of coarse jokes, jibes at the innocents under his command who could not talk back, and bad grammar. The warrant officer had previously risen to warrant rank in both the army and the navy. He told us to stick to one service and not change about in search of adventure, starting over from the bottom each time.

The method of instruction was simple. Each student was issued with a copy of *Canadian Air Publication No. 16*, Stores Instructions for the RCAF, and told to memorize it. CAP 16 was written in bureaucratize, largely copied from the stores regulations of the Royal Air Force, which were cribbed from those of the armies of Wellington, which were in turn cribbed from those of the armies of Pontius Pilate. No attempt was made to explain the meaning of the words used in it. For exampled, we were told that vouchers had to be posted to the stock ledgers, but we were never told what the word 'posting' meant, nor the meaning of the word 'ledger,' until one of the more erudite members of the course, who had done some bookkeeping before he joined the air force, let us in on the secret. There were no training aids at all, such as blown-up copies of the vouchers we were to use, which the instructor could fill in as watched. There were no mock storekeeping exercises to give us practice in what we would be doing when we reached the field. Some of the instruction given was highly impractical. For instance, we were made to memorize the procedure for taking an aircraft engine apart to prepare it for storage, although no storekeeper was allowed near an engine with a wrench; such tasks were reserved for mechanics, and any storekeeper trying to muscle in would have been in danger of his life.

The flight sergeant was intent on having his students do well on examinations, however. To make sure of this, he walked around the barracks every Friday evening and told the men what questions would be on the Saturday morning examination. Needless to say, we all did well.

As the course progressed we were given practical training. This consisted of going to the actual stores section at the Trenton station, where NCOs were to put us to work. The work consisted of sweeping the floor and dusting the bins, with a prohibition of touching any of the storekeeping forms for fear we might screw something up. Actually this was not bad training for what we were to do when we graduated, when we would spend most of our time sweeping the floor and dusting the bins.

To those of us who questioned the value of the training, the response of the storekeepers was always the same. "It's all done differently once you get on a squadron." None of the old sweats had ever had any formal storekeeping training, but had learnt on the job. They appeared to be coping, however, which encouraged us all; even if we graduated knowing nothing, we would be no worse off than our predecessors.

There existed an institution known as 'Duty Watch,' in which a quarter of the airmen were confined to barracks every fourth week and used for odd jobs in the evening and during the weekends. The work included all the tasks which always have been the bane of a serviceman's life— cleaning latrines, mowing lawns, polishing floors, waiting on tables at the NCO's and officers' messes, peeling potatoes, washing dishes and sweeping floors; all the 'joe jobs.' We knew there was no escape.

Non-commissioned officers always handled the Duty Watches, officers having more important things to do. They had a free hand. One warrant officer at Camp Borden, who was responsible for the training of aircraft carpenter riggers, used the duty watch all one summer to build a house for him on a lot adjoining the air station. The station expanded to take in his lot and his house, and he sold both of them to the Air Force. Then he had the house classified as a married quarters, and lived in the house. During the war he achieved commissioned rank, continuing to scrounge anything which was not nailed down, and retired after the war full of years and honours. He considered himself hard done by, since somebody else by then was living in his house.

We were made to keep clean and tidy. Our uniforms had to be pressed, our brass buttons polished, with Brasso or more often with Silvo, and our boots shining. We were not required to go through the 'spit-shining' routine of the army, but our morning inspections were quite severe. In the winter, with greatcoats buttoned up to the chin, some brave souls would tempt fate by appearing on parade without their tunics on underneath their greatcoats. Sometimes this worked; once in a while a perceptive or sadistic sergeant would order the men to open their coats, and woe betide those improperly dressed underneath.

Cleanliness was insisted on, but not godliness. Only once in six months in Trenton in 1937 was there a church parade, and we had no chaplains. It took a war to bring religion in the Air Force.

Storekeepers took a six-month course. When we graduated we had some theoretical knowledge of storekeeping but no practical knowledge. Our instructors were proud of the job they had done on us.

We went on to win the war.

CHAPTER THREE

In November 1937 I was transferred, together with a half-dozen other recent graduates of the stores course, to No. 2 Equipment Depot in Winnipeg. When we reported for duty on a Monday morning, we found ourselves in a different world from the one we had known in Trenton.

The depot, which qualified as an RCAF Station, had previously been a rubber warehouse, and before that had been used for growing mushrooms. The aura of the horse manure used to grow the mushrooms still remained in corners. There was a flagpole at the front, but no other signs of the military presence, There was no parade ground, no sentry-box with a smartly-turned out airman in it, no guardhouse.

Since there were no barracks, everybody 'lived out' somewhere in Winnipeg. We AC2's welcomed that, since without barracks there were no compulsory lights-out times, no weekend barrack-cleaning parties, no Saturday morning inspections, and no possibility of confinement to barracks for our sins. There was no petty harassment from corporals or sergeants after hours, and the landlady cleaned our rooms and made our beds. Best of all, we were paid living-out allowances which raised our pay to some ninety dollars a month— big pay for that day and age. There was no duty watch, no stints of duty in the non-existent sergeants' mess or officers' mess. We thought we were lucky.

One of my first tasks was to find a boarding house. I settled for one run by a woman had operated a similar establishment in Folkestone during the First World War, where she had catered to Canadian soldiers on their way to the trenches in Flanders. Her husband had been a sergeant in the Dragoon Guards, who had lost his stripes and his future due to drink. In the Twenties she had immigrated to Canada, and had been boarding airmen since then. She understood the niceties of military life better than her boarders did; for instance, she told of those who had boarded with her five years previously. Airmen still wore breeches on ceremonial occasions then, and she woke up her charges five minutes earlier on Fridays so that they would have time to wrap their puttees around their legs.

My choice of a boarding house did not, however, elicit the approval of our sergeant major. He was a well set up man in his forties, who looked good on parade, and had a good record in ground crew in France during World War I. He was also a hard drinker, although he never appeared looking the worse for wear. He admired lechers, and showed his contempt for those who did not indulge in such recreations. These characteristics having ruined his marriage, and left him paying alimony, he was living in a rather sleazy hotel near the depot, where he had run up a considerable bill in the beer parlor.

The hotel manager forgave part of his indebtedness if he persuaded airmen to live at the hotel. He solicited all newly-arrived airmen to stay there, pointing out all its opportunities for drink and venery. I was not interested in either, being 18 years of age and still in the milk-shake stage, having a profound distaste for beer and believing in romantic and courtly love. When I opted for the boarding house he never forgave me.

My job at the equipment depot was mostly dusting bins and sweeping the floor. It was there that I learned the art of using a push-broom; bang the broom on the floor at the end of each stroke to shake the dirt out of it so that lines of dirt would not be left on the floor. I also put equipment away, labelled bins, and did odd jobs. There were two of us Aircraftsmen Second Class in the stores group, the arrangement being that for six months I would do the bull-work and my colleague would do the paper work, and then we would change places. Unfortunately at the end of the six-month period he was transferred and his place taken by a corporal. It was beneath the dignity of the corporal to do the menial jobs, and I was condemned to continue at low-technology tasks.

We did have some slight contact with flying. A time-expired Gypsy Moth biplane was wheeled into the building one day with its wings folded, to be stored for some esoteric purpose. On the way in one of the AC2's managed to bash in the end of one wing. He was properly horrified and duly punished, even if the aircraft was not to fly any more and damage did not matter. Discipline had to be maintained.

From where we sat is seemed that we were not doing anything useful. No.1 Aircraft Depot in Ottawa received all stores from contractors or from the Royal Air Force which supplied the RCAF with spares for British-built aircraft. It could easily have sent everything directly to the user units. Nevertheless, equipment was shipped out to Winnipeg, unpacked, binned, tended, accounted for, and then selected, packed, shipped, and again accounted for under cover of multiple documents to such units as RCAF Station Vancouver. It seemed that a lot of unnecessary work was being done. Actually the exercise was a dry run for the war that was to come two years later, when No. 2 Equipment Depot operated as it should have, with Winnipeg supplying the many stations which sprang up on the prairies. This unusual effort of the Air Force brass to think ahead actually worked.

Sometimes, of course, things went awry. The Canadian government had detected a threat to the West Coast from such people as the Japanese, sitting malevolently on their islands on the other rim of the Pacific, and decided to protect the country with six Blackburn Shark aircraft, which would have been world-beaters in the First World War. Paradoxically, when used over the seas for the Navy, it flew as a landplane, with wheels. When working for the land-based RCAF it flew with floats.

The Sharks, to be flown by No. 6 Torpedo Bomber Squadron, were to carry torpedoes between the floats. This meant that the country would have to invest in torpedoes, and the RCAF duly ordered two of them from Britain. Presumably, the six Sharks would have to share them. No. 6 TB was still at Trenton in early 1938, although it was scheduled to go to Vancouver. The two torpedoes were therefore to be shipped to the depot in Winnipeg, and kept there until 6 TB was ready for them. Winnipeg was 1500 miles from the water, and there were all sorts of good places to keep the torpedoes at the naval base at Esquimalt near Victoria, where there were also many people skilled in the art of caring for them. But this would have required co-operation with the Navy, which no decent airman would consider.

Thus it was that a dozen of us junior storekeepers were told off to ride to the Canadian National Railways freight shed in the back of a stake truck, to take possession of the two torpedoes. Two great crates, built out of inch-thick planks, awaited us. Our party pushed and pulled them onto the back of the truck, under the command of our corporal We drove back to the depot, proudly sitting atop the cases, and pushed and pulled some more to get them into one of the stores groups behind a protective barrier of chicken wire. There they reposed, waiting for 6 TB with its Sharks to reach Vancouver.

They were objects of awe to us all. We had read stories of the havoc torpedoes had wrought at sea as submarines launched them on their evil progress against helpless merchant ships, of destroyers dashing in among enemy battle fleets to send cruisers and battleships plunging to their deaths in the icy depths. We had seen movies and read magazine articles which showed torpedoes in action. We discussed the fact that a torpedo cost $10,000. But none of us had ever seen one of the sleek and deadly weapons themselves.

Curiosity was too much for one of us. One of our airmen looked at the crates, walking around them to note that they were about twenty feet long and five feet wide, with a large screw every six inches holding the top down. At last he could contain himself no longer. He took a large screwdriver and began to unscrew every one of them on one crate. It took him an hour, but he finally had them all out, and he could lift off the top of the crate and look inside. He pushed the lid to one side.

There was nothing inside. The crate was completely empty. The flabbergasted airman rushed to his corporal to report, who rushed to the sergeant, who told the sergeant major, who called in the flight lieutenant commanding the depot. Soon a gaggle of NCO's and officers was standing beside the empty crate amid a clamour of excited voices. The sergeant conscripted every airman in the vicinity, armed them with screwdrivers, and set them to work unscrewing the top of the other crate. It was just as empty.

We rolled in a platform scale and weighed the crates, and compared our results with the weight on the shipping documents, which the railway had charged for. There was a disagreement of fifteen hundred pounds.

Two empty crates had been prepared for shipment at an English stores depot, trucked to a railway, loaded aboard a railway car (in England a 'goods wagon'), hauled to dockside, loaded aboard a ship, taken across the Atlantic, unloaded at Montreal, placed on a CNR freight train, carried to Winnipeg, and trucked to our depot. At every stage and change of freight-charging carrier they were recorded to have been weighed, with the weight agreeing with the waybill. It was obvious that every handler had simply taken the word of the previous handler that the weights were in agreement.

Telegrams were soon flying to Ottawa, and from Ottawa cables were being despatched across the ocean. The Royal Canadian Air Force was obviously not going to pay $29,000 for two crates full of English air. At the English stores depot some hapless airman or some luckless NCO, perhaps even some officer, was undoubtedly catching hell, as were others all down the line. Meanwhile, all Canada lay naked and undefended to the foreign navies threatening it.

The airman who had taken off the lid was commended gruffly by the Officer Commanding for having brought the matter to light. The man's corporal was not so commendatory, since the airman had had no authority to mess with anything like a torpedo crate, and he should never have opened it. Such technical work should have been done by a skilled tradesman such as an armourer.

Furthermore, a shortcoming of the corporal, and worse, his sergeant, had been exposed by the airman's daring act. The NCO's should have weighed the cases when they came in to make sure that the railway was not overcharging them, and they had not. But the fact that the Flight Lieutenant had praised the man protected him from their malevolence, and he heard no more about it. He got off easy.

The sergeant major called us together and swore us to secrecy. "Keep it under your hats," he told us. "It will only make us, and a great air force, look ridiculous." He was referring to the Royal Air Force, which was the great air force; he had served in the RAF during the war in France, where he had salvaged aircraft between the lines at night. It was dear to his heart. We obeyed orders, and the incident remained a deadly secret.

The empty crates probably spent the war shuttling equipment back and forth across Canada. After having been shipped at great expense across the ocean and then halfway across the continent, they were the most costly crates the RCAF ever owned. They were built of excellent wood, and it is highly likely that someone managed to have them struck off charge so he could convert them to part of a summer cottage. Perhaps, during their lives, they were even used to transport torpedoes.

Later in my career, after I remustered to aircrew, I volunteered for service in torpedo bombers. It was dangerous; 95% of the crews had to be replaced in combat every three months. But when I reported to Operational training Unit in Patricia Bay on Vancouver Island, I was given instruction on torpedoes—how they worked, how they were aimed, how they cut through the water on their way to sink a ship. We were shown torpedoes. I was happy. Ever since I had been one of those conscripted to take out those hundred wood-screws I had wanted to see one. And now I had.

There was an ironic footnote to it. Late in the war a group of airman were detailed to cleanup a pile of ostensibly empty crates in one corner of the Repair Depot at Jericho Beach, in Vancouver. At the bottom of the pile they found two crates with torpedoes in them. Happily by that time relations with the navy had improved. The RCAF shipped them to the naval base at Esquimalt. Perhaps they were the same two torpedoes.

CHAPTER FOUR

In the fall of 1938 I was transferred to Vancouver, to the air station at Jericho Beach. There I was put in charge of Section 28 of stores, consisting of nuts, bolts, washers, and split pins—the official title was Aircraft General Spares—and after I had proved myself, Section 29 as well—General Hardware, such as nails and wood screws. My place of work was an ancient wooden shack, a hand-me-down from the 1920s when Jericho Beach was the RCAF's chief seaplane training base. It had been built in the unjustified assumption that there was no need for insulation in the West Coast's benign climate, with the result that drafts blew through it, as did sand from the beach. I had to keep sweeping the sand out, but at least I could now do the paper-work as well as the bull-work.

The base at Jericho Beach was undergoing expansion, and the hangars were new, as was the hangar apron, a great concrete expanse upon which flying boats were pulled up by way of slipways. The station was equipped with Vancouver twin-engined biplane flying boats, Vedette biplane flying boats with one pusher propeller, and a Fairchild 71 seaplane. Sometimes the aircraft were left bobbing at buoys out on the water, but this was not a good practice since the salt water corroded the aircraft and everything in them, while enterprising citizens passing in boats would board the aircraft at night and steal instruments, particularly clocks, as well as any tools left aboard by incautious mechanics.

When I arrived in Vancouver the barracks were not completed, and again I had to look for a boarding house. The one I chose had four airmen already there. We were well looked after, but the family had obviously come down in their previously-well-off West Point Grey world. The man of the house was a reserved businessman type, who was obviously ill at ease with us paying guests. One evening, feeling homesick for my own family, I offered to help dry the dishes. He quietly but firmly pushed me aside, and did them himself. Looking back on it, I can sympathize with him.

LAC Emmott, Vancouver, 1939.

One evening he happened to pass the partly-completed barracks when he saw me on the porch. He stopped to inspect the place, considering that as a taxpayer he was entitled to check on anything the government was doing. He was very unflattering on the building's workmanship. Later on, however, he introduced me to a friend of his who had designed most of British Columbia's schools, a fact he was very proud of. Having gained my education in these desperately unattractive buildings, I lost faith in his architectural judgment. The barracks is still in use, as a youth hostel now, in good repair and in fine shape after more than half a century.

We embarrassed him for only a few months before the barracks opened, and I was allotted a bed in it. Barrack-room life in Vancouver was pleasant, since we were out of the "boot camp" atmosphere. (The phrase is an Americanism which was unheard of at the time.) We were exposed to Friday-night clean-ups and Saturday morning inspections, duty watches and guard details, but the senior NCOs let us alone after hours.

There were six of us to a room, under a corporal. Sometimes the corporal turned out to be a married man, who lived with his wife, and left us pretty much on our own. Knowing we were well off, we kept the floor clean and the beds made. Official reveille was at 6:15, but nobody got up before seven. The mess hall was in the basements of the barracks, so that we did not have far to go for breakfast. Just before eight we would form up outside the barracks to march a quarter mile or so to the hangars and shops at the water's edge. The hangar area was fenced in but the barracks was not, and ordinary auto traffic drove around it. Nobody worried. The days of spies and terrorists were far away.

After hours we headed for the night spots of Vancouver, if we had enough money to do so. If we were out of funds we lounged around, mostly in our barrack rooms, reading or listening to radios. When lights-out came we would tune in a radio station which played soothing music until we fell asleep. At one stage a bugler was commissioned to sound the "Last Post," which was defined as a call to wake us up to tell us to go to sleep, but then he was transferred and we could drop off to sleep to the music again.

Barrack life suited some of the more feckless airmen down to the ground. If they spent all their money on fast women or slow horses there was still a bed to sleep in, three meals a day, and a uniform to wear. Besides, the barracks were close to Spanish Banks, loaded with nubile young women in bathing suits.

Airmen were allotted barrack rooms according to squadrons. The men of No. 4 flying Boat Squadron were housed together, six to a room, and so were the men of No. 6 Torpedo Bomber Squadron when it reached Vancouver in 1939. Because I belonged to Headquarters squadron, I was bunked with other storekeepers, clerks, motor transport drivers, service policemen, cooks and motor-boat crewmen, who lived in my room or the one next to it . This scheme gave us a good deal in common, since we shared officers, NCOs, and problems. In the barrack rooms devoted to the flying squadrons the discussions were about aircraft, engines, flying and cleaning the hangars; ours were about paperwork problems, the orderly room and our NCOs.

The non-commissioned officers controlled our lives. They enforced the rules we lived by, and made a good many of them. All but one or two of the sergeants were married, and went home at night, but there were a good many single corporals, who kept us on a fairly tight rein. The war was not completely one-sided, however; one of the men in my room lived in Vancouver, and spent his nights at home when he was not on duty watch, coming in early in the morning. When he arrived he always brought a handful of flowers which he picked on the way, and placed them on the table beside the bed of the room corporal, whom he knew had hay fever. The poor man would wake strangling and coughing. He was a cook, however, who had to rise early to prepare breakfast, and his tormentor simply kept out of his way until he was safely in the kitchen.

There was a tacitly-recognized pecking order in the ranks. The airmen with the most prestige were the mechanics, the fitters (engine mechanics) and riggers (airframe mechanics), who had the most highly-skilled jobs with the most responsibility, since upon their work depended the lives of the pilots. They also were chosen as crewmen, which allowed them to fly, and qualified them for an extra seventy-five cents a day, big money in those times. Furthermore, the four or five airmen who were chosen to be trained as sergeant-pilots each year were almost always chosen from the mechanics. A sergeant-pilot had incredible prestige among the airmen, and even among his fellow sergeants. Radio operators (the term was "wireless operators" in those day), ranked next. They had a long, gruelling course, their technical skill was high, and they worked with high-technology devices. Motor-boat crewmen did a macho job, worked with marine engines, and sailed the sea. The administrative airmen—storekeepers, clerks, and medical orderlies—came next. Service policemen and disciplinarians (drill instructors) ranked a little lower. At the bottom of the totem pole were the "general duties" airmen, who did the janitorial work and other labouring jobs.

Promotion worked on a different basis. Clerks got the fastest promotion, because an orderly room demanded responsible men to handle confidential papers and minister to the Commanding Officer's wants. A storekeeper had quite a good chance of becoming a stores officer, while a mechanic had little chance of becoming a technical officer, because that demanded an engineering degree. Service policemen got their corporal's hooks fast because they needed authority to do their job.

Disciplinarians needed stripes to give drill instruction, and to carry out the master-of-arms duties required for the smooth running of the station. Their job was low-key at operational stations like Vancouver, which had other things on its mind besides drill. They were responsible for guarding the station, but that was not taken too seriously. During working hours the station defence consisted of one airman standing guard at the main gate with an unloaded rifle. At night the guard was increased to four men and a corporal, still without any ammunition for their rifles. They did have bayonets, however. Any such warlike appurtenances as machine nests or anti-aircraft guns were, of course, unheard of.

Our relations with our officers were strictly formal and distant. The station commanders and the senior officers were usually First World War veterans, often aces, who were considered by the airmen to live in a distant Valhalla, which ordinary mortals could never enter. The junior officers were men of our generation who had college educations. The men who had joined the air force with me to learn how to be skilled tradesmen envied them, but felt themselves essentially their equals, considering that they would have been officers too if their parents had been able to afford to give them a college education. We never thought ourselves "groundlings to their godlings," and indeed a high proportion of the airmen recruited in the years immediately preceding the war went on to become officers.

We were something less than militaristic. Rather than looking on ourselves as warriors we considered that we had a uniformed job that called for a certain amount of discipline. Nobody ever left the base in uniform if he could help it, and those who did so were viewed with suspicion. The brass did not consider us as warriors either. They emphasized that we were a technical, not a fighting service.

We took our duties seriously, however. In 1939 the senior military officer in British Columbia was the General Officer Commanding, an army general who took himself very seriously indeed. One Sunday he had occasion to visit the air station. The airman on guard duty stopped him, asking him for a pass.

"I haven't got one, but you should know me," the general said.

"Sorry sir, but I can't allow anyone in without a pass," the airman said.

"Look man! I'm the G.O.C!"

"I don't care if you're the G.O.D.," the airman replied. "You can't get in without a pass."

CHAPTER FIVE

In Vancouver I served three stores officers. The senior was the son of a First World War general. The junior was Flying Officer William Mackay Smith, the son of the Chief of Police of Winnipeg, whom I consider the best officer I ever served under, and whose treatment of me was such that I would have walked off a cliff if he had ordered me to do so. The middle officer was crazy. We will call him Flying Officer Jones.

He was a man who wore wings but had not been allowed to stay on flying status, for reasons which soon became obvious. He had a fierce moustache, drove a little English car when nobody drove little English cars, and had a trace of an English accent. Having been taught to fly, he considered himself a cut above ordinary stores officers. He also had weird ideas about how the stores section should be organized, much to the disgust of Flight Sergeant Dinny Reilly, who really ran it. Flying Officer Jones treated us enlisted men with the kind of rough humour that a medieval lord of the manor would use to his villiens, asking sharp questions which left us embarrassed, and accusing us of great feats of womanizing and drinking. We preferred our officers to be formal and rather distant, and our first impulse when one of them treated us familiarly was to look for a catch in it somewhere.

Mr. Jones was always embarking on some scheme which meant work for us, like changing the location of the paint stores and then putting all the paint back where it came from because the altered location was too close to the armament section. He was not malicious, however, and on the whole we rather liked him.

Being single, he lived in the Officers' Mess, a beautiful mansion which once had belonged to one of the first families of Vancouver. We airmen often got to visit it—we were allowed to polish the floors, clean the windows and act as bar-tenders during the Officers' Mess dances, which were a big thing in Vancouver's upper social circles. We kept our eyes open during these affairs, and thus it was that when Flying Officer Jones escorted one of the nurses from as military hospital in the other end of town into the garden, and made a determined pass at her, that all of us AC-plonks knew all about it the next day. The moonlight had struck black fire from the roses and the night-wind was heavy with the breath of the dreaming sea, but the same wind was cold as it caressed the branches of the weeping willows, and the lady preferred to keep her clothes on.

It was logical, therefore, that a couple of days later Flying Officer Jones called me into his office and told me to order enough panes of glass to build a greenhouse in a corner of the grounds of the Officers' Mess. Greenhouses are warm even in winter, they are redolent with the perfumes of flowers, and they have things like piles of sacks which come in handy. He had a sketch with him, which he commanded me to translate into sheets of glass. Since my guardianship of Section 29, Miscellaneous Hardware, encompassed window glass, it was obviously my job.

I knew as much about greenhouses as I knew about bawdy houses, having never visited either, but I sought out a corporal who was an expert in both, and he came up with a bill of material which included some hundred dollars' worth of glass. A hundred dollars was a month's wages in those easy days.

"Now go to Flight Sergeant Reilly and get him to buy that glass from Local Purchase funds," said F/O Jones. I did so with trepidation, knowing that Reilly would promptly blow up, and that any unwary Leading Aircraftsman in the neighbourhood might be badly hurt in the explosion. The whole Air station had a local purchase allotment of only fifty dollars a month, and Jones' glass would bankrupt the fund for the rest of the summer.

"Jones! Jones! That crazy bastard! Skincock! Skincock!" spat out Reilly, quivering with indignation. I made myself scarce before he had time to transfer his rage to me and give me some unpleasant task. Reilly disappeared into Jones' office, to reappear madder than before, sputtering fire and brimstone. He went back into his own office, peered into a number of mysterious books he kept, the contents of which were unknown to all but him, and emerged swearing fiercely. A week passed, and then Reilly told me to phone downtown to the Wilkinson Glass Company to order the glass, and then to accompany a transport truck to pick it up.

I rode downtown in the back of the stake truck, smart and glamorous in my khaki overalls. They were six sizes too big, as was the custom with overalls, which were issued allowing for shrinkage from washing. That worked for mechanics who got their coveralls dirty, but not for storekeepers who did not have to cope with greasy engines and thus did not have to wash them every week. It looked as if my coveralls belonged to my big brother.

We threaded our way through downtown Vancouver and came to a stop before the premises of the Wilkinson Glass Company. I presented my Local Purchase Order to the man in the office, who led me to a back corner of the warehouse. Several cases filled with glass leaned against the wall.

Standing beside them was a young man of about my age, about my height and weight, about my build, like me with dirty-blond hair and undistinguished features. He took my slip of paper. "I've come to take the glass," I said. I checked the number of sheets of glass and their sizes. Everything was correct.

"Okay. I'll take it."

"Hold on," said the young man. "How about the case?"

"What about the case?"

"The case the glass comes in. It's specially built, and it's expensive. It's not listed on your bill."

I stepped back, shattered by this unexpected setback. I needed the case to get the glass back to the station; without it, the glass would reach its destination in tiny shards. If I returned without the glass, F/O Jones would kill me, and if I brought it back in pieces Flight Sergeant Reilly would kill me considerably more painfully.

"But holy smoke!" I protested, "I've got to get the glass there somehow—and I never thought I'd need a special case. Anyway, we haven't got any special cases out at the air station, nobody told me about them—"

The young man looked at me. "But that case cost a lot of money. If it gets lost we have to pay for it ourselves."

Disaster loomed. I considered telephoning Flight Sergeant Reilly, but dismissed the thought. The purchase of the glass had bankrupted the local purchase fund, and the air station had no more money. The thought of telephoning Flying Officer Jones himself never occurred to me; we airmen never spoke to our officers except through our NCOs. I looked at the young man in total dismay.

Then, grasping at a straw, I said, "Look—lend me the case long enough to take the glass back to the air station. I'll unload it and send the case back to you as soon as I can."

"Gosh," he replied, "I'm taking an awful chance. I've never seen you before—how do I know you'll send it back?"

"Heck, I said, "I'm in the air force. You know where Jericho Beach air station is—I can't leave there—if I did it'd be desertion. You know where to find me." Casting myself on his mercy, I told him of my difficulty. He was skeptical at first, but gradually he became a little sympathetic. "Okay," he said, "You can take the case, but remember—you've got to send it back. It's worth money."

"Thanks a million," I said with a sigh of relief. I signed for the glass, and the truck driver and I trundled it into the stake truck. We rode back to Jericho Beach, where we unloaded it into the back of the stores building. I left the glass in its case, since there was nowhere else safe to store it while we waited for the greenhouse to be built.

I returned to my storekeeping, busily issuing out nuts, washers and bolts, and sometimes screws and nails. I knew that nothing would happen instantaneously with the glass, and resigned myself to fending off the queries of the glass company about what we were doing with the case.

My friend the corporal who knew all about greenhouses came in one day and made some notes on the back of an envelope, and a sergeant who was far from being a friend came in another day and made notes on the back of a cigarette package. A couple of days later the sergeant marched the duty watch up to the officers' mess, where we cleared off a section of the ground where the greenhouse could be built. I had mixed feelings as I laboured with hoe and spade. I didn't like working when I could be relaxing, it being after hours when we were volunteered for the task, but I wanted to get rid of the glass so that I could send the case back where it belonged.

The next morning there was a buzz of excitement around the stores section, with many covert glances being cast in the direction of Flying Officer Jones' office. The previous night, after keeping a barrack-room comrade of mine who was employed as a bartender awake two hours after legal bar-closing time while he demanded exotic drinks, he had retired to his room. At three in the morning he had come charging out of it, brandishing a sword he had inherited from a cavalry ancestor and kept on a shelf over his bed, to make a desperate attack on a large oil painting of a First World War ace which hung just above the stair landing. Shouting that he was repelling an attack by Indians, he dealt it many grievous wounds, and would very likely have despatched it had he not tumbled over a banister and landed up in a sofa at the foot of the stairs.

The crash alarmed the Orderly Officer, who dashed out of his room, arrayed in full uniform with the badge of his office—a black armband with the letters "O.O." emblazoned on it in scarlet—and enquired what the fuss was about. Jones, mistaking him for his erstwhile antagonist, took after him with his sword, but tripped over a standing lamp which the orderly office cleverly threw in his way, and knocked himself unconscious when he slid into an end table. The Orderly Officer called in a half-dozen of his fellow officers to truss him up.

When he regained consciousness he construed his bonds as evidence that he had been captured by the Indians and was about to be burned at the stake, but he bore his impending fate bravely as he was carted off to the psychiatric ward at the military hospital. Rumor has it that he recovered well enough there to entertain his girl-friend, the nurse, in his hospital bed. The partitions between rooms did not, however, reach to the ceiling, and two army privates watched the goings-on and reported them to us. We wished him well. He was an interesting man to work for.

Jones was replaced by another officer. He entered my storehouse, where he asked, "What's this?"

"Glass, sir," I replied. "To build the greenhouse."

"Greenhouse! That goddam greenhouse! We haven't got the men to build it—we haven't got anybody to look after it when it does get built! We haven't any money to buy the flowers! Nobody wants that damn greenhouse!" He stormed off.

He was right. With Jones off the scene nobody was the slightest bit interested in the greenhouse on the grounds of the Officers' Mess. It had been Jones, and Jones alone, who wanted to stroll through the scented rows of flowers in the drowsy warmth of the building, as he led the fair lady toward the pile of strategically placed burlap sacks behind a thick growth of rhododendrons. The greenhouse never got built; the glass never got used. It stayed in its case in my storehouse, getting in the way, demanding to be dusted, to be kept out of harm's way, to be accounted for under the heading "Not in Vocabulary."

At intervals a call would come for me from the glass company. I put the man off with far words, width insincere promises, with outright lies. Then letters started coming in, dunning us for the cost of the glass case. We could pay the invoice for the glass, since there was proof of its delivery, but not for the case. Anyway, the glass had used up all the money in the Local Purchase fund. I apologized, I cringed. I wished I had never heard of the glass or the case it came in.

Then the war broke out. I was transferred away from the station, leaving the glass still in the back of the stores building. I presume the letters stopped coming. I never found out what happened to the glass. I forgot all about it. In due course Flying Officer Jones was discharged from hospital certifying that he was recovered. He later used to pull the certificate out at parties to establish the fact that he was the only officer in the RCAF who could prove he was sane.

I fought the war behind a stores counter for a couple of years, and then I left storekeeping and learned how to navigate an aircraft. I went overseas, where I dropped bombs on Germany and helped to smash up the French railway system in preparation for D-Day. Much to my surprise I survived the war and was shipped back to Canada on the Queen Mary.

I was sent to an operational station at Patricia Bay on Vancouver Island, my "Canada" badges (which only those who had served overseas were allowed to wear) on my shoulders and my medal ribbon that showed I had seen combat on my chest.

These badges of honour, visible evidence that I had flown through the shell-torn skies over Germany, would make me a valued addition to the coastal reconnaissance squadron that I was to join. My new commanding officer, I knew, would be overjoyed to see me. He himself had no overseas service, but I would be understanding, and downplay my exalted position as a battle-scarred veteran.

He welcomed me warmly. "One of you tour-expired guys from overseas, eh? As if I didn't have enough troubles! You guys can't get along with anybody but yourselves—you think we should be all down on our knees thanking you. All my own aircrew that have been here with fighting the war off the West Coast for three years,

CPL N.W. Emmott, 1939

flying in all kinds of weather, having to dodge around among the mountains, getting no goddam thanks from anybody—and now they're getting insulted right and left by you bastards that think they're King Shit because you got a free trip to England. You don't know anything about West Coast flying and you're too dumb to learn. But I guess I gotta take you. Well, I got an answer for that too. Luckily we got a new pilot just got posted in from England. I'm forming a leper colony for you overseas bastards, and you can join it. Go meet your pilot."

I sought out my new pilot. He was a man of my own age, with my kind of undistinguished features, my own shade of dirty-blond hair. He had flown light bombers out of Lincolnshire. I had flown in heavy bombers out of Yorkshire. I welcomed him as a friend, as a comrade, as a member of the most exclusive club in the world—the club of those who had seen air combat.

He took my hand, shook it, and then peered at me. Then he stepped back and said, "Where's my packing case?"

CHAPTER SIX

In 1939 the world changed, and the Royal Canadian Air Force with it. The war started.

In common with all other leading aircraftsmen at the time I was promoted to corporal. It meant nothing much for me, since I was employed at Western Air Command Headquarters, housed in an office building, first the Post Office in Vancouver, and then in a building in Victoria. One of my jobs was to meet the thousands of men who were rushing to apply for enlistment in the Air Force. One of the applicants was a dwarf only four feet tall. However, he was noticed by one of the senior officers, who sent him off to the Boeing Company's factory at Sea Island, where he turned out to be invaluable because he could crawl inside wings to do assembly work.

In Victoria we were exposed to an instance of military bureaucracy which left us wondering. At the time it was assumed that poison gas would play a big part in the war, and orders came that all military personnel in the Victoria headquarters would be issued with gas masks. We received them, and dutifully tried them on. All the clerks, however, were civilian, most of them women, and they were not entitled to any such luxuries. Under as gas attack we would either have to don our masks and let our girl companions choke to death, or hold our breath while we shared gas masks with them. Luckily the occasion never arose.

Early in 1940 I was sent back to Jericho Beach, where I found that my exalted rank required me to become the corporal in charge of a barrack room. Most of the airmen in the room were older and far more worldly-wise than I was, but they had been used to the ferocious discipline of the civilian market place, where an instant's disagreement with a boss could mean discharge and starvation, and they were fully co-operative. One of them who had been a Canadian National Railways station-agent in the late

Twenties gave me detailed instructions on how to issue railway tickets so that could keep the money yourself. I have never been able to put these precepts into practice. Another was a medical orderly who was bitterly resentful because he had served in the American Army, and later in the Chinese Route Army, as a male nurse, entitled to commissioned rank. There was no provision in the RCAF for male nurses, and he had to be enlisted as an airman. Eventually he deserted. Sexual discrimination existed in those days too.

The airmen were a pretty good lot, although there were some rough diamonds among them. Our officers included more oddballs. As soon as the war started anybody who could fly a plane was enticed into the force, including several bush pilots. One of them, whom we shall call Tommy Boys, had a personality not well adapted to military discipline. Taking off in a seaplane from Jericho Beach one Sunday afternoon, he dived down on every sailboat in English Bay, caught their sails in his slipstream, and upset every one of them. Such was his sense of humour, and so frequent were his punishments, that a letter addressed to "The Orderly Officer, RCAF Station Vancouver," was duly delivered.

One day Tommy, with fellow officers, was drilling on the hangar apron at Jericho Beach, with one of their number detailed as flight commander. He got them into motion very well, but after he had started them marching toward the seawall and the salt water, he forgot the word of command to stop them. As they neared the briny deep Tommy called out, "For God's sake say something, if it's only goodbye!"

Pilots were in short supply, so Tommy was despatched to Trenton to pick up a Shark aircraft and ferry it back to Vancouver. He took with him one of my fellow airmen, a fitter (i.e., an engine mechanic) as his crewman. Their flight took them north of Lake Superior, where Tommy had flown during his bush-pilot days. He knew everybody there, and his flight was a series of reunions with old friends. This involved extensive detours to airports nobody had ever heard of. The reunions required considerable drinking, which even in those easy days cost money, so Tommy took to freighting supplies to prospectors at standard rates. He also carried people aloft on sight-seeing trips at five dollars a flip. Tommy explained his slow progress to the air station at Jericho Beach by complaining about the weather.

At Fort William (now Thunder Bay) Tommy made a rendezvous with one of his friends at a downtown hotel. As he waited for him in the lobby, jacket open, without a necktie, cigarette ashes dribbling down his front, he was spied by the Inspector General of the RCAf, who by chance happened to be in the same hotel. The senior officer, apoplectic with rage, strode up to him. "You!" he shouted.? "You—Flying Officer!"

"Hi," replied Flying Officer Boys.

The senior officer pointed to the many rings on his sleeve that bespoke his exalted rank. "Do you know who I am?"

Tommy looked at the man's sleeve and nodded. "You got a good job, mate—hang onto it," he said, and departed for the beer parlour.

My friend the crewman returned to Jericho Beach in a state of shock. With three years of air force discipline instilled in him, teaching him that officers were exalted beings, Tommy Boys was too much for him to take. It required years for him to get over it.

Not all the odd-ball officers at Jericho Beach were retreaded bush pilots, however. Squadron Leader F. J. Mawdesley, who was one of the air force's original characters, a pioneer Arctic pilot, and a fairly good seaplane pilot (although he was accused of being blind) was the Officer Commanding No. 4 Bomber Reconnaissance Squadron (previously No. 4 Flying Boat Squadron) in 1940.

One of my mechanic friends was detailed to fly as Mawdesley's crewman in a Vancouver flying boat. He climbed out on the wing to start the engines. The moment the second engine started Mawdesley began his take-off run, without waiting for the man to climb down to safety in the cockpit. My friend was nearly blown off the wing into the water, and when the plane landed he furiously refused to fly with Mawdesley ever again. To his credit, Mawdesley did not stand on his rights.

Mawdesley was very proud of his navigational skill, which included arriving at a destination exactly on his pre-computed Time of Arrival. He hedged his bets by approaching the destination early and then orbiting long enough to make his touch-down time exact.

One night when I was on duty in squadron stores Mawdesley walked into my storeroom. He poked an accusing finger at a pile of heavy rubberized garments. "What are these?"

"Seaplane wading suits, sir," I replied. "They just came in."

"Hold one up." I extended one of the heavy suits, designed to allow men to wade out into the sea to fit wheeled beaching gear supports to the flying boats to allow them to be hauled up the ramp.

"Put it on." I obeyed.

"Now let's see how it works in the water," he said. "Wade in." I closed the stores lock-up, waddled out onto the hangar apron, and walked down the ramp up which the flying boats were trundled. I walked out into the chill water until it rose to the top of my wading-suit. I stopped.

"Keep going!" Mawdesley yelled at me.

"This is as far as I can go, sir," I called back.

"Keep going? Keep going? Go deeper!"

"But the water's pouring in--"

"I don't care? Get in deeper!"

With no choice—to a permanent force corporal a squadron leader was higher than God—I walked in deeper. Water poured over the top of the wading suit, soaking my uniform."Deeper! Deeper!" Mawdesley kept yelling, until I was swimming. He stood on the slipway, doubled up with laughter. Finally he waved me in.

I returned to the lock-up, removed my wading suit, and stood there in my soaked uniform. Just them a group of airmen came in to return special tools they had borrowed, and I had to stand dripping as I signed them in. Two hours later I shut up shop. The next day I had a cold.

Such behaviour gave him a reputation throughout the whole air force as being as nutty as a fruit cake. He had his finer feelings, however. One day he was walking to his office past an airman who was practicing semaphore signalling, waving his flags at another airman a few hundred feet away. As Mawdesley approached the airman sent a message telling his colleague who was coming. Mawdesley looked at him, and then called the airman over. He said to him, "The word 'Hatter' is spelled with two T's," and resumed his walk to his office.

CHAPTER SEVEN

During the "Phoney War" period the Canadian war effort was low key. Europe was a long way off, and we had a lot of allies—France certainly, what was left of Poland, and Belgium and Holland if we needed them. Then came the Battle of France, and all our allies fell. Suddenly we felt ourselves naked to the world. With Britain and her empire fighting alone, there was an actual danger now that hostile forces might actually attack Canada. The order had gone out earlier that military bases were to be built along the West Coast. Now they took on doubled urgency.

One of these bases was at Ucluelet, on the seaward side of the south end of Vancouver Island. No. 4 Squadron was sent to this half finished "bush station" in August 1940. The airmen were less than overjoyed at the prospect, since they much preferred the fleshpots of Vancouver, where there were nightclubs and beer parlours and young ladies who admired men in uniform.

Ucluelet could only be reached by air or water, and the pitiful handful of aircraft on the West Coast were too busy to fly us there. We took the CPR coastal steamer to Nanaimo, caught buses to Port Alberni, and then crawled into launches to take us another forty miles to our destination.

We were an odd mixture. The airmen were a combination of teenage recruits and skilled tradesmen, often in their thirties and forties. There were first-class garage mechanics transmuted into engine technicians, highly-skilled carpenters and metal-workers who were now airframe technicians, long-distance truck drivers who were motor transport men, seamen who were motorboat crew-men, and trained accountants. Some of them had had their own businesses. Too old, or not in good enough physical condition to join the army, they flocked to the air force, where their skills could be put to much better use.

The corporals were almost all men like myself, in their early twenties, who had been in uniform two or three years, and who knew the service fairly well but that was all. The sergeants were old sweats, the ten and fifteen-year men who were tough and cynical and knew how to scrounge and find loopholes in the regulations, and tended to have an unquenchable thirst for beer.

We all worked well together. The station had to be completed with roads and docks and modifications to the buildings to make them livable, which meant that the civilian skills of the men were extremely valuable. The young corporals, respectful of their older subordinates' expertise, treated them with consideration. The sergeants were swamped with administrative work and had no time to be petty tyrants. There was no time for parades or square-bashing, and nobody bothered about spit-shined shoes or No. 1 uniforms. It was a happy station.

Cabin built at Ucluelet, B.C. by Sgt Mel Martin, 1940

We storekeepers did not have to join in the building projects. Even if nobody flew the two Shark aircraft bobbing at buoys in the bay, and the enemy submarines in the Pacific remained undiscovered, every item of equipment reaching the half-built base had to go through stores. They had to be unloaded from the ships that brought them, unpacked, counted, put into bins, labelled, vouched for, issued to the users, cared for while they were in stores, and demanded from the equipment depots when supplies ran low. We were frightfully overworked, but since there was nothing to do after hours, overtime was not much of an imposition. Besides, work was a cram course in storekeeping in all its aspects. Those of us who had specialized in one aspect of the job, as I had when I was in charge of nuts and bolts at Jericho Beach, learned how to do everything.

The air force recognized this increased expertise—and its shortage of NCO's—by promoting me to sergeant. This had one unpleasant result—I had to "wet my hooks" in the sergeants' mess. The catch was that I hated beer. Bravely, however, I took hold of the bottle and sipped at the nauseating stuff, trying to hide my distaste. It was going down very slowly. Then, screwing up my courage, I tilted the bottle and drank the whole mess down. As I set down the empty bottle some helpful sadist stuck another bottle in my hand. I had to fake drinking this one until I could hide the bottle behind a chair just before I left.

The amity and efficiency shown on the station did not extend to the higher levels of air force administration. One day an airman reported to Ucluelet—a grizzled man who had been recruited as a shoemaker, a trade in which he was expert, and sent to Ucluelet on the ground that there were no civilian shops nearby capable of repairing the airmen's shoes. To do so, of course, he needed tools, and I forthwith sat down and typed out demands for the tools carefully listed in a document entitled "Establishments," and sent them off to the Equipment Depot in Winnipeg. They all came back acompanied by a vitriolic letter stating that the demands were unjustified, that nobody needed a special shoe-repair capability at Ucluelet, and that we should be more careful in future. The shoemaker, reduced to janitor work, was loud in his denunciation of the air force, and had to be posted before he ruined everybody else's morale. The officer who cancelled the demands, of course, went on to high rank as a tough-minded administrator who stood no nonsense.

Some of the postings to the station made sense, however. The sergeant cook in charge of the kitchen was an old sweat who was expert in the careful preparation of all the forms demanded by the proper administration of his kitchen, the keeping of the place clean, and the proper dress and discipline of his handful of men. He had only one chink in his armour. He could not cook, and the food he served would have given dyspepsia to a pig. One day some men caught a number of beautiful salmon, of the kind served as delicacies at expensive restaurants. He served them as fish-cakes.

Then the powers that be posted in a man who had been given two stripes upon enlistment, because he had spent twenty years as a chef on a Canadian National express train travelling across Canada. He could actually cook, and when he was given salmon he prepared them and carved them artistically, finishing by placing a mirror behind them so that they looked twice as big. The food improved immensely as he cooked and directed the junior cooks, while the sergeant filled out the papers. The officers dined in a separate room, and the sergeants ate at a separate table in the dining room, but the food was the same for all of them. They were all happy about it.

Then one day a sergeant in the British Columbia Provincial Police appeared in his police launch on one of his periodic patrols. The young-middle-aged senior NCO's welcomed him as a contemporary, and invited him for dinner at the mess. He accepted gladly; food aboard his two-man-crew boat was nothing to write home about. He relished every mouthful. Then, at the end of the meal, his nose was observed to wrinkle. He thanked his airmen friends and went back to his boat.

The next day he returned, inspected the mess hall, and climbed into the attic. There he found a complete still, well built and in full operation, and completely illegal. A few shrewd questions established that the guilty man was the ex-CNR chef. The policeman took him away in handcuffs.

The quality of the food immediately plummeted as the sergeant had to return to active preparation of the rations. Selected members of the station's personnel were also bitterly unhappy to see the corporal go. They had been sharing the booze that the good chef had made; like the food he cooked it was of excellent quality. Their chagrin was increased when they found that the inhabitants of prisoner-of-war camps were running stills of their own, without interference from the Veterans' Guard which stood watch over them. It seemed bitterly unfair. The police sergeant was not invited to the mess again.

No. 4 B.R. Squadron remained at Ucluelet until August 1944. During that time it gained no victories, sank no submarines nor did it ever see any, suffered no operational casualties, and gained

Stranraer Flying Boat, Ucluelet, B.C. 1940

no battle honours. The Sharks were phased out in 1942, to be replaced by Stranraer flying boats (their crews referred to them as "Strainers,") and then by American PBY flying boats which the RCAF called Cansos.

I was with them only about four months, after which I was posted to Patricia Bay.

CHAPTER EIGHT

Patricia Bay, British Columbia, lies at the north end of the Saanich Peninsula; in turn it lies on the south end of Vancouver Island. The setting is so beautiful that all the promotional brochures extolling the Cote d'Azur, Big Sur, and the Riviera actually describe Patricia Bay. The mountains of Vancouver Island frame it on one side and the Gulf Islands on the other. There are great Douglas fir trees standing beside the roads, there are fields filled with reflective cattle, and snug hostelries tucked into out-of-the-way places within easy distance. The air station was seventeen miles from Victoria, a city filled with beautiful women conditioned to set high values upon military uniforms, Victoria having been a bastion of the military since 1843, when it was founded.

For me it was rather a sink-or-swim situation, since I was the senior stores NCO, and my officer was a former truck-company executive from Ontario who came to work at eleven in the morning, left at one, and took two hours off for lunch. He let me run the place. I soon learned to forge his signature so that I could get things moving (the chief duty of a stores officer is to sign vouchers) and since I knew what the vouchers were supposed to do, and knew how to tag the equipment when it was put into bins, I managed quite well. What really made my reputation was that I was able to put web equipment together.

When the Royal Air Force was founded, Lord Trenchard decided that he would make it a smart service by importing drill instructors from the Grenadier Guards. These leather-lunged drillmasters knew that no real soldier was worthy of the name unless he could march twenty miles wearing full web equipment—knapsack, packsack, haversack, waterbottle, bayonet frog, ammunition pouches and cross belts. In due course the daughter service, the RCAF, took the same line. Infantry-style web equipment was sent to Patricia Bay to fit the airmen for the war.

The catch was that nobody knew how to put it on. Faced with this dilemmas, I took a despicable action—I asked assistance from the army. An old friend of my father's who lived in Victoria had served in the infantry in the First World War. I bundled up a set of the web equipment and took it to him, and he showed me how to put it together. Some time later my stores officer, in company with the station commander, walked through the clothing section, to find me busy draping straps and haversacks and water-bottles around the form of an airman to whom they had just been issued. They were mightily impressed—there I was, a hard-bitten experienced non-commissioned officer, quite twenty-one years old, with more than three years' service, demonstrating my expertise by assembling a complete set of web equipment.

Shortly thereafter I was promoted to the rank of flight-sergeant. The officer congratulated me. He did know that the stores section ran smoothly. He did not know that I was forging his name.

It was wonderful being a flight sergeant, especially at Patricia Bay. The weather was good, the scenery was good, and Victoria was a good place to visit during my off hours. I was able to afford a Model A Ford car. Best of all, I had a great deal of impressive insignia on the sleeves of my tunic. On each sleeve near the shoulder was the eagle that all airmen wore (or was it an albatross?), then a great big white cloth crown, then my three stripes. I looked highly important.

Other people thought I was important too. I went to a dance put on by a group of patriotic ladies, where I found a highly attractive girl who obviously preferred me to the man with whom she had been dancing before I cut in. I nodded to the table where he was sitting, rather disconsolately. "Do you know him?" I asked her.

"Yes," she said, "but I like you better. You're a lot higher rank-- aren't you—look at all those things on your sleeve!" She fingered the eagles on my sleeves, the eagles that every airman wore. "And you've got your wings too—I just love pilots!" I nodded happily. "That other fellow—he's nothing compared to you—all he has is a little narrow ring around his cuff." I nodded happily again. The man was a flying officer, four ranks higher than I was. I never enlightened the young lady.

I saw her again a couple of months later. Somebody must have enlightened her about military ranks. She was very cool to me, and when she left she had her arm in that of the flying officer.

Of course, beside flight sergeants storekeepers we also had aircrew at Patricia Bay too.

A great deal of army training took place on Vancouver Island. The land abounds in mountains for training mountain troops, beaches on which to practice landings, valleys for digging trenches, and uninhabited areas to shoot artillery shells into. Besides, the weather is mild, without blizzards to disrupt training or clog roads with snow. Men do not freeze their feet, suffer frostbite if they lose a mitten, or need special winter clothing. Training can take place all year round outdoors, as the promotional literature from Victoria tells the tourists.

The thousands of troops being put through their paces practiced attack and defence, bridged rivers, dug fox holes, followed up artillery barrages, fired off trench mortars, and made co-ordinated attacks with tanks. What combat veterans objected to was that no attention was paid to threats from the air. The soldiers neglected camouflage, marched along in full view of anybody overhead, took no cover if aircraft did appear, and in general behaved as if aircraft had not been invented. In battle this would be suicidal, as experience in France, the Western Desert and Russia proved only too clearly. The army brass decided to do something about it.

A detachment of three Lysander aircraft, with five pilots, was formed at Patricia Bay. The Lysander was a two-seater monoplane with a high parasol wing, which gave it startling short-take-off and landing characteristics. It had been designed during the Thirties as an army co-operation aircraft, and at the army and air force staff colleges in Britain the received wisdom was that the aircraft was so maneuverable that no fighter would be able to shoot it down, and that its derisory defence of one drum-fed machine gun on a Scarfe ring in the rear cockpit, and one gun firing forward to be operated by the pilot, would keep it safe from harm. Put to the test in France in 1939 and 1940, however, it turned out to be a death trap, with the German fighters shooting Lysanders down like pheasants. They were good enough to fly over Vancouver Island, though, and in 1942 they were even armed with depth charges and used for anti-submarine patrol.

The three-plane detachment was given one-pound bags of flour, which were hung on bomb-carriers on the sponsons which spread out on either side of the wheels of the fixed undercarriage. The flour bombs could be dropped three at a time, or all twelve of them could be salvoed at once.

With these powerful weapons, the pilots were told to make mock attacks on the troops, swooping down on anybody careless enough to expose himself. Troops in convoy were the best targets, but platoons or even squads on maneuvers were attacked, and sometimes individual soldiers on motorcycles. Whenever the detachment was told something was going on—maneuvers, the movement of a convoy, a route march, or a training exercise—up to three Lysanders, properly bombed up with flour, would take off to track down the brown jobs.

When a quarry was sighted, the Lysander would swoop down, drop the flour bombs, make another attack if possible, and then fly away, leaving the unhappy soldiers cursing the flour bombs, the air force, and their luck. The Canadian Army was very sticky about smart-looking soldiers in clean, pressed uniforms, and the flour left the men looking like clowns, the object of jibes from their compatriots and criticism from their sergeant majors. Catching a convoy was the most fun for the airmen, especially if it was raining. In the rain the flour would turn into a sticky paste that befouled uniforms, weapons, trucks and equipment. With practice, the pilots became so accurate that they could pick off a single man on a road. Airmen liked the game a lot more than soldiers.

The generals thought this was splendid training. The soldiers did not share the generals' enthusiasm as they washed flour out of a freshly-pressed uniform, dug it out of the recesses of a Bren gun carrier, or picked it out of the action of a rifle. They did become quickly aware of the threat from the skies, and became adept at scattering, camouflaging, hiding from air observation, marching along the sides of roads under trees, and otherwise doing the things that would save their lives in combat.

No special permission was needed. If there were soldiers in sight they could be bombed, to teach them to keep their eyes open at all times. Nevertheless the pilots kept their jobs a deadly secret, to protect themselves from army vengeance. Too many of the soldiers were husky gentlemen adept at unarmed combat.

The practice came to its climax one day when two Army Commanders, General Potts and General George Pearkes, VC, held a ceremony to take over an auxiliary airport at Cassidy, near Nanaimo. There was no air force detachment there, since the airport was only a landing strip to allow liaison aircraft to fly in and out to serve the army camp. After all, General Rommel in Africa used aircraft to ferry him around, and it was only right that Canadian generals should have the same privilege.

A staff car bearing the two generals, all decked out in their red tabs and other military finery and with swagger sticks, drove up to the podium, appropriately decorated with flags, where the airport would be officially taken over from the contractor who had built it. A guard of honour, all blancoed and polished, with rifles lined up as if with a micrometer, marched onto the runway. Commands crackled through the air, rifles came down to the "Present," and the two generals strode confidently forward to accept documents from the contractor.

Then they looked up. Racing down the runway at a height of six feet were two Lysanders. They pulled up just as they reached the guard of honour and loosed their flour bombs. The guard scattered, their military perfection smothered in flour. The two generals dived underneath the staff car. The contractor rose shakily to his knees, daubed with flour, and began to search for the papers he had so carefully prepared. The platoon sergeant had to be restrained from ordering his men to load with ball and fire.

The telephones at Western Air Command Headquarters were soon ringing off the hook. General Pearkes had a few thousand well-chosen words with the Air Officer Commanding. Not even an Air Vice Marshal talks back to a general with the Victoria Cross. The two pilots involved were soon on the carpet.

However, it was soon discovered that everything that they had done was perfectly legal. They had carte blanche to flour-bomb any group of soldiers except those in such sanctuaries as fixed camps, and the honour guards and the generals were legitimate targets. As far as the pilots were concerned they were just following orders.

Nevertheless, they could not be suffered to remain unscathed—not when they had strafed two generals, one of whom, General Pearkes, was to go on to become a Member of Parliament and later Lieutenant Governor of British Columbia. They were transferred to a Mosquito Operational Training Unit on the East Coast, which they wanted to go to anyway. An Army major, however, who had been unfortunate enough not to inform the air force of the ceremony, was banished to outer darkness.

The detachment was disbanded shortly thereafter, the feeling being that the army, and especially the generals, had gained enough experience with air attack. But it was fun while it lasted.

In the fall of 1941 I was posted to Claresholm, Alberta, a Service Flying Training School, where pilots who had learned to fly elementary Tiger Moth and Fleet Finch aircraft were introduced to bigger twin-engined Avro Anson aircraft.

Just before I left I found something that shook me rigid. Inspecting a voucher, I saw that some dishonest person, blind to the dictates of honour, had had the nerve to forge my name on it.

CHAPTER NINE

Claresholm was a new station, which a few months before I arrived had been notable chiefly for great ditches along the sides of the roads, where it was rumoured that several people posted as missing had fallen in and never been found again. When I got there, however, it was well organized, and the biggest station that I had seen. It was the first station for me which had streets and avenues like a city. The number of people on it was larger than the neighbouring town of Claresholm, a farm distributing center with a heavy percentage of Scandinavians.

The West Coast stations had been run rather amateurishly, with the operational flying being done in outmoded, unsuitable aircraft, by men with no clear idea what they were really trying to do, against an enemy and a threat that we were convinced was imaginary. The chance of a German submarine travelling all the way to the West Coast, where most of the ships at sea were mostly under the flag of the United States with whom the Axis was not yet at war, was vanishingly small. Nobody took our task seriously. It was a matter of showing the flag, of persuading the citizens of B.C. that they were being protected, of towing targets for the artillery and the navy to shoot at, and of making token patrols

Claresholm was another world. Everything done there was aimed single-mindedly at one target—turning out pilots for the shell-torn skies over Europe. Everyone was conscious that the survival of our country and our way of life depended on what was done there, and that our contribution was not merely important but vital. Work went on every day, with no breaks for Sundays or holidays; a sunny day when men could fly could not be wasted. The school was a big, well-managed company which ran like a clock, with well-trained classes graduating on time, with the aircraft well-maintained, and the housekeeping necessary to feed and clothe and house the staff and the students being conducted with quiet efficiency. The military aspect of life was played down, except for the students, who had received their elementary training at civilian schools where they were exposed to no discipline except that in the air, being led back onto the military straight and narrow with drill and inspections. Commanding a Service Flying Training School successfully made the air force careers of many officers. Hugh Campbell, who commanded Claresholm as a Wing Commander while I was there, for one, went on to become the Commander in Chief of the RCAF, and his successor, Fred Carpenter, died as an Air Vice Marshal.

The staff, as usual, was a mixed bag. Some of the pilot instructors were dashing young men who bemoaned their fate in being teachers on the prairie, others were Americans who had learned to fly before coming to Canada to get into the war and were unhappy about being employed as instructors, and a good many who welcomed the chance to get more flying time in before they were sent into battle.

There were others who were overjoyed at being in a respected uniform but far from the guns, and who pulled every string to avoid being sent overseas. The cadets at first included a fair proportion of older men, but became younger and younger as time passed. The airmen just took what came and did their job; not a few of them had joined the air force to escape the infantry, and they were not inclined to rock the boat. There was a fair leavening of mature men among them, who kept things on an even keel.

Training stations tended to be concentrated on the prairies, because the dry climate provided long stretches of good flying weather with few interruptions. The wet winds blowing from the Pacific Ocean lost their moisture as they climbed up over the mountains, but they kept their strength. Indeed, when I first arrived at Claresholm I saw airmen stationed at the side of the runways to dash out and catch the wing-tips of the aircraft as they landed, because the Ansons, which would fly at forty miles an hour, refused to stop flying after they landed, and the men had to man-handle them back into the hangars.

High winds, however, were found about thirty miles south, at Fort MacLeod at the eastern end of the Crowsnest Pass. There it was rumoured that a dog had been blown up against a hangar and had starved to death before the wind let up. Instead of a windsock a logging chain was attached to a pole. When the chain stood straight out in the wind the pilots were told to be careful; when the links of the chain started to snap off flying was cancelled.

The foothills were the home of the *chinooks*, the warm winds which could drive winter temperatures up by twenty degrees within minutes. A farmer, it is said, was driving a two-horse sleigh which was overtaken by a chinook. His horses were struggling through three feet of snow while the rear runners of the sleigh were dragging on the bare ground. At any rate, the clear weather and the rugged Ansons, some of them with patched bullet-holes from Coastal Command service, allowed a no-fatality record to be set up until the station changed over to fly Cessna Cranes.

This happy record continued despite the fact that there were a good many of the instructor pilots (especially the Americans) who did not have the approved respect for Air Force rules and regulations. It was strictly forbidden to perform aerobatics with Ansons, which were plodding old planes, withdrawn from active Coastal Command service because they were slow and clumsy, but at intervals a pilot, bored with flying straight and level, would loop one. The wings were supposed to break off, but the Ansons did not know this and the aircraft stayed together, although there were always strained spars and loosened joints (the pilots said they had flown through heavy turbulence.) There was also a good deal of 'shooting up' (the term later became 'buzzing') anybody or anything that could be suitably harassed. One pilot flew down the length of a freight train, bouncing his wheels off one car after another. One night a pilot saw a train approaching along a straight stretch of track. He came down to the level of the telegraph poles, flew toward the train, and switched on his landing lights. The engineer of the train, thinking he was heading into a head-on collision with another locomotive, threw on his emergency brakes and flattened every wheel on the train. The pilot who did it bragged about his feat discretely in the sergeants' mess, and the Canadian Pacific Railway complained bitterly, but it was impossible to prove anything— nobody could read aircraft serial numbers in the dark.

During my stay at Claresholm I achieved something that shortly before I would have believed impossible—I was promoted to the rank of Warrant Officer Second Class. That made me a sergeant-major. I was the senior non-commissioned man in the stores department, with about forty people on my staff. I had two officers above me, but the airmen had little to do with them—I was the boss they dealt with. I flatter myself that I did not presume upon this authority, the greatest amount that I have ever had in my life.

WO2 N.W. Emmott, Claresholm, 1942

The men called me "Major," as was the custom.

While I was there airwomen arrived, the first the RCAF had had. I had twelve of them. Being a confirmed romantic, I never used my exalted position to take advantage of any of them. Besides, I thought it would be bad for discipline. After all, I was Permanent Force, and had principles to uphold.

It was at Claresholm that I learned how beer can save life.

Like any well-run station which in the daytime resounded to the roar of Jacobs engines in Cessna Crane aircraft, it closed its eyes after Lights Out, and slumbered through the prairie night. The airmen and airwomen slept secure in the knowledge they were guarded by the service police. All night long the service police patrolled the streets and avenues, alert for crime, insurrection, treason, spies and rabid coyotes and gophers. The nights were long beneath the light from western stars, but the service police carried out their patrols and all attacks were beaten off.

Morning inevitably came, and the night patrols reported to the guard house and went off to their barracks for their rest. Although it was strictly forbidden, more than one SP secreted a bottle of beer in his locker to drink before he turned in for the day.

One man did exactly this. He stripped down to his shorts, drank his hoarded beer, and turned in, soon to drift off to dreamland. Meanwhile, the air station awoke, and the morning's flying began. The Cessna Cranes took off with their youthful students at the controls. They made a predictable amount of noise, enough to drown out the hammers in the workshops and the typewriters in the orderly room. The tired service policeman slept through it all—he was used to it. Then he stirred to the nemesis of all who drink beer before retiring—hydrostatic pressure. He put off the evil moment as long as he could, but at last he had to swing down from his upper bunk and head for the ablution room.

He was just returning to his barrack bed when he heard a shattering crash. Still half-asleep, he continued on his way, to halt abruptly, with one foot in the air. There, nestling in his bed, was the port engine of a Cessna Crane. The student pilot had misjudged his approach and flown the plane through the roof of the barrack-block. The service policeman took one look, and suddenly the enormity of what could have happened, and how narrowly he had escaped death, seized him. He turned and dashed out the building's door, tales of how crashed aircraft burned and exploded giving wings to his feet.

The barracks was next door to the airmen's mess, filled with men at lunch. Dressed only in his shorts he sprinted across the road and ran into the mess, which was build with a central cooking area surrounded by counters. He hurdled one counter, ran through the domain of pans and pots, hurdled the counter on the other side, ran through the dining area, scattering plates and cups, burst out the door, and was far down the road when he ran out of breath. Fortunately he stopped before he laid himself open to charges of desertion.

When he collected his wits one of his fellow SP's gave him a blanket to cover him and drove him back to the scene of the crash. His next stop was at stores, to draw a new uniform. He was given a bed in a different barrack room. The war ended, and he went back to civilian life.

But one wonders—does he still chug down a bottle of beer at bedtime? And if he does, when he gets into bed, does he look carefully to see if there is an aircraft in it?

It was at Claresholm that I heard the radio broadcast by President Franklin Roosevelt telling of the Japanese attack on Pearl

56

Men and women of the 15 SFTS, Claresholm, ALTA, Equipment Section, 1942.

Harbour and the United States' declaration of war. At the end of the broadcast the Star-Spangled Banner was played. Those hearing it stood to attention, the first time we had done so for a foreign anthem. This was a special case. During the long years of the war so far, there were many times when I had feared that we would lose; indeed, once or twice I had said, "After all, it's their turn to win." But now, with a sense of profound relief, I knew that with the USA on our side the enemy had no chance. There would be rough days, deaths and disasters ahead, but we would win.

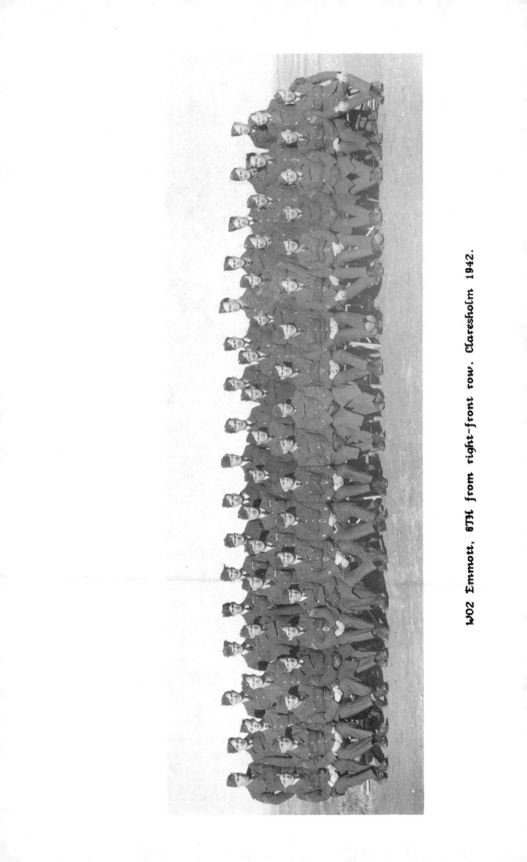

WO2 Emmott, 6TH from right—front row. Claresholm 1942.

CHAPTER TEN

At Claresholm I remustered to aircrew.

When I enlisted I wanted to fly, but the regulations forbade it. To fly, you had to have a college education, and I had only high school. I enlisted as a storekeeper.

Two years later the war broke out. The RCAF signalled it by promoting me, along with every other Leading Aircraftsman, to corporal. The Air Force also memorialized the outbreak of war by recognizing the fact that it was not really necessary to have a college degree to fly effectively, especially when aircrew would be required in large numbers. Before 1939 was out I found that I was now educated enough to take my place in the sounding skies. There might be danger there, but it was unlikely that it would be greater than that which I faced with airmen to whom I had issued ill-fitting uniforms. I took pen in hand (actually I sat down before a typewriter) to write a memorandum to my stores officer as follows:

"The undersigned NCO respectfully requests that he be remustered to aircrew, since his education now qualifies him for this trade."

My flight-sergeant marched me in before the stores officer, who fixed me with a steely glare. His eyes dropped to my memo on the desk in front of him, and after a lengthy pause he spoke.

"Corporal," he said, "this is the one of the most disgraceful memos I have ever seen, and the most indefensible request. Here you are a trained storekeeper—" his voice choked and broke off. "Why, you're even a corporal. Not only that you're trained and experienced, you're even an NCO!"

He paused for breath.

"Here we are, trying desperately to build the very foundation of an Air Force, and you want to quit? Nothing can happen on this station—nothing, I tell you—until the equipment to do it with is obtained—demanded, received, unpacked, issued, accounted for!

You can't even tell that a man is in the Air Force until Stores—" he capitalized the word—"issues him a uniform! If we train you as aircrew, we have to train somebody else to take your place. We have recruits coming here, classed as storekeepers, who don't know an issue voucher from a ledger sheet! We have to train them—and that's where you come in. We haven't enough trained men anywhere, and the Stores Section is vital!

"Now you want to desert? You want to leave this stores section, this air station, the whole air force, in the lurch? You're a traitor— a coward—a scoundrel! While better men are struggling with the hard realities of life, trying to get the equipment that's so vitally necessary to defend our country, you want to bore holes in the sky, ignoring your responsibilities!" He lifted my memo as if he were retrieving it from a sewer. "I'm going to be easy on you, corporal. Instead of recommending your court martial on grounds of dereliction of duty I'm just going to rip up this memo and put it where it belongs—in the wastebasket! Flight, march this worthless excuse for an NCO out!"

"Attention? About turn? Quick march!" the flight sergeant yelled. I marched out quickly, in a state of shock. As I left I heard the officer call to the flight sergeant, "Watch him carefully, Flight! We don't want any more of this behaviour!"

I went back to work, licking my wounds. A few weeks later I was transferred to Ucluelet, where I had to work fifteen hours a day. There was a desperate need for storekeeping sergeants, and they made me one. A new stores officer took over, and I got along fine with him. That is, I got along fine until submitted a memo to him asking to be remustered to aircrew.

He called me in. "What's all this?"

"Well sir, what with Dunkirk and things getting tough, I thought they'd be needing pilots—"

He sprang from his chair.

"Pilots? You thought they'd be needing pilots? Don't you know that pilots are the end product of a process that starts with stores? You know how hard we've been working lately—everybody working overtime, including me—all of them tired—no time off for months. And now you want to quit, to leave us in the lurch—quit, and throw a heavier burden on your comrades? You want to jeopardize the proper operation of this station, of the whole Western Air Command? Now, with Dunkirk behind us and the forces of the enemy on the upsurge, you want to ignore your true responsibilities? You're a traitor, sergeant—probably in league with the enemy? Get out of my sight before I lose my patience, and never let me see you doing anything like this again? Get out!"

With the immediate appreciation of the situation that I considered made me a natural for aircrew, I decided on a course of action. I snapped out a witty answer. "Yes sir!" I said, turned, and marched out the door.

Another year passed. I put a crown above my stripes and became a flight sergeant. I was transferred. I got another stores officer. I submitted another memo.

The officer called me in. For fifteen minutes he discussed my background, my intelligence, my probable military prospects, and my moral fibre with emphasis on my proclivity for treason, vile desertion of my comrades, self-seeking ambition, and shirking of duty, together with blindness to every precept that had made our country great. The floor heaved beneath me as his invective flowed over me, the curtains became a dirty brown, the pictures fell off the wall, and the carpet caught fire. I stood before him in a state of admiring shock. His command of the English language, his air of command, his superiority to all my other officers in the art of denunciation, all drew forth my envious awe. When I left his office I was only four feet three inches tall. It was good to serve so capable an officer.

Another year passed. I became a warrant officer. I was transferred again. I had a new Stores Officer. It was time to submit another memo.

The previous New Years Day the officers had invited the sergeants to visit the officers' mess, where it became obvious to my eye that they had rugs on the floor. The sergeants didn't.

I changed my tactics. This time I wrote a memo applying for selection to Commissioned Rank. (The words are always capitalized in the Air Force.)

My officer called me in. He looked up from my memo. "I'm glad to see this memo, sergeant major," he told me. "You have performed well as warrant officer in charge of stores here, and we need stores officers with your kind of practical experience. I'll be glad to recommend you for a commission, and I'll push it in every way possible."

A month later I received a lengthy application form to fill out. It instructed me to take a physical examination. I called the hospital to make an appointment. The doctor examined me. When he had finished I retied my necktie and stood before him, smart and clean, my uniform knife-edge creased, my boots brilliant, my heels together, the very model of a modern sergeant major. "Did I pass, sir?"

He looked me up and down. "Yes, you did. But I tell you, sergeant major, I haven't much use for you."

"Me? Why not?"

He looked down at the form he had just filled out. "Here you are—trying to become a stores officer—when you're perfectly physically fit for aircrew? You—with dozens of men less fit than you volunteering for aircrew—deliberately trying to evade your responsibility to defend your country? You're a coward, sergeant major—a traitor! I'll sign this, but I don't want to! Now get out of here!"

I looked at him. I met his gaze. "All right. Make me aircrew."

They did.

When I had been promoted from Flight sergeant to Warrant Officer I had removed the stripes and moved the crown down to the cuff of my sleeve, whereupon some of my acquaintances commiserated with me because I had lost my stripes. When I remustered to aircrew I had to revert to sergeant, which meant that I put up three stripes again and took off the crown. My friends were glad to see that I had mended my ways and got my stripes back.

Two years afterward I was navigating a Halifax heavy bomber over the Kammhuber defence line in Holland when a Junkers 88 night fighter poured cannon-fire into our starboard wing. The pilot corkscrewed just in time, and he lost us. But for several minutes I wished devoutly that I was back in my stores section, issuing out ill-fitting uniforms.

CHAPTER ELEVEN

From Claresholm I was sent to No.4 Initial Training School at Edmonton, located on the grounds of the University of Alberta. Its purpose was to introduce us to a host of things like air force law, air force history, some purely academic subjects such as mathematics, and air force skills such as navigation and sending and receiving morse code. We were taught the phonetic alphabet, which started out as the old British Ack, Beer, Charlie, Don, and then changed halfway through the course to Able, Baker, Charlie, Dog to allow us to communicate with the Americans. Years later an international phonetic alphabet was devised that began Alfa, Bravo, Coca, Delta (two syllable words that are understandable even if mispronounced), but I never really learned it. Now I can say that I know that phonetic alphabet from A to B.

Our instructors were high-school and college teachers brought in from civil life, and many of them were first-class. The speed of instruction was intense; once I dropped a pencil on the floor and missed a year of college algebra when I bent over to pick it up.

I wanted to train as a pilot—everybody did—but the experts selected me as an observer. I was pretty downcast at the time, but afterward I realized that they had done exactly the right thing. I became a good navigator, but it is extremely doubtful that I would have become anything more than a very average pilot. Furthermore, when I got on operations later I realized that my dreamy personality over enemy territory would have resulted in me letting my mind stray when complete absorption in what I was doing was absolutely necessary. As a navigator I had no such worries. The ITS selectors saved my life.

From ITS I was posted to an Air Navigation School at Prince Albert in Saskatchewan. There we took instruction in navigation, plus the allied subjects of photography, meteorology, and something about armament. We were taught nothing about what makes an aircraft fly, how the engines worked, how to turn on a radio, or anything but the barest tools of our navigation trade.

Navigation training was centred around *Air Publication 1234, Air*

Navigation, A Royal Air Force publication which was supposed to be the last word. It was written in eighteenth-century English, with words like "Wind" and "Course" capitalized, possibly in emulation of German, which capitalizes all nouns. There was nothing in it about the nuts and bolts of navigation, such as what kind of a pencil to use, how to use a straightedge or a pair of dividers, how to fold a map properly, or even how to use a hand-held computer. We were given instruction in how to use the computer, being taught a method which later on turned out to be wrong; I was forced to the indignity of learning the right way from my operational pilot. A good deal of instruction was given in celestial navigation (the Air Force called it "astro") but the written words were confusing and the illustrations unclear or missing. There was a list of instructions devoted to the Distant Reading Gyro-Magnetic Compass, which we never saw until we got overseas, and therefore never studied. The real reason for all this was that the art of air navigation was in its infancy, and the instructors had to do the best they could, bolstered by the fact that experts had written the book, and experts never bother to explain the simple things.

Flying over Saskatchewan in Avro Anson aircraft was educational but spartan. We spent our time learning how to map-read, getting "pin-points" off the map to find out where we were, drawing lines on our charts to plot the aircraft's position if there had been no wind, and then comparing the "no-wind" position and the pinpoint to find out the velocity of the wind, meanwhile keeping lengthy logs of what we were doing. Our instructors put great stress on log-keeping, perhaps because it was easy to assess. During a flight, of course, the log invariably fell onto the floor and got stepped on, leaving the marks of rubber flying boots all over it. We did a lot of our navigation by taking radio bearings of broadcast stations. We also took drifts to find out how far the wind was blowing us sideways. We had no drift sights, but had to make do with a wire stretched from the front of the bomb-aimer's window in the nose to the rear of the position. We would move the wire until the objects on the ground were tracking down it, and read the drift off in degrees from the scale.

We also took observations of the sun and stars by means of the Mark IX sextant, which gave results of startling inaccuracy. The Ansons did not have an astrodome, but a hatch in the roof of the cabin which we opened to shoot the sun or the stars. That was not bad in the summer, although it did leave a film of oil from the engines in one's hair, but it was horrible in the winter. During our first night flights none of us could see the stars in the sextant at all, since it took a knack to recognize them, and this threw us into the depths of depression until we learned how. Celestial, which was greatly stressed during our training, was valuable for coastal and transport crews, but for bomber navigation it turned out to be almost useless.

One of my instructors shook us to the core one day when he told us that our navigation had only to be accurate to five miles—"Five miles is good enough navigation for anybody." Previously we had been conditioned to think we had to be accurate to a few feet. Actually he was the only realistic instructor we had. The sad fact was that in those early days the navigation instruments that were essential to give even passable accuracy had not yet been invented, and only the barest essentials could be taught. We did get a good grounding in the basics, however, and when we were exposed to advanced techniques later we could use them.

After Air Navigation School we were sent to Rivers, Manitoba, which previously had been the school which specialized in training navigators in celestial navigation. We were bunked in a hangar which contained several hundred beds, and in which the water in the toilets was hot and the water in the showers was cold. It gave us raw material for complaints, which made everybody feel good.

While we were stationed in Rivers I visited Winnipeg, a couple of hours away by train. During my visit I called in at my old stamping ground, No. 2 Equipment Depot, where I had served briefly four years before. An old friend of mine, Stormy Southward, was a warrant officer storekeeper there, and I called on him. I noticed one of the young ladies who worked for him, a tall redhead.

"I'd like to know her better," I told him. "Ask her if she'll go out with me."

He came back a few minutes later. "She says if he can't ask for himself the heck with him."

I stepped back, and then I mustered up my courage to ask the lady for a date.

Two days later I asked her to marry me. She turned me down.

After a brief stay at Rivers I was posted to Dauphin, Manitoba, for a bombing and gunnery course. During my stay I went to Winnipeg every time I had the chance, seeking the lady out.

At the conclusion of the bombing and gunnery course I was

graduated and presented with my wing—a single "O" with as half-wing attached to it, which was described by envious aircrew of other trades as a "flying asshole." At the New Year I was promoted to a pilot officer. I was not a pilot, but the screwy Air Force nomenclature indicated that I was. I never told the uninitiated that the rank did not mean the trade.

As a trained navigator, my next posting was to Summerside, Prince Edward Island, to take a General Reconnaissance course to learn how to navigate over the sea. There I practiced a technique known as "track crawling," which required drawing a required track on the map, and staying on it by measuring the drift continuously and altering course to offset it. The students were taught what submarines do, and how to report on the ships and other features in an enemy harbour (we practiced on Campbellton, New Brunswick).

P/O N.W. Emmott and wife,
Winnipeg 27 February, 1943.

Before I left I stopped at a jewelry store in Summerside and bought an engagement ring. It was the best investment I ever made in my life.

On my way west after the course I married my love in Winnipeg, in Trinity Anglican church. My wife had paid to have the bells ring out our happiness, but I was in such a state of shock that I did not notice them.

CHAPTER TWELVE

At Summerside we were asked to volunteer for whatever task suited our fancy. I still wanted to see what a torpedo looked like, so I volunteered for torpedo bombers. Contrary to long-standing Air Force policy, which dictates that nobody is ever sent to the place he asked to go to, I was posted No.32 Operational Training Unit, back at Patricia Bay, a Royal Air Force unit at the other side of the field from the one I had whipped into shape when I was a flight sergeant.

On my way there with my new bride I stopped at my home town, Nelson. While I was there I reclaimed my old 22-calibre rifle and said to my bride, "Come for a walk with me in the hills. I'll show you how to shoot this rifle." She dutifully followed me, and we went up into the bush, where I set up an old tomato can on a stump and showed her how to take aim. Then I threw another tin can into a little stream that burbled its way along, and said, "Shoot at that." She aimed and pressed the trigger; the can jumped a foot. She worked the bolt and fired again; the tin can jumped another foot. It turned out that she had been the crack shot of her rifle club at Winnipeg. I have never talked back to her since.

We went on to Sidney B.C., the closest village to Patricia Bay. One of the friends I had made in my flight-sergeant days rented us a gardener's cottage, which consisted of one room, a bed, a chair, a table, and a little stove. It was located in a beautiful spot near the beach, beneath tall fir trees, and the climate was perfect. Outside our window was a stump on which a bantam chicken laid an egg most mornings. We had the eggs for breakfast. It was a wonderful introduction to married life.

No.32 OTU was an RAF unit, not an RCAF one, and the staff was at pains to keep things as English as possible. The meals were labelled with names like 'tea,' whose hours conflicted with the desires of the young men to head off for Victoria, 17 miles away, to

67

savour the night life there. At a mess meeting a brash Canadian got up to suggest that the meals be served at "more sensible hours." The temperature fell to zero, the Commanding Officer looked at the offender as if he had snubbed the Queen, and the RAF officers at the meeting agreed as one man that the existing hours were very sensible indeed. However, they did decide to lay on a 'high tea' which would meet the Canadian desires.

At Bomber Command OTUs the aircrew chose their crews themselves, but there was no such nonsense at a Coastal Command OTU where I was. We found a list posted on a noticeboard which told us who we would be flying with. I found my pilot to be Sergeant D.J. Linklater, my wireless operators were to be Sergeants Frank Russell and "Avro" Hansen, and that was it. It worked out very well, and all of us survived the war.

At the OTU we were introduced to the Hampden aircraft. It was a twin-engined plane that had originally been designed as a bomber, and had been used as one early in the war. Its fuselage was deep and very narrow, and more or less rhomboidal in shape, with a skinny structure sticking out the back on which the tail surfaces were supported. There were two gun-positions, one atop the fuselage and the other at the lower rear corner of the quadrilateral, with a single Vickers gas-operated gun on a Scarfe ring. The pilot had a fixed gun, and the observer another Vickers G.O. in the nose.

The aircraft were battle-scarred and unreliable, and the engines too often quit on takeoff, leading to a crash. Several times during my three months at the OTU our crew came back to base to find a pillar of smoke at the end of runway, with a pyre at its base, and four dead men in it. A rumour was extant that if the aircraft found itself in a certain attitude the flat fuselage would blank off the tail control surfaces, whereupon the aircraft would become uncontrollable. Whether this was true or not it was widely believed, although the crews continued to fly the aircraft without complaint. We comforted ourselves by thinking that when we got on operations we would be flying in Beaufort aircraft, which had been specifically designed for torpedo bombing and therefore would be better. In actual fact they were worse, but ignorance was bliss, and we soldiered on.

Flying training, after the pilots had been checked out on the aircraft, was largely navigational exercises and mock attacks on the ships that plied the sea-lanes around Vancouver Island, particularly the Canadian Pacific "Princess" boats which sailed between Vancouver, Victoria, Nanaimo, and Seattle. Torpedo operations called for low flying, and most of the flights were as close to the water as possible. Even for a navigator, perched in the two-foot-wide nose of the Hampden, it was a lot of fun. Usually aboard an aircraft there is no sense of motion, but there certainly was in a Hampden dodging islands at low level.

Flying low was a macho thing to do. One of the pilots on our course was very macho indeed—he feared neither God nor devil, had a mouth like a sewer, and delighted in bragging about his flying ability—which, to be honest, was good. Another pilot was a man called Bill Rodney, whose father was a clergyman, who never swore under any circumstances, and led his life by the precepts of the Good Book. The other pilot had nothing but hard words to say about him. Then one bright day over the waters of the Strait of Georgia the macho man got down as slow as he dared. Bill Rodney flew under him, his propellors creating a wake in the water. The macho man was strangely subdued in Bill Rodney's company after that.

My own office was in the nose of the aircraft, under the pilot's feet. I had a tiny navigation table, a bombsight, and a Vickers gas-operated gun (when it was actually fitted.) From the right side of the fuselage there stuck out a number of metal pegs to hold the drums of ammunition for the gun. During my navigation exercises I spent most of my time measuring the drift, using a drift recorder that stuck out from he left side of the aircraft. The compartment was only eighteen inches wide after you subtracted the pegs sticking out from the side.

On one trip the pilot practiced firing his fixed machine gun, which was set into the nose above my head. He dove down at the water, picked out a convenient whitecap to shoot at, and pressed the firing button. As soon as he did so the deflector bag, which should have caught the expended shells, came loose and all the redhot cartridge cases streamed down the back of my flying suit. I am the only man in history to have performed a strip-tease in the nose of a Hampden aircraft in flight.

We has to learn a lot of things about naval matters. One of them was ship recognition. If we flew on a reconnaissance mission and saw a ship, from any navy in the world, we had to be able to recognize it and report it accurately. We did it by practicing on little ship models, photographs, slides projected on the screen, and flash cards. The British navy was fairly easy, because we were familiar with the ships from the magazines and books we had read; the American navy was not bad, because the ships were distinctive; the German navy was easy to learn because all the ships seemed to be designed to look like one another; and the Japanese ships carried pagodas. It was the French navy that was hard to learn, because there was nothing distinctive about them. I kept mistaking French ships for those of another navy. It worried me. I took a pack of flash cards home and got my wife to go over them with me. Finally, after hours and hours of work, I felt I had the problem mastered. I could recognize ships of the French navy.

The morning came when we were to take the final examination in ship recognition. We filed into the classroom. As we did so the sergeant in charge of the subject said, "You can forget about the French navy. They sank the fleet in Toulon harbour last night."

We did practice torpedo runs, sometimes with live torpedoes which we dropped on static targets, and sometimes we did dummy runs on the Princess boats. These runs involved a low-level approach, a simulated drop, and then a pull-up over the ship. On one flight we had an experienced torpedo-bomber pilot who had flown in the Mediterranean, battering away at the ships trying to supply Rommel's Afrika Korps. After we had finished the exercise and landed, we gathered by a coke-machine to discuss the flight.

He looked at us with compassion. "If you fly like that on operations you won't last one trip. The Jerries will shoot you out of the sky like ducks. If you don't change your method of operating you haven't got a chance." Our mouths fell open. We were supposed to be completely trained torpedo crews, and here was a combat veteran telling us that we didn't know anything. He and Jim Linklater, my pilot, kept talking, Jim to find out what he should do to stay alive. I withdrew from the conversation. As a navigator I would take the plane out and back, but the actual torpedo drop had to be done by the pilot. I shrugged my shoulders, and after a few hours dismissed the matter from my mind. Like all my comrades, I knew very well that I would live forever. Other people would be unlucky, but not me. Even when we flew through the smoke from a crashed Hampden at the side of the runway we knew that we were invulnerable.

At length the course was over and we were graduated as fully operational torpedo-bomber crews. We took our embarkation leave, and I said goodbye to my wife at the railway station in Winnipeg. I reported to Halifax, to board the liner Louis Pasteur.

The voyage to England was without incident. Everybody aboard was in good spirits. Whenever a call was made on the public address system for someone the cry would arise, "Gone overseas!" A group of wireless operators, who would have made a good country and western music group, gathered on the deck to entertain us with country music. At night the ship echoed to the strains of such songs as "Frigging' in the Riggin" and other nautical ditties. I was not with my crew. They were sergeants, and I was an officer. I slept in a two-person cabin with eight berths in it. They had more fun.

In due course we reached Liverpool, the port from which my father had left England for Canada thirty-four years before. We were marched off the ship and packed aboard trains to travel through the night to the reception center at Bournemouth, on the south coast. Late at night two men came through the coaches carrying a big container from which they ladled out stew. Later they came around with another container, saying, "For the cooks." We didn't know any better, so we filled this pot with money. The crew of the train obviously knew a bunch of naive newcomers when they saw them.

When we gathered a few days later on parade in Bournemouth, one of the men said that he had been listening to "Calais One," the German English-speaking propaganda radio station. The woman announcer had said, "Another group of Canadian airmen had just landed in Liverpool. Germany is not worried. The Luftwaffe will take care of half of them and the rest will kill themselves on motorcycles." We did not know how right she was.

CHAPTER THIRTEEN

Bournemouth, where the RCAF Reception Depot was located, was a seaside resort town. It was full of elderly retired generals, valleys turned into parks (they were called "chines,") and dozens of hotels. We were billeted in these hotels, which bore names like "Royal Bath," and usually had lofty ceilings, rococo exteriors, and the marks of luxury as viewed in the time of Edward VII. With two or three officers in a room, now equipped with spartan military furniture, living was quite pleasant.

Because it was a resort town, it was full of entertainment facilities. There were movie theatres, legitimate theatres, a pavilion in which a tea-dance was held every afternoon, a bath complex with an Olympic-sized swimming pool, libraries, and first class shops (not that there was much in them.) The chines were lovely places, all landscaped and filled with flower-beds, ponds filled with goldfish, and tree-shaded walks. The beach was blocked off with barbed wire and the approaches to it were decorated with skull-and-crossbone signs and the word "Mines," a heritage from the days when invasion was feared, but except for that Bournemouth was an ideal vacation spot.

For us it was very nearly a vacation. It took time for the military bureaucracy to find places for us in the war machine, and the brass kept us in a holding pattern until they did. We gathered in a car park or sometimes in a byroad for morning parades, and then were sent off to take classes in ship recognition, aircraft recognition, the history of the Battle of Britain, or some other aspect of Air Force lore. During the afternoon we were usually left to our own devices. Movies and the tea-dance were very popular.

I enjoyed going to the tea-dances, since the music, two years behind North America in keeping with British custom, was more to my taste than the latest music I had heard before I went overseas. I also found it easier to dance to. Although conscription of women for factory jobs was in full blast, there was a sprinkling of women,

72

all of them with highly exotic and slightly decayed good looks, available as dancing partners. I found out later that prostitutes were not conscripted for factory duty because they demoralized the other girls they had to bunk with. Wholesome girls in that pavilion were in rather short supply.

At intervals we were sent off for various courses. One of them took me to Oxford for two weeks, I where I stayed in a room which had been in use for five hundred years, and was as comfortable as when it had been built. I guess you can get used to anything. After two weeks, I was able to style myself a graduate of Oxford.

P/O Emmott, battle course, Sidmouth, Devon, 1943.

Later I was sent off to take part in a commando course at Sidmouth in Devon. We were quartered in a luxurious 19th-century manor house near the beach (which as usual was sown with mines.) When we entered the house for the first time we saw a cartoon clipped from "Punch" magazine tacked on the bulletin board. It showed a fearful little soldier standing in front of a chasm over which he was to swing himself with a rope, while an officer exhorted him, "There's nothing to it!" The officer's arm was in a sling.

The next morning we were paraded outside the entrance. The officer in charge said, "You will now meet Flight Lieutenant Entwhistle, who will be your chief instructor in commando tactics." Out marched an officer. His arm was in a sling.

We were marched around the Devon countryside with rifles on our shoulders, given training in estimating distances and in describing terrain. (The army has only two types of trees, pine trees and bushy-topped trees.) It was a lot of fun, in the open air exercising every muscle, and the only fly in the ointment was that we were always hungry, and since we were not on aircrew rations because we were not employed on aircrew duties, we never had enough to eat. We took to salting the bread and eating it to supplement the meals, which were mostly brussels sprouts. We did, however, have access to rough Devonshire cider, which was insidiously pleasant to drink and had a kick like a mule. We soon learned to treat rough cider with respect, especially after we drank too much of it during a break in a route march and had to march home in a state of grievous illness.

Ever since I had enlisted I had been exposed to bayonets, and had carried one for many months, but I had never been taught how to use it. One of the scheduled lessons was in bayonet fighting, and I was bloodthirsty enough to look forward to it. However, on that day I was told off to be the guinea pig for a group of WAAF trainee dental technicians taking an examination, because I had 32 teeth, unusual in England. I never learned how to bayonet.

While all this was going on, those of us who had come from Canada as fully-trained torpedo-bomber crews wondered what was happening to us. Some of the more bloodthirsty among us wanted to get into action a soon as possible, although I admit that I looked on another day in Bournemouth as another day of life. Then one day we were paraded and informed that RCAF Headquarters Overseas had seen fit to transfer us from Coastal Command to Bomber Command. We would all be sent to another OTU to learn how to fly in bomber aircraft at high altitude over land rather than in torpedo aircraft at low altitude over water.

It turned out that we had been trained as four-man crews, one pilot, one navigator-bombardier, and two wireless-operator air gunners, to crew Beaufort aircraft. The Beaufort was a fine aircraft, except that it was slow, unmaneuverable, underarmed, underpowered, would not hold height on one engine and was prone to engine failure. It had suffered such heavy losses on operations that it was pulled out of service, to be replaced by Beaufighters, which were faster, more maneuverable, more heavily armed and more reliable, but which needed a two-man crew, consisting of a pilot and a radio-operator navigator. The two WAG's were no longer needed, and our navigators were not radio-qualified. The most cost-effective way to recycle us was to send one of our WAGs to Coastal Command to fly with crews which for some reason or other needed another radioman, and to send the three remaining members of the crew to Bomber Command. On our way to operations we would pick up two gunners and a flight engineer, as well as a bomb aimer.

Nobody consulted us. However, on balance it turned out to be lucky for some of us. The additional training time meant that when we went onto operations we would be considerably more experienced than the average crew, straight out of flying training schools in Canada. Besides, the five-month training cycle at Bomber Command meant that we would not get onto operations until the next spring, missing the long dark nights when aircraft were sent on long and horribly-dangerous missions into Germany almost to the Polish border.

The additional time in the air was important. It meant that we had more time to become familiar with all the niceties of flying that are not taught in formal courses. We could make mistakes under conditions where we could learn from them and not die from them. We had time for in-flight actions to become automatic. We could gain that extra judgment that allowed us do assess the worth of an action instinctively and smell out errors. The losses of our group who had taken the torpedo OTU at Patricia Bay and then been sent to bombers were considerably below average.

We were sent to Pershore in Warwickshire, in the Vale of Avon where Shakespeare had been born. There we were given billets in Nissen huts and told to make ourselves comfortable. That in an RAF training station in 1943 was impossible.

The training aircraft were Wellingtons, twin-engined bombers which were built with geodetic frameworks covered by fabric. The geodetic frames were interlocking triangles of metal which were of the same design as Buckminster Fuller used to build arena domes at such places as Palomar College, California. The aircraft had a reputation for coming home despite shattering battle damage, but they had their shortcomings. On landing the tanks had to be switched from the mains to a small tank which contained forty gallons; unfortunately it was possible for an inexperienced airman to switch the fuel off completely instead of just switching tanks, with the result that both engines would quit during the landing and cause an inevitable crash. Between the rear turret and the wireless operator's position was a diamond-shaped hole around which it was necessary to step carefully when in flight. On more than one occasion an unwary crew-member had simply stepped through it and fallen to his death.

The OTU aircraft were war-weary ones which had been used on operational squadrons during the earlier years of the war, and they were not particularly well-maintained. This is not to be wondered at, since the mechanics were usually boys who had only a year's training or so. There were a good many mysterious crashes, which contributed to the fact that nine percent of the men who served in Bomber Command were killed in non-combat crashes, a high proportion of them at Operational Training Units.

Our instructors were tour-expired aircrew who had struggled through their own courses a year or two previously, survived a tour, and been posted for a tour of instructional duty. In keeping with military tradition they set up a pecking-order in which they kept us students in our places, reserving such amenities as comfortable billets and seats in the mess near the fire for themselves. I told myself they deserved their perks, but it irked me that they should kick us around the way they did, knowing that a good many of us had only months to live. We consoled ourselves that when we returned after our own tours we could inflict the same indignities upon our own juniors.

At Pershore we acquired a bomb-aimer and a rear gunner. Crews generally were allowed to sort themselves out at OTU, pilots, navigators, bomb-aimers, gunners and wireless operators milling around in some common gathering-place until they coalesced by some occult means into crews. We arrived as partial crews, however, and there were some bomb-aimers left over from a previous course, and we were simply issued one per crew to bring us up to strength. The same was true of gunners. We received Bob Bamford from Montreal as our bomb-aimer, and Neil Burgess from the West Coast as our rear gunner. We must have been a good crew; we all survived. Later, at our next unit, the Heavy Conversion Unit where we would be introduced to four-engine aircraft, we would pick up a flight engineer and a mid-upper gunner.

Our quarters at Pershore were quite a comedown from the luxury hotel we had occupied in Bournemouth. We lived in cement-block Nissen huts, lined up in rows near the instructional school. The buildings unfortunately were not inherited from the Crimean war, as building standards had deteriorated since then. All the buildings looked the same, and airmen in their cups often continually staggered into the wrong one by mistake. Indeed, one night another pilot on the course stumbled into the building occupied by my pilot, my bomb-aimer and myself, threw himself down on a bed, and then under the influence of hydrostatic pressure, arose and urinated on some clothes of Jim Linklater, who had laid them on the floor for lack of a better place to put them. When Jim came in a little later hell understandably broke loose.

The huts were heated by British stoves. Britons complain about their weather, which actually is mild and often pleasant. Their difficulty with personal comfort stems from the fact that their winter is not cold enough.

Because Britons, even in Scotland, do not freeze to death in the winter if their houses are poorly heated, they do not heat them properly. Canadians, who do freeze to death if the house gets cold, keep warm in the winter. It came as a shock to Canadians in England during the war to find how drafty and generally miserable the buildings were.

The root of the problem lay in the unshakeable English belief that fireplaces will heat houses.

Fireplaces are good to look at while one is sitting down, holding a drink in one hand and petting the cat with the other, or while hunched up chin on fist while dreamily listening to muted music, and they come in handy for burning scraps of garbage or roasting chestnuts. But they will not heat a house worth a hoot. All the pioneers, once exposed to Canadian winters, always blocked up fireplaces and installed stoves.

The officers' messes always had great manorial fireplaces, but they were always surrounded by senior officers standing with their hands out to the fire or their backs to it with the tails of their jackets spread wide. I was a junior officer, however, and I never got near the fire. Our quarters were little rooms, each of which was heated by a tiny stove.

The stoves were a tribute to the English belief that a stove, even if not actually a fireplace, should at least look like one. They were squat devices, with the front left open to expose the fire. The chimney was placed squarely in the middle of the top, cleverly designed to make balancing a can or a kettle to heat water for cocoa or coffee impossible, and also to make sure it conducted most of the heat straight out of the room. The stoves theoretically burnt coal, but a frugal RAF did not give us any, except once in a while apparently by mistake. A good deal of our time was spent in a frantic search for anything that would burn. Each room had a washhandstand (the official nomenclature) inherited from a standard officer's equipment list as used in the War of the Spanish Succession. It was made of wood, and few of them survived a winter. We did not need them anyway, since we had ablution rooms where the water was actually sometimes hot.

There was a station coal-pile, but it was fenced off, guarded and whitewashed to expose the depredations of thieves. We never managed to steal any coal. At one time several grand old English oaks were cut down to clear the approaches to one of the runways, and we descended upon them to try to chop off some firewood. Unfortunately all we had was a tiny hatchet (called a 'chopper' in England) and the trees were of the kind of wood used to build sailing warships, impervious to shot and shell. All we could hack off were a few twigs.

Even if we managed to find something to burn, the problem was to light the stove. The fact that the front of the stove was open kept the fire from getting a draft. We started the fire by placing a newspaper over the open front, kneeling down, and blowing our lungs out at the feeble flame. As long as we puffed, the flame would burn, but the moment we stopped it died. At intervals it would flare up and set fire to the screening newspaper, which would blaze up and disintegrate, shooting showers of burning paper all over the room while the occupants took up a frantic dance as they put them out, trying to keep from getting holes burnt in their uniforms.

The stoves also lay in wait for the unwary. A stray ember at the bottom of the pile of coal, twigs or screwed-up paper in the grate would lie quietly, contemptuous of our huffing and puffing, until we left in defeat and despair, and then blaze up merrily after everyone had gone. When it got going, the stove would glow cherry-red, and there was no way to damp it down to economize on our hoarded fuel until it burned itself out, to leave the room as glacial as before.

One evening our crew tried to warm up our hut. We had managed to scrounge a little aviation gasoline, which we poured over our collection of twigs, slate disguised as coal, and pieces of a board of a packing crate which we had found on the roadway, and puffed at it until our faces were red and our lungs bursting. Nothing worked. We gave up and crawled into bed.

At two in the morning that buried ember burst into flame and set fire to the rest of the fuel. The stove grew red-hot and the temperature in the room reached tropical levels. We threw off our bedclothes and lay soaking up the grateful heat until we went back to dreamless sleep. After an hour the fire burnt itself out, the temperature plunged, and we woke up in the morning shivering furiously. We all caught colds except the bomb-aimer, who caught pneumonia.

Meanwhile the Englishmen seemed impervious to cold. In the morning we would see the men of the RAF Regiment (the ground-defence men who were called "rock apes" by their comrades) jogging about at military exercises in their shirtsleeves, while we Canadians, used to cold weather, huddled in our greatcoats, perishing with the cold. We understood then why the British have always done well as Arctic explorers.

Later during my stay at Pershore I rode my bicycle to the local village. There at the railway station I saw crates piled on the platform. They were filled with a shipment of those same misbegotten stoves, manufactured in the village, and on their way to other RAF stations. I gave up hope that efficient stoves would ever be introduced into the Royal Air Force. The brass considered that they would rot the men's characters.

CHAPTER FOURTEEN

We lived through the winter at Pershore, and were graduated along with the rest of our course, having lost nobody, though Wellington OTU's were notorious for fatal crashes in training. Two or three crews had been lost from other courses which had trained at Pershore at the same time we did, but we had been lucky.

We went from Pershore to No. 1659 Heavy Conversion Unit at Dalton in Yorkshire, where we learned to fly four-engined Halifax aircraft. For a navigator things did not change much, since a navigation training trip was the same no matter what kind of aircraft was doing it. But we did pick up our flight engineer, Ron Ashelford, a member of the Royal Air Force, who came from Jersey in the Channel Islands but had been working in London, and our mid-upper gunner, Gordon Adams from Thunder Bay in western Ontario. We now had a complete seven-man crew.

We were quartered in a Nissen hut which was the coldest place I have ever lived in. We had to sleep in our flying suits, and even then we were cold. When we complained we found that the housing was under control of the army, who said, "You Air Force types are hothouse flowers," and told us that in comparison to soldiers who had to sleep under hedges we were living in luxury. We consoled ourselves with the thought that it was March and the winter would not last forever.

At the HCU we met evidence that we were getting closer to the sausage machine. One of our instructors was a sergeant air gunner who had survived a tour on bombers, and who said that he was looking forward to repatriation to Canada, but "Not ops again—not that!" shivering as he said it. We knew in the back of our minds that we were going in harm's way, but we had resolutely kept the thought there. Now we were forced to look the facts in the face. Nobody mentioned it; nobody talked about our chances of survival, although the grim butcher's bills coming in from the night raids on Germany were reported in the newspapers every morning. In any case discussion of the odds against us would have been bad form, although they were in the forefront of everyone's mind. We took heart from the fact that so far we had survived two Operational Training Units, with none of us falling by the wayside, and we trusted in our luck.

In due course, graduated from Heavy Conversion Unit, checked out as trained crews for Halifax heavy bombers, we were gathered in a crew-room to hear our fate, and to be told where we were to be sent. As we sat and waited I noticed a man from my previous home town in British Columbia, Fernie, who had come as an air gunner via a different route to the HCU. He had been an eight-year-old when I had been thirteen or so, and I had looked on him as a little kid. Now here he was, getting up from his chair to poke at some balls on a miniature pool table in the crew room. As I saw him get up I had the sensation that I was an observer, watching him and watching myself at a ceremony performing some strange ritual, almost like a sleep-walker in a dream, and the impression came over me that he was doomed. Three months later I saw his name in a casualty list. Then somebody called the names of our crew, and the moment passed. From then on it was a matter of putting one foot in front of the other, as I imagine soldiers going into battle have done since time immemorial.

Bomber Squadron No.433, RCAF.

81

Halifax aircraft of No.433 Squadron, with ground crew, Skipton-on -Swale, Yorkshire, 1944.

We were posted to No.433 Squadron based at Skipton-on-Swale, a little village about five miles from a medium-sized village called Thirsk, which in turn was twenty miles from York. 433 Squadron was the last bomber squadron to be formed in No.

6 Bomber Group, the Canadian group of Bomber Command. It had no particular prestige, no distinguished alumni, and no particular coverage in the Canadian press. The Officer Commanding was an Englishman, since few Canadians had achieved enough rank and experience to be sent to command squadrons.

The station held two squadrons, 433 and 424. 424 was an older squadron which had served in the Western Desert, and had been around since October 1942. It had more seniority, more "time in," and its members let us know that we were the new kids on the block. The hardened aircrew on our own squadron were distant at first, although friendly enough, in the style we had become familiar with during our aircrew careers; every time we changed stations we were rookies again. There was no particular ceremony as we reported for duty. New crews came in nickels' and dimes' worths, and were welcomed with forms to fill in and that was all.

RCAF Station, Skipton-on-Swale, Yorkshire, 1944.

We were given quarters in cement-block buildings which were spartan in the extreme. There were no lockers, but there was a length of water pipe upon which coat-hangers could be hung to keep our uniforms. Theoretically we were entitled to batman service, but the batmen (usually batwomen) were few and far between, and we polished our own shoes. It seemed a bit unfair to me. When I had been an AC2 I had been set to work to polish officers' shoes, and now that I was an officer myself the rules had changed. Still, there was a war on. I considered it unwise to complain, since my crew-mates were violently democratic, and considered that nobody should have to shine anybody else's shoes. In retrospect, they were probably right. The officers' mess was a Nissen hut too, but it was comfortable enough.

Once on the squadron we were introduced to radar. The set was called H2S, a number of fanciful reasons being given for the name; it turned out that it was just another abstruse code-word designed to keep the set's existence secret as long as possible. It became our prime navigational aid, and was largely responsible for the improvement in bombing accuracy that occurred in 1944. It also served to alert the German night-fighters to our presence, and to home onto us from fifty-five miles. Mercifully we did not know this at the time.

We did some cross-country flights to get us used to the aircraft, and then Jim Linklater flew his second-dickey war-experience flight with an older crew. A couple of days later I walked down to the navigation section as I did every morning. The navigation leader spoke to me as I entered, gesturing at a blackboard. "You're on tonight." The name "Linklater" was written on the order of battle for the night's operations. I looked at him without surprise but with something approaching shock. "We are, eh?" I answered, trying to look nonchalant. "I was wondering when we'd start."

"This is your first op, isn't it?"

"Yeah. Guess I'll know all about it this time tomorrow."

"You're not kidding. Well, see you at briefing."

I walked over to the flight office. The rest of the crew was already there, standing with strange, self-conscious, half-unconcerned smiles. Linklater looked at me and grinned half-heartedly. "Guess you already know, eh?"

"Yeah. Where are we going?"

"You'll know before we do. You go to the navigator's briefing an hour early."

"I guess so."

"We better go out to the kite and check everything," Linklater said. "It's V-Victor."

We cycled out to the dispersal pan where the big black Halifax was waiting. As we set about our various businesses, the warm rather sickly-sweet and vaguely unpleasant odour of gasoline and spilled oil and ether-smelling hydraulic fluid was strong in our nostrils until its very prevalence familiarized it into oblivion.

Linklater and Ron Ashelford, our flight engineer, held a conference regarding the engines. The wireless operator (a spare for this operation, since Frank Russell, our regular WAG, was temporarily out of commission) was seated behind his radios, checking out all the dials. Bob Bamford, the bomb-aimer, checked the H2S and the bombsight. Gord Adams, the mid—upper gunner, climbed into his turret and began to clean the perspex, stretching to reach the awkward corners. Neil Burgess, the rear gunner, checked his four Brownings. I checked the distant-reading compass and made sure the Gee box worked.

Linklater called down to me. "All your stuff OK?"

"Yes—so far."

He leaned down from his lever-enclosed position. "Say—make sure you get outa the way in a hurry if I say "Bale out! All you're gonna see of me is a whoosh!"

Bamford laughed. "I'll be outa there before you take time to finish the sentence."

The WAG looked out from behind his radios. "That's all I'm going to hear. If we get out of this kite you're going to see something move faster'n lightning."

"Remember, " I reminded them, "I get out first."

"Don't be so cheerful," said Ashelford.

We climbed out of the aircraft and cycled back to the flight office. By some unspoken agreement we talked of the armament, of the equipment, of the aircraft, but never of the risks we were about to share. Link was a little more matter-of-fact than the rest of us. He had already undergone his baptism of fire.

At 5:30 I reported for my navigator's briefing, held earlier because we had more work to do, working out tracks and distances and working out the take-off time by computing backwards from the Time on Target. We found we were going to bomb a railway marshalling yard in the suburbs of Paris called Noisy-le-Sec. Compared to a trip over Germany it was rather like a visit to the nursery slopes. The really stiff opposition was over Germany, not over France.

Our maps prepared, we began on our flight plans, pencilling in the tracks we had measured between turning points and the distances between them. At 6:30 we joined the rest of the crews in the main briefing room. The squadron commander welcomed us, and then the chief pilot lectured the pilots, the flight engineer leader spoke to the flight engineers, the wireless leader laid down the law to the WAGs, the gunnery leader told the gunners to "keep 100% watch at all times," and the bombing leader told the bomb-aimers what kind of pathfinder markers they would be expected to aim at. We navigators had already been talked at by the navigation leader, Don Simpson. The meteorologist briefed us on what the winds were going to be, and we worked out the headings to fly. I religiously worked out the wind to the closest degree for my flight-plan. Later I found that the wind could only be estimated to the closest twenty degrees or so, but I was young and keen. The intelligence officer went over the dangerous spots to avoid. "There are approximately fifty guns here..." A nervous laugh went round the room and some of the men squirmed in their seats.

In a moment of calm a man named Hatcher came up to me and shook my hand. I remembered him from my ground-crew days at Patricia Bay where he had been a corporal storekeeper in one of the squadrons on the station; we had been reasonably friendly—at least as friendly as a flight sergeant could be with a corporal. He had remustered to aircrew about the same time had, but had not followed my torturous course to battle, but had gone straight to bomber command to do a tour, followed by six months as an instructor. Now he was on his second tour. He was a happy, debonair chap who enjoyed life and had not an enemy in the world.

"Paris," he told me, "a piece of cake. There is no flak there to speak of, and the Jerries will keep their fighters in Germany—they don't give a damn if Paris gets bombed. Not like my first tour—the targets were really hot there."

I looked at him with deep respect. We were both flying officers now, but he was a battle-tested veteran with a tour behind him while I was still a sprog. I treated him as my superior, which indeed he was. But seeing him there, I took heart. He had survived a tour, and if he could so could I. Then the briefing officers called us back to attention, and we parted.

The briefing over, the crews lined up for their operational supper; eggs and bacon, which we never received at any other time. As the queue moved up to the counter, there was an undertone of tension, of grimness, in the banter that was being exchanged. I had expected some of the light-hearted skylarking I had read about in books about World War I. There was none. Here and there some men made feeble jokes. A few made grinning references to the *Stalags*, the German prison camps. Nobody spoke of death; nobody mentioned any of those who had stood in this identical spot a few days before and had not come back, but we were thinking of them.

I found that I could eat my meal with queer relish, despite the fact that a few hours before I had had absolutely no appetite. When I finished my big mug of tea I muttered, "Better get going," and went off to the briefing room to make a few last-minute preparations. I put on my flying clothing carefully, undoing my collar and loosening my tie as a last touch.

We climbed into the back of a lorry, driven by a WAAF who ground the gears as she started. As she had come around to the back to shut the door, there was a quick babble as the men gave the letters of the aircraft at which she should stop. "P-Peter—O-Oboe."

Our crew got out and clumped together under the port wing of the aircraft, all puffing cigarettes but me. I followed the rest of them in the ritual of urinating on the tailwheel. Everybody did it; omitting to do so would have been an offence against unwritten air force law. The padre came around, handing out cigarettes. The squadron commander came round to wish us luck.

Linklater flipped away his cigarette and climbed into the aircraft, which suddenly took on the aspect of some prehistoric monster engorging its brood. We went to our positions. The pilot started the engines, the flight engineer at his side. "Starboard outer! Port Outer! Starboard inner! Port inner!" All four propellors vanished as one by one the engines coughed, spat out a gollop of black smoke, and steadied down to their familiar roar. The bomb-aimer buckled himself into the jump seat beside the pilot. The wireless operator and I took up our seats in the rest position behind the pilot. "In case the kite crashes! What a happy thought!"

A green eye winked at us from the control van, parked near the end of a runway. Linklater pushed the throttles open and the Halifax began to waddle to the take-off position. The eye winked again, and the aircraft suddenly became a thing of grace as the wheels left the ground. "Wheels! Brakes!" Linklater called, and Bamford applied the brakes and retracted the undercarriage. Suddenly I was happy; we were embarked on the mission for which we had been trained. I crawled forward to the navigation position in the nose and pencilled the take-off time in my log. "Your first course is one sixty true—one six zero true."

"One six zero true it is," Linklater confirmed, and I plunged into the mass of work, a crowding successions of jobs that had to be performed desperately against time, leaving me no time to think of anything else. I turned to the Gee set to get my first fix. That was when things started to go wrong.

The Gee set was a radio navigation aid which depended on a master station on the ground sending out a pulse of energy which was picked up by three slave stations, each of which then sent out pulses of its own. The pulses were received by the aircraft, and displayed on a cathode-ray tube, the ancestor of the TV tube. After a series of calculations position lines were plotted on a special multi-coloured map and a fix obtained where they crossed. I had never had trouble with as Gee set before, but this time the information given made no sense at all.

I leaned over to Bob Bamford. "Can you get me fix with the H2S?"

"I'll try." Then he shook his head. "I can't pick up a specific town— we're flying over the industrial part of England; it's all built up, and I can't tell one town from another." I looked at his radar screen. It was a plate of mush.

"What's wrong?" Linklater asked.

"The Gee-box is unserviceable."

"What are you going to do?"

"Fly my flight plan courses until I can get an H2S fix."

"Okay." Jim never said much in the air.

We flew down the length of England, Bob and I trying to make sense out of the radar picture. We turned north of London to head for the continent. The coast came into view on the H2S set, but not clearly enough to let me fix my position. We flew out over the North Sea. The enemy coast appeared on the radar, and I saw two cities come up. I looked at my map, and jumped to the conclusion that they were Calais and Dunkirk, and that we would fly between them—almost on track. A load fell from my shoulders. Suddenly I knew where we were, and I could navigate the rest of the way to the target with confidence.

I gave the pilot a new heading to steer. Then Bob jabbed my arm. "Those cities weren't Calais and Dunkirk—they were Dunkirk and Ostend!"

I looked at the radar screen. He was right; I had misidentified the blobs on the screen. Bob and I conferred quickly, and then I replotted our position and gave Linklater another heading change. We headed back onto track. Suddenly the aircraft bumped, and Link said, "Slipstream." We were back in the bomber stream. I worked frantically to correct my log, find a wind I could trust, check my ETA at the target, and get things back on the rails.

"That's the target ahead," said Bob as he picked up Paris on the radar. "I'd better go ahead into the nose to drop the bombs." He pushed the curtains aside and disappeared as he crouched over his bombsight. I checked the ETA. We would be over the target in a few minutes.

"I can see the target indicators," Link's voice came. "I've got 'em," Bob answered. We swung onto the final course for the run-in over the target. "Left-left—steady," Bob's voice came, as soon as Link reported "Bomb doors open." I stayed at my table, working frantically .

I called up Linklater to give him the course out of the target. Bob's voice came, "Bombs gone!" as the plane lifted when the bombload fell free. We swung north out of the target area, and then turned west, back towards England.

"Wasn't much," Linklater commented laconically. "Hardly any flak, no fighters." We flew through the night, the gunners swinging their turrets, Link and Ashelford swivelling their heads as they searched for prowling fighters. The coast came up before us, and the enemy territory fell behind us. We relaxed.

We headed up towards Yorkshire again, with me depending on the H2S for navigation. As long as we knew where we were we could distinguish between the blobs of light on the screen and tell which blob meant which city. After a while I turned on the Gee and plotted a fix. It was in the right place. After its rebellion earlier it was working perfectly now. I treated it with reserve, but after several fixes had proved correct I used it to home over the station, and we came back right over the runway.

Flying control stacked us up, and we circled the field, with the wireless operator and me in the rest position. We landed and trundled off to our dispersal, where a lorry picked us up to return us to the briefing room. We were given big cups of coffee—terrible coffee—laced with rum as we waited to be questioned by the intelligence officer.

"It was a pretty easy trip," a group of us said as we drank our coffee.

"We lost a kite, though."

"One of 424's kites came back with a machine gun stuck in the H2S blister. Mid-air collision."

We nodded, each of us guiltily thinking, "Better them than us." We were interrogated, and then went back to the mess for our post-operational meal; bacon and eggs again. I was too keyed up to sleep for a while, but when I finally drifted off I slept like a log.

The next morning we found that the serial number of the machine gun found in the aircraft H2S blister verified that it had been a 433 squadron aircraft which had gone down over Paris.

One of the crew had been Hatcher, my old ground-crew friend who had been relieved that last night's trip would be an easy one.

We had received our baptism of fire. I had never looked out; I still had not seen flak-bursts or bomb-bursts or fighter flares or tracers. But I had been blooded.

The crew discussed the trip when we got together. "Pretty easy trip after we got organized," I said.

"Shaky at the end," said Linklater. "The hydraulics packed up and we had to land with the bomb-doors open."

I nodded sagely. Sitting relaxed in the rest position after I had navigated the aircraft home, I had known nothing about it. It would have done me no good if I had. Anyway, that was the department of Linklater and Ashelford.

CHAPTER FIFTEEN

Shipton-on-Swale, 1944.

Our second trip came two days later. When we went out to the aircraft—V-Victor once more—we saw that the armourers were loading 500-pound bombs again, and this indicated that we would be attacking a French target. It was a relief; German targets were far more desperately defended. My navigator's briefing confirmed this. Our target was the railway marshalling yard at Lens, which had been the scene of one of the battles of the World War I. Although nobody told us, the bomber war was changing from German cities to smashing up the French railway system in preparation for the Normandy invasion.

After our briefing we went out to V-Victor, where we gathered under the wing after Link and Ashelford had completed their ritual walk-around inspection of the aircraft. When it was time to climb aboard, I said, "Once more into the breach, dear friends," misquoting from Shakespeare's *Henry the Fifth*. I was careful to leave out the next line, which had to do with filling the breach with English dead. Nobody recognized the quotation.

The moment we took off I ducked under the legs of Bob Bamford who was sitting in the jump seat beside Linklater and acting as second pilot, to start navigating the aircraft the moment I could spread out my maps; I did not want to see my difficulties of the previous flight occur again. But the Gee set worked perfectly, the radar fixes that Bob got me agreed with the Gee fixes, and the aircraft stayed on track. We had been hectored to keep on track, since that concentrated the bomber stream and got us through defence zones quickly with no isolated aircraft as easy meat for fighters. Everything was going well. Except for hearing Link say, "Look at that crazy bugger—left his navigation lights on. Somebody always does that," nothing untoward happened. The wind changed over the Channel and we had to increase our airspeed to stay on time, but that was a minor adjustment.

We crossed the French coast and flew on. Over France I was in control of things well enough to stand up and climb up the steps that led to the wireless operator's compartment. For the first time I looked out over enemy territory. There were a couple of search-lights probing the sky, but they were miles away, white beams of light that wavered slowly back and forth in a dignified dance. They seemed anything but threatening. The Halifax flew steadily on-ward, undulating slowly as the gunners swung their turrets first one way and then the other as they kept up their search of the skies for enemy fighters. I knew there were fighters aloft, hunting for us with murder in their hearts, but the consciousness never soaked in. I was happy standing there looking out at the French countryside beneath, dark and remote and seemingly peaceful.

After a few minutes I went back to my position in the nose and resumed my navigation. As we neared the target I remembered a conversation with a tour-expired navigator who had told me that he always put on his parachute over the target, in case the aircraft blew up. That happened frequently enough, when an anti-aircraft shell exploded the bomb load. Lens was ahead, so I reached over to the stowage near my left hand on the bulkhead, took the para-chute pack out of the elastic bungee cords that held it in place, and clipped it onto my harness. When Bob ducked through the curtains to reach his bombsight I turned out my light, pulled the curtains aside, and stood looking out at the scene ahead. I could see the multi-coloured target indicators, the occasional pin-pricks of light that were flak guns firing at us, the bright splashes of light from the bomb-bursts. I stood fascinated for perhaps five minutes. Then Bob said, "Bombs gone!" and I had to go back to work.

We went in at 4500 feet, low enough for light flak guns to shoot at us. Rumour had it that the Germans had rolled up a train of flak-guns mounted on railway cars. They were giving us a hot reception. The light guns fired tracers. The red and white balls of light rose leisurely from the ground, and then sped up ferociously as they passed us. After the war, when I was driving along a highway with lanes divided by a dashed white line, I would look in the rearview mirror of my car and see the white dots flashing away behind me. They looked just like the tracer shells did after they had passed us.

Linklater told the debriefing officer that we had seen one fighter, but we were not attacked. One of our thousand-pound bombs hung up, and when we landed that night we found that one of the five-hundred-pounders had not gone either. Of course, if we had ground-looped on landing the plane would have gone up in a beautiful blast of explosive. But that would not have been my responsibility. My navigation had been good, and I was happy.

We had a day without operations, although we were sent on a practice cross-country, and then we were on the battle-order again. When we went out to check the aircraft we found the ground-crew winching a 2000-pound "cookie" aboard, with cans of incendiaries to go with it. We knew we would be going to a German target, where the opposition would be far greater that we had met in bombing railway targets in France. One of the ground-crew looked at me as I peered into the bomb-bay. "Strictly women and kids tonight, eh?" I nodded without answering. The butterflies started churning in my stomach.

The target was Dusseldorf. My navigation was good, and we stayed on track all the way. When I slipped on my parachute and looked out at the target the sight of the city below in flames fascinated me. There were big patches of flame from the fires already started, with bursts of light from the bombs, smaller white eyes winking from the flak guns firing at us, and a myriad of twinkling lights which were the incendiary bombs catching hold, mixed with the Christmas-tree ornament red and green target indicators.

Around us were bursts of light from exploding flak shells. Just as we were running up to the target a blast jolted the Halifax upward fifty feet, and the sky was filled from horizon to horizon with a blinding flash. An aircraft directly below us had been hit by a flak-burst which exploded its bombs, and it blew up in mid-air.

We dropped our two-thousand-pounder, with the boxes of incendiaries that fell apart in mid-air and dropped hundreds of small incendiary bombs on the city below, and turned north to leave the target. I had just given Linklater the course to fly to get us back home when the urgent voice of the mid-upper gunner came, "Fighter starboard quarter—corkscrew starboard—GO!" Linklater kicked the rudder and shoved the nose down and went into his spiral evasive action, turning thirty degrees and pulling out five hundred feet lower, turning sixty degrees back the other way, climbing to regain the height he had lost, and then repeating the maneuver, all the time chanting what he was doing to make sure he ended back on the right course. "He's lost us," the gunner reported. We straightened out. I went back to my navigation. Bob Bamford crawled back from the nose and seated himself in front of the H2S set. The wireless operator continued to sit just behind me on the steps to the main fuselage, stuffing bundles of aluminum-plated strips—"window" to us and "chaff" to the Americans—to confuse ground radars. Now and again Linklater would check with the gunners to make sure that they were alert, and at intervals he and Ashelford had a brief technically-worded discussion about the aircraft. We had begun to vibrate badly, although we had no apparent damage. Except for the rasp and burble of the gunners' breaths—they left their intercom switches on at all times—the intercom was quiet.

One of our thirteen cans of incendiaries hung up. Linklater shook some of the little bombs loose just after we crossed the Dutch coast, but the rest stayed in the bomb bay. We lost height slowly over England, until at ten thousand feet, Bamford, Linklater and Ashelford took off their oxygen masks and lit up cigarettes. I could navigate by Gee, and Bob did not need to feed me any more radar fixes. The gunners had to stay in their turrets, alert, but the wireless operator could stop throwing out window and get back to his radio sets. I had to work as hard as ever.

We landed, turned in our parachutes and our escape packets filled with benzedrine, chocolate, French and German money,

For bogus documents
(if sho t down), 1943.

maps of Europe, and little phrase-books which were doled out to aircrew before each flight and carefully collected after. We also carried passport-sized photographs of ourselves in civilian clothing, so that the underground could make up phoney documents for us if we had to bail out and evaded capture. I carried a pencil with a compass built into it; in a moment of carelessness I used it to navigate with, and it broke at the compass.

We usually flew in battle dress, with a heavy sweater under it. Our flying boots were knee-high, with tops that could be ripped off to make the bottoms look like ordinary Oxfords, except that they were big and clumsy. I doubt if they fooled the Germans. We also wore whistles tied to our battle-dress collars, to attract attention if we had to ditch and were floating around in dinghies in the dark. For a few trips I carried my revolver, which I had learned to shoot fairly well when I was a sergeant, but then I decided it would only get me into trouble if I was shot down, and I left it at home.

At debriefing we were asked if we had seen any flares at sea—Verey lights from ditched crews. Linklater reported one or two, which I had carefully logged, with their positions. After my tour was over I discussed the matter with Air-Sea Rescue crews, who were forever being sent to search for dinghies after lights had been reported at sea; they practically never found anything. Later I wondered if those incendiaries we had jettisoned had led some other bomber crew to report lights, which were religiously searched for. The Air-Sea Rescue boys always moaned when they were briefed to look for "flares reported by Bomber Command."

Nonchalantly confident of myself, I was talking to another navigator, newly arrived at the squadron, in our dormitory. Linklater was lying on his bed at the other side of the room. "You know," I said grandly, "When we were over Dusseldorf I could hear the bombs going off in the city beneath us."

Linklater sat up. "You clot!" he hissed at me. "That was flak!"

With three trips under our belts, we felt we had some time in. We were a good crew; we could put the bombs where they belonged. The next trip taught us differently.

CHAPTER SIXTEEN

Everything was routine on our way to Mannheim for our fourth operation, with our regular wireless operator, Frank Russell, back with us. The gunners turned on their oxygen on the ground, and as soon as we were airborne Neil Burgess said, "Better turn on your mike, Gordy," to the mid-upper. The scratchy neutral background noise of the intercom was drowned out by the magnified wheeze and gurgle of their breathing. My Gee set worked perfectly down the length of England and over the North Sea as we approached the Dutch coast. The green match-sticks marched across the face of my Gee indicator, changing appearance on command as I followed the sequence of settings needed to get a reading. I looked out as we crossed the English coastline, to see it lying below us like the lace edge of a crumpled handkerchief.

The German radio interference stretched out toward us until the Gee signals were submerged in a sea of 'railings.' I computed what the readings should have been and moved the 'pedestals' on the display along the base line to where the signals should have been, and a couple of times I was able to eke out another fix, but then the indicator was hopelessly blocked by solid interference. I turned my head toward Bob Bamford, who was twirling the multifarious knobs on his H2S set. "Gimme a fix, Bob," I said.

He handed me a scrap of paper. I looked at it, plotted the fix on my map, and handed the paper back. A couple of minutes later I thumbed my microphone and said to Link, "We're two minutes early. I'll have to dogleg to waste time. Alter sixty degrees starboard—now."

The pilot wrestled the plane into the time-wasting maneuver. We felt ourselves shoved roughly down into our seats as centrifugal force multiplied our weight, and I felt my hand too heavy to lift as I tried to print something in my log. I waited for the aircraft to straighten out.

"How're we doin', navigator?" Link asked.

"Not bad. We're bang on track, and within half a minute of our timing at the concentration point. That means we'll cross the Dutch coast at the right place."

"Good show." The intercom went back to its faithful transmission of the unnoticed sigh and puff of the gunners' breaths.

The enemy coast lay before us, a long, slightly-curving white line that the pilot and flight engineer could see, but was hidden from Bob and me as we sat blind behind our blackout curtains. Bob twirled his knobs. "You're all right, Norm," he told me.

On either side of us a sparkle at our altitude with a glow beneath it told of German flak pumping up at other aircraft. "Are you sure we're on track, Norm?" Link's anxious voice came. "We're heading straight for that stuff to starboard of where we ought to go in."

"Yeah. We gotta seventy-mile-an-hour wind, though, and that gives us fifteen degrees of drift. The wind'll blow us over far enough to miss it even if we seem to be heading straight for it."

"Okay," Link replied, assent making a poor try at hiding the anxiety in his voice. "Didn't know there was such a strong wind."

V-Victor flew on through the velvet darkness. Sure enough, the two defended areas with their livid excrescence of gunfire passed slowly and safely on either side, while ahead of them stretched blackness unrelieved by the faintest glow of light. The carefully-plotted route we were to follow tonight avoided all the hot spots. As long as V-Victor stayed on track flak would hardly be more than a worry until we neared the target.

Beside me Bob was wriggling about, tugging at a strap on his parachute harness. Eyes still glued on his green disc of light, he pushed down in his narrow seat, shrugged and shook his shoulders, and settled himself or another hour. He was just pulling down his heavy sweater when his hands left his chest as if they had been scalded.

"Hey!" he exclaimed, "my H2S here's gone for a Burton!" The green glow of the strange eye leapt into emerald flame before him and then collapsed into a tiny afterglow which slowly faded to total darkness. He twisted and pulled at knobs and switches with hurried, nervous fingers.

"Engineer—go and see if the generator's still working for this thing—I can't get a spark out of it."

There was a brief silence as Ron Ashelford crawled to the generator housing with a flashlight. Finally his panting voice came over the wire. "You've had it, Bob—the whole lead to your receiver is burnt in half. Can't do anything to fix it here."

"Oh boy—this'll be fun," I said. "Looks like we're going from here to Mannheim and back on astro and intuition."

"How about your Gee-box?" asked the pilot.

"The Germans jammed that long ago. Won't be any good to me until we cross the coast on the way out."

"Are we on track now?"

"Yes—bang on when we crossed the coast. I've got a pretty good wind so far, and according to the met man it won't change much to the target. The trouble is it's a lot different from the forecast wind, and with a seventy-mile-an-hour wind a small error in my estimate will make a great big screaming error in position."

"God—what a happy thought! How about direction-finding radio?"

"Ain't got some. They took out the equipment to make room for the H2S that just went for the big hairy chop."

"Hope your intuition works right." The pilot switched off his microphone and left me to my calculations.

"Can you get me a pinpoint, Bob?" I asked.

Bob pushed through the curtains to the nose. His answer came shortly. "Hopeless. Hundred per cent cloud cover."

"Okay. How about an astro shot?"

"You've had that too, Norm," the pilot's voice broke in. "Can't see the stars. There's a layer of cloud at about 25000— four thousand feet higher than we are."

"Can't you climb over them?"

"Not with bombs on."

"Oh joy, oh ecstasy! Okay—I'll go on there on dead reckoning and the old wet finger." I turned to the wireless operator, as if I could see him through the aircraft structure. "Hello wireless operator. Be sure and give me those broadcast winds Bomber Command Headquarters is sending out every half hour. They're the only navigational aid I have."

"You bet I will, Norm."

I kept drawing lines on my chart and computing courses. My big problem was the wind; the fickle, changing, heart-breaking wind that never stayed the same for a quarter of an hour. And the course was not straight either; my route, from which I was not supposed to deviate by more than three miles, or be in error by more than four minutes in timing, doglegged all over Holland and Germany to avoid defended areas. My signposts, the stars, were hidden behind the clouds, which were getting thicker and uglier and more ice-laden all the time. Halifax aircrew had no de-icing equipment; some boffin had calculated that the extra weight would reduce our bombload, which would lengthen the war. Link and Ron carried on a brief, worried conversation about the ice. Since I had my own worries, I scarcely heard them.

I drew a little square on my map; it was perhaps half an inch from my red-pencilled track lines. I plunged into an ocean of figures and emerged with a new course. The plane swung onto it and levelled out. Jiggling and slewing slightly as the gunners swung their turrets, the plane flew on through the gloom. Now and then the dim shape of one of the scattered clouds slid up to us and broke in misty vagueness against the pilot's windscreen, hiding the view of the night's nothingness with a cloak that was darker than the darkness. The advance guards of the great cloud-bank ahead began to draw together until they were brushing against the plane's camouflaged sides in steady ghostly succession.

"That cloud's buildin' up pretty thick," said Link. "We better try to climb over it now that we've used a few hundred gallons of petrol."

"Okay," I answered. "Tell me when you level off—I'll have to dream up a different wind and figure out a new course."

The plane nosed up to a different angle of attack and began to fight its way up to the clearer air above the clouds. "Levelling off—23000." Link reported.

"Can we see the stars yet?"

"No—we're still under cirrus clouds."

"I see. Alter course six degrees starboard—now."

"Six it is—starboard."

The plane slewed briefly and then droned on as before.

"Look skipper—the next course is up to the target. According my D.R. we're okay— but keep your eyes open in case I'm off track."

"I'm going into the nose," the bomb-aimer said. He turned down the lights in our compartment and crawled through the curtains, putting up the collapsible padded bomb-aimer's chair as he reached the transparent nose. Behind him I carefully buttoned up the curtains, turned up the lights again, and went back to work.

I calculated the time it should take the big bomber to plow its way to the target. "We'll be there within the wave, alright," I said, "if my D.R. is right."

"That won't be bad," the pilot replied, "but I can't see anything. This soup we're in is pretty thick. How about you, Bob?"

"Visibility is only a couple of hundred yards out in front here. Nothing so far."

"Well, keep your eyes open. How about you, gunners?" Link's tone was beginning to acquire a note of anxiety. "Any flak or anything?"

"All we saw was another kite about a couple of hundred yards away, ten minutes ago," the rear gunner replied.

"That's good news!" I exclaimed. "We're probably in the stream anyway."

"Was it another bomber?" asked Link hurriedly.

"Yes— I think it was a Lancaster."

"Good show."

"We oughta be over the target in six minutes, skipper." I fingered my oxygen mask nervously. There was nothing I could do but wait for the target to approach. Apprehension grew in my mind. If we missed Mannheim and started wandering alone over Germany we would be duck soup for the fighters; if we ran over flak positions by ourselves we wouldn't have a chance. I chewed my lip behind my mask and rubbed my hands together. Four minutes— three.

"I'm going to lose a couple of thousand feet and see if we can see anything," Linklater said. The plane nosed down.

"Two minutes to go. See any markers yet?"

One minute to go. I felt a sick emptiness in my stomach. My second-hand swept off another minute. "We ought to be there now—think we're anywheres near it?"

"We might be right over it. Can't see nothing for this cloud."

"Stay on the same course for six minutes more, and then turn south. Hope to hell we see something soon. Are we still letting down?"

"Yes—we're at eighteen thousand feet now. I don't want to go down too low—the flak around us is getting thick."

"If it's that thick we must be somewhere near the target area, anyway—"

"Yeah—I don't think you missed it by much."

100

"The six minutes crept by, and the big plane turned south, still losing height.

"Levelling off at 17000."

I recorded the information in my log with fingers that were shaking slightly. I calculated a new course. The Halifax turned west.

"'What's this below us?" Bob called, his voice tense and excited. "Looks like what we're looking for!"

"Naw—it's just a fire—no, it's some town or other!" the pilot responded.

"I'm gonna let the load go now—can't carry this block-buster around all night!"

"Okay—pull the plug!"

"Left-left—steady—bombs gone!" The plane jumped. "Had the fire right in the cross-lines!"

"Stay on the course you're on," I told the pilot. The plane droned on for another couple of minutes.

"Gimme an alteration, Norm," the pilot's words came, thin and unsteady. "We're headin' for the biggest bloody raid you ever seen!"

I cursed. "That must be Mannheim? If only we'd hung onto that bomb for another two minutes!" I was white-hot with anger at the perverse fates that had brought me so close to a successful completion of the job I had risked so much to do.

I looked at my map. "Go onto one-seven-five—now!" I scribbled furiously in my log. "Bomb-aimer, gimme a bomb-sight bearing on the raid, willya?"

"Gotta wait until the turn's completed—she's steady now—okay—one-oh-two relative—about six miles."

"Thanks." I turned to my map and my instruments, frantic fingers flying, my brain striving madly with the speeding second-hand of my watch. I read a course off the computer, looked at the time, scribbled briefly in my log. My cold hands were sweating; beads of salty water were trickling down the sides of my helmet; my heart was pounding madly inside my heaving chest. I switched on my microphone with fumbling fingers and panted to the anxious pilot, "Three-one-four—now!" The plane swung around, one broad wing pointing at the burning city only a few miles away. I did not even have time to look at the scattered bomb-bursts and markers and gun-flashes, like an eruption of fiery smallpox among the wheeling searchlights.

"You couldn't 'a' missed that by two miles, Norm," said the pilot. "Damn these clouds? If only we'd been three thousand feet lower we coulda seen that raid and put our bomb right in the middle of it!"

"Anyway, I know where we are now," I answered, calming my frantic emotions. "Hope I can get something to work with on the way home."

"You and me both," agreed the pilot with all his heart. The aircraft steadied for the long ride home.

In the rear turret Burgess, enormous in his electric flying suit, swivelled back and forth, up and down, in his untiring, rhythmic search of the hostile sky. He shoved his tiny control stick over as far as it would go and the turret followed. Faint in his ears he could hear a tiny whistle that grew deep and full-throated, and then shrilled and died as the questing steel and perspex bubble swung back. It was the cold night air, blasted back from the roaring propellors, using his outthrust gun-muzzles as organ-pipes like a child blowing across the neck of a bottle. To the eerie accompaniment of his four murderous voices Burgess rode backwards across part of Germany into France and on into Belgium.

Beneath the aircraft, on the resentful ground, garrisoned by enemy gun-crews, there appeared to be no activity. The route avoided flak positions, and the fact that V-Victor was not being shot at implied that we were pretty close to track. I breathed easier. A few minutes earlier, when we had overflown our estimated time of arrival the thought that we were wandering lost and lonely over Germany has clawed at my throat in terror. It had not been the immediate danger that had frightened me so badly, for the flak and the search lights had not been very near; it was the sense of being swept to destruction by a power out of my control, with the maps and instruments that should have guided me to safety useless in my shivering hands. To be trepanned to death without being able to do anything to fend it off, like a sheep prodded to the slaughter—that was what was so terrifying, so mortifying. As I looked at the little cross on my map, labelled with a time a few minutes back, I felt a release from apprehension that was physical. At that crudely-pencilled time I had known where I was, and that was why I, as a navigator, was there. The shadows of searching night-fighters were not even a ripple across my happiness.

What worried Link was not our navigation troubles—he was calmly sure that I could get us home. What alarmed him was the black and forbidding bank of fantastically-battlemented clouds that barred our path. They were thunder-clouds—ice-laden cumulo-nimbus clouds full of terror and sheer malice. Link looked to either side, to see if he could go around the seething misty heights. There was not even a gap; everywhere the clouds stretched like a demented wall. He decided to climb over them. The aircraft began to claw its way upward, engines straining. The pilot watched the inching movement of the altimeter with anxious eyes, shifting his worried gaze from the engine gages to the altimeter to the compass to the clouds outside. The slow movement of the needle stopped; the aircraft had reached its ceiling.

"This kite must be picking up ice," Link worried. "She oughta be able to get another three or four thousand feet yet, specially with no bomb load."

"Something's wrong," agreed the engineer anxiously. "She's using too much petrol too."

I looked at my compact bank of instruments. "Say, skipper, what's happened to the airspeed?"

Link's gaze jerked to the indicator; the green-glowing needle had sagged from the luminous "180" and now was jerking back and forth just before the "160" mark. "Holy smoke!" he exclaimed, "this kite must be loading up with ice faster'n I thought!" He looked at the pitot heat switch, leading to the electrical heating circuit which kept the airspeed indicator from freezing into uselessness. It registered "On."

The needle moved back. "All I can do with the kite is 145," he told me a moment later. "Work out a new ETA."

I called up the new arrival time. Link conferred with the engineer. "We won't make it to Skipton," Ashelford said. "We'll have to land at Woodbridge in southern England."

"Navigator—what kind of a groundspeed we got?"

"I got an eighty-mile-an-hour wind—that cuts our groundspeed to about 75 or 60 miles an hour."

"Are you sure that's right?"

"No—I'm just using a bomber command broadcast wind. I don't know how good it is."

"Are we on track?"

"According to my D.R. we are, but I don't trust the wind."

"Jesus— what a shaky do!" Link clicked off his microphone.

Back in England a group of meteorologists, working from information collected by strange and devious means from half of Europe, were forecasting the wind velocity. They received reports from other aircraft, averaged them, added a factor for expected changes, and sent out their figures. Tonight, the aircraft were in a rapidly-changing wind field, and the reports varied so much that the ground-based experts were totally confused. They did the best they could. It was not very good.

The wireless operator handed me a new wind. I calculated a new course, and told Link to alter. As he bent to set the course on the compass he saw that the airspeed needle had moved backward. "Work out a new ETA, navigator," he said.

I did. The engineer said, "We haven't got enough fuel to get to England. We'll have to ditch."

"I'll lean the mixture out a little," said Link.

The needle moved further back. I worked out another ETA for the Dutch coast. My figures showed that we would run out of fuel before we got there. "Anyway, we won't have to ditch," said Bob, "we'll be out of gas before we get to the coast."

"Looks like we're going to have to bale out," Linklater said, his voice tight. "God damn it, everything's going wrong tonight!"

I did not answer. I looked at my map and kept working. The Halifax droned on through the night and the clouds. Then from the rear turret Burgess' voice came to my worried ears. "Say—are we supposed to be over water?"

"Shouldn't be—we still have an hour according to my D.R. before we hit the coast."

"Well, we sure got water under us now—I can see it through breaks in the clouds."

The pilot's voice, excited, broke in. "Say—this airspeed's coming right up—it's a hundred and seventy and still goin '!"

"The engine settings are the same as ever," said the engineer.

"Those settings shoulda kept it at 180 the whole time—you know," said Link with suspicion dawning in his voice, "I bet that pitot head was on the fritz all the time!"

I looked at my Gee-box. There was still interference but I could read it well enough to get a fix. Three minutes later I knew where we were. The fix was so far from my dead reckoning position that I calculated another one. It told the same story.

"Say—something is wrong, but everything's okay now. We're right over the Dutch coast, about seventy miles north of track. Lord, was my navigation out tonight!" I worked out another course and gave it to Link.

"Then we got enough petrol to go home on!" the pilot called, almost gayly.

"That broadcast wind wasn't worth a hoot," I said.

"All's well that ends well," broke in the rear gunner.

"We ain't home yet," rebutted the mid-upper. "Wait till we get home."

Below us the coast crept past as the English one had done hours earlier. Far off there was a sparkle of flak, and a wavering searchlight; then as we flew farther out to sea even these small signs of enemy effort faded into the gloom. We descended below 10000 feet. Bob lit a cigarette. Far ahead a pinpoint of light stood up toward the sky. "There's your landfall beacon," Link told me. The aircraft kept on toward the headland where the homing searchlight stood waiting for us. Just before we reached it I called up to the skipper the course that would take us home.

"Right through the searchlight belt—right through the fighter belt—right through the flak belt—and we didn't have a shot fired at us!" My voice was rueful as I condemned myself for having done so poorly my job of navigation.

"That sure was a shaky do," commented the pilot wearily. "I thought we had it."

I did not answer.

Technicians replaced the radar set the next day. The night after that we went to Essen. Everything worked. No bombs hung up. Two fighters attacked, but vapor trails made them easy to detect and avoid. There was heavy flak in the target area, but in my blacked-out cubicle I never saw it, and when I clipped on my parachute to look out at the target things were so interesting that I forgot to be frightened.

We attacked three French targets and then went on leave. We were veterans now.

CHAPTER SEVENTEEN

Going to war is touted as an exciting business. A Canadian parliamentarian once said that politics was the most exciting thing next to war. So it is for many. My trouble is that although I did go into battle—every flight was a battle—I hardly ever saw any of the war.

Some of my trips were pretty hairy, with aircraft being shot down on either side, exploding in mid air, crashing into the target, going down in flames, being hit by bombs dropped by another aircraft, or spinning down with a wing blown off. Even over friendly territory we ran into danger, as when a Lancaster, clawing for height in the same stretch of blackness we occupied ripped off the radio antennae from our fuselage.

While this was happening, the pilot kept switching his gaze from his instruments to the black world outside; the gunners kept swinging their turrets as they searched the skies; the flight engineer climbed into the astrodome over the target to watch for fighters; and the bomb-aimer left his seat at the radar set as we approached the target, to crouch behind his bombsight and watch the target approach in all its bomb-tormented, flame-struck glory.

The navigator, however, sat at his position, facing the port side of the aircraft, poring over his maps and making cabalistic lines and marks upon it, and entering cryptic references into his log. He was curtained off from the rest of the crew, except for the bomb-aimer who sat at his side operating the H2S radar until it was time for him to drop the bombs.

The aircraft had to be totally blacked out, but the navigator needed light to work. With his chart thumbtacked down on the folding table hinged to the aircraft's port side, his log-sheet on whatever part of the chart he was not working on, his handheld E6B computer (actually a sort of slide-rule that also worked out the effect of the wind), the cigar-box in which he kept his spare pencils and erasers and a spare pair of dividers at the edge of the table, he drew lines on his chart and made entries in his log. He was the most furiously-working member of the crew. Every alteration of course, change of airspeed and change of height had to be logged, as well as fixed obtained from the "Gee" radio-navigation set. After the aircraft flew far enough toward enemy territory that the Gee set was jammed, radar fixes, which could not be jammed, were plotted. The wind direction and speed were computed every six minutes, and every twenty minutes the course had to be altered to keep the aircraft on track. There was scarcely a moment that was not consumed with copying figures down from the Air Position Indicator (a device which received heading from the distant-reading compass and true airspeed from another computer and read out the latitude and longitude of the aircraft as if there had been no wind), twisting the knobs of the Gee set, stepping off distances with dividers from a scale at the edge of the map, measuring wind vectors with a square Douglas protractor, and writing down every action in the log, as well as recording anything unusual seen by other crew-members, such as flares seen at sea, aircraft shot down, or attacks by enemy fighters

Thus the navigator had no time to look out, and no window to look out of. He was closeted in his little cubicle in the nose of a Halifax or in the body of a Lancaster, beavering away, too busy even to eat his flying rations. The constant activity was actually an advantage, since the navigator always had something to occupy his mind, and the work kept him so busy that it drove fear into the background. Fear there was, of course, when the target was announced and the intelligence officer told about flak concentrations and fighter bases, and during the ride out to the aircraft in lorries that were occasionally referred to as 'tumbrils,' but once airborne and the frantic activity commenced, the fear was overborne by the immediate necessity of the navigation tasks.

Thus it was that because of my job I saw very little of the war. The gunners' description of tracers being exchanged in air combat, the despairing comment of the pilot as he said, "Jesus! that Jerry fighter just shot down four bombers one after another!" the description by the bomb-aimer of what he thought were aircraft on fire but were actually the first V-1 buzzbombs launched against London, I heard, but saw nothing but the rivets on the inside of the fuselage.

On my first trip my Gee set malfunctioned and I did not get my navigation sorted out until we got a radar fix as we crossed the south coast of England. As a result I was so busy that I never looked out at all during the trip. Things went better the next trip, and when we got to the target I had things well enough in hand to decide to look out. I turned off the lights and peered over the bomb-aimer's back at the scene in front of me. I saw the dark city, its pitiful attempts to hide itself in the blackout betrayed by the bomb-bursts and the brilliant splashes of colour of the Pathfinders markers, red and green and yellow, renewing themselves as the PFF aircraft backed them up. It looked as if a handful of gunpowder had been dropped onto a panorama stretched on the floor, with each grain exploding as it touched. I stood transfixed for a couple of minutes, and then closed the curtains, turned the lights on again, and went back to work.

After that, I looked compulsively out over each target, no matter how urgent the navigational task might be. This was the climax of our trip, what we had risked our lives to do. Once we had dropped the bombs our danger might be no less, but we had carried out our task.

Sometimes *en route*, if things were quiet and were on a long leg with no immediate change of course, I would look out briefly once or twice, climbing up the steps leading to the wireless operator's position, to see the German searchlights swinging lazily but murderously as they looked for us. Except for them, everything always looked peaceful over open country, with never a light showing, but here and there a twinkle of starlight reflecting from the winding course of a river or the surface of a lake.

My experience was not confined to me. An ex-bomb-aimer forty years later told me that his navigator had looked out at the target once, seen the bombs and the flak, and had rammed the curtains shut and never looked out gain until his aircraft was shot down over Osnabruk. He had his first good look at the German countryside as he swayed back and forth beneath his parachute.

On the journey back home (we always said, "On the trip out you're working for the government; on the trip back you're working for yourself") I always homed to the air station on the last leg, using Gee. This involved setting up the cathode-ray tube so that two lines of light ('blips') were positioned along a base line. They looked like match-sticks on one scale, and like skipping ropes, frozen when the rope was highest, on another. As we neared base the two blips would come closer and closer, until they merged into one single skipping-rope over the base. I had a chart carefully drawn out and scotch-taped to the lid of the cigar-box in which I held my navigational tools, which told me which way to direct the pilot in response to the behaviour of the blips, one procedure for each quadrant of the compass. To the pilot homing seemed a little like magic, and I tried to keep it that way. Letting down through cloud directly over the runway always impressed him.

Once over the base, we would join the circuit. The pilot would call up the control tower, and would be told, "V-Victor, aerodrome eight thousand." We would orbit at eight, and then six, and then four thousand, until we were cleared to land.

After the pilot told me he had seen the drome I would take the thumbtacks out of my map, fold it and my log-sheet together, put my dividers and protractor into their cigar box, and put them all in my canvas navigation bag with my computer. I would remove my parachute from its bungee cords and with it in one hand and my navigation bag in the other I would crawl under the feet of the bomb-aimer as he sat as assistant pilot in the jump seat at the pilot's right, and sit down in the rest position halfway down the fuselage. The rest position was the official landing position for the navigator and the wireless operator, since nobody was to be in the nose during the landing, in case the aircraft went up on it. The trapdoor under the navigator's position, which made getting out of a crippled Halifax in flight much easier than getting out of a Lancaster, would be of no use to a trapped airman on the ground.

In the rest position—the only aircrew who actually rested in it were those who had been wounded—I could not see anything either. I would plug my headset into a jackbox, wait for the thump of the wheels and the voice of the pilot crying "Brakes!" to the bomb-aimer beside him after he touched down, and look at my watch, so that I could complete my log with the time of landing. I didn't care that there was no window in the rest position. I was always too tired to roam around the aircraft, and since the rules said that I should remain seated, strapped in, and as I was a disciplined regular, so I did.

Thus it was that one night we lost an engine and had trouble getting the wheels down, since the engine which had stopped was the one that fed hydraulic power to the undercarriage retracting mechanism, and we had to fly around among the cluster of aerodromes in the Skipton-on-Swale area while the engineer struggled to extend the wheels manually. The rear gunner later declared that he was looking up at the tree tops as we flew, unable to gain height with the undercarriage down and one engine dead. I did not remember the incident. The gunners, who had to stay in their turrets for fear of German intruders, the pilot, the engineer and the bomb-aimer knew what was going on, but I was paying no attention to the conversation on the intercom. I had done my job, and as far as I was concerned that was that.

Things changed a bit after the Normandy invasion. We flew several daylight trips in support of the armies on the ground. Navigation was easy. We flew in a gaggle, not a formation, since our pilots had not been trained in formation flying nor were they practiced in it—it was impossible to fly formation at night. The sky was thick with friendly fighters who had driven the Jerry fighters out of the sky. When we climbed out and set course the sky looked as if it was infested by a swarm of midges, and when we saw how they were cutting across one another's' paths the pilot turned white and said, "Jeez! How did we ever do it in the dark?"

"Good thing we couldn't see each other then—we'd 'a' been shit scared if we had."

The pilot flew my courses, but he might as well have followed the crowd. I did not work very hard. If the other aircraft were close we were on track.

There was no need to keep the curtains closed, so I looked out through the transparent nose of the aircraft at the unfamiliar world in front of me; the English countryside, the city of Luton where microwave hospital therapy machines always played hob with radar and Gee, London off to one side—we never flew over it— and then the Channel. The pilot asked me for a course.

I answered, "See that lighthouse ahead?"

"Yes."

"Steer for it."

"And you call yourself a navigator!"

We flew over the beachheads—if they were hot enough for the pongos they looked all peaceful to us—we crossed our own lines, and then the flak started. None of us had ever seen flak in the daytime. The heavy flak made big black ragged clouds like pieces of storm-wrack, and white flak bursts left the sky marked with woolly flocks of sheep. We could not see the fiery hearts of the flak-bursts in the daylight, and they looked rather innocuous, but when the flak got closer the pilot dodged away. Ahead of me I saw a plane go down in flames, and hoped it was a German fighter. The Pathfinder markers went down ahead of us, and we bombed the red and green splotches of light. The pilot stuffed the nose down to get some speed, and we swung out onto our course to leave the target. Back over our own lines the Channel looked like ground glass covered with ships. We flew at ease up the spine of England admiring the view. The air was smooth, and this time I ate my lunch. I liked daylights. I had a chance to see something for a change.

We did one trip all by ourselves, to a buzz-bomb launching site one afternoon. We were briefed to bomb at 20,000 feet, but the site was covered by cloud. "We'll take a look at ten thousand," said Link, and came down. "Flak just behind us," said Burgess, his voice cool. "Flak burst ahead," said the bomb-aimer, his voice not so cool. There was a sharp crack, a smash as if a giant were hammering the fuselage with a sledge, and a piece of flak drove through the aircraft. The world revolved and I rose halfway to the roof as the pilot kicked into a diving turn. "Bastards!" he shouted, "One short, one over, and the third right on the nose!"

"Bomb-aimer—can you see the site?"

"Think so."

"Okay. We'll go in and bomb."

We did. Bombing buzz bomb sites was unrewarding, since they were hard to hit, and hard to destroy if we did hit them.

"They're good gunners, aren't they?" I remarked to the pilot as we crossed the French coast.

"Too bloody good.? How is it down there?"

"Okay. A bit drafty." I had not been very frightened, since the incident had been over so quickly. What made me happy was that I had actually seen a little bit more of the war.

A couple of months later I was speaking to a fellow navigator who had returned to the squadron after having been wounded. "Flak never used to scare me before I got wounded," he told me, "but it sure as hell does now." I nodded sagely. I still had the valour of ignorance.

I did have a grandstand seat at a spectacular fireworks display. We attacked shipping in the port of Le Havre, and a German ammunition ship was set on fire. It lay shooting up a display of exploding pyrotechnics like a Chinese New Year, the streams of multicolored lights going up to five thousand feet.

Then the Air Officer Commanding-in-Chief of Bomber Command, Sir Arthur Harris, sent us back to the cities of Germany or out to drop mines again. I was back in my black hole, working over my log and chart, looking out for five minutes every trip.

So it was that although I went to war I didn't see much of it. If you want to know what happened, ask the pilot or the gunners. They saw it all. I stayed ignorant.

CHAPTER EIGHTEEN

Just before I went on leave, the adjutant called me in. He shoved a cheque I had written towards me. "Whadda ya mean, Emmott?" he snarled. "Writing cheques that bounce!"

I looked at it with disbelief. I had never had any trouble with money. I had always paid my debts. Nobody had ever dunned me. A good airman should be responsible financially, he should spend no more than he made, he should pay his debts promptly, he should live no higher on the hog than his rank entitles him. So I was taught, so I believed and so I behaved for the first seven years of my Air Force life.

When I first joined the Air Force I was paid $1.70 a day, a princely sum in those piping times, especially when it was considered that the army boys drew only $1.10. Then war broke out and put stripes on my sleeves, and before long I was making no less than $70 a month to spend as I saw fit, plus board, room, and uniforms. In those days it was good money, since a cashier in the Hudson's Bay store in Victoria drew only $15 a week. You could run a car on it. I did: a Model A Ford.

Then I remustered to aircrew, and when I received a commission my pay shot up to $6.25 a day and keep (I had to buy my uniforms.) I thought I was rich. When I was made a flying officer my pay went up to $7.50 a day, plus the marriage allowance going to my wife. I thought I was filthy rich.

When I was shipped overseas I arranged for my pay to be deposited in an English bank so that I could write cheques on it. In between operational flights I spent money with a lordly hand. I bought a bicycle. I attended plays in Harrogate, the watering-place of northern England (the female parts were good, but the male parts were bad, since all the young men were off to war.) I bought snacks at night—beans on toast, Vienna steak (made out of beans), sausages (made out of bread), and rock cakes (made out of rocks). Occasionally I ate beefsteak (made out of horses.) I patronized pubs, where I drank 'arf and 'arf, shandy, mild 'n' bitter, and sometimes the aristocratic tipple of gin and lime. Once I even had some black market Scotch.

Then the cheque bounced. There was no money in my account. I could not understand it—I had not been spending that much money. The adjutant sent me to the accounting officer. There the mystery deepened. The reason was that no money had been deposited in my account by RCAF Overseas Headquarters. The accounting officer could not enlighten me why I should not be paid. After all, I had carried out my duties in navigating Halifax V-Victor, and if I was not the best navigator in the world my crew had been good enough to keep the fact quiet.

P/0 Emmott, Mrs Marian Emmott
Robentson, P/0 A.H Emmott
(brother), London, 1943.

I decided to go to London to enquire. I still had enough money to do that, particularly since I was given a railway warrant to get there. I sought out overseas headquarters, and wended my way through the labyrinthian proper channels to the pay officer.

I got the attention of a lofty and condescending accounts officer. He explained things to me. It was all very clear to him after he had thumbed through my file. "You were a permanent force airman," he told me. "That means you have to contribute to your pension." He looked up another regulation. "When you got your commission, you were supposed to go on contributing. But for some reason you were treated like hostilities-only airmen, who don't contribute because they're not eligible for pensions for long service—they get pensions only if they become casualties. So your pension

114

deductions didn't get made, and nobody noticed it until a little while ago. That left you with a negative balance, which has to be recovered., The sum is quite considerable—you've been an officer for a year and a half now, without making those pension payments."

"Holy smoke!" I burst out, or words to that effect. "But it doesn't make any sense to take it all back at one crack? That doesn't leave me with a penny!"

"You don't understand," he said, as if speaking to an errant child. "You're not eligible to draw pay if your account is in deficit. You can't draw pay and allowances you haven't earned."

"But that's incredible? How am I supposed to live? After all it was your fault, not mine!"

"Watch your tongue, young man? I certainly had nothing to do with it!"

"Well, if it wasn't your fault, it was the fault of pay accounts! Not a nickel!"

That rubbed his fur the wrong way. He looked at me with complete disapproval. "The error is perfectly understandable. When you got your commission you got a new regimental number, beginning with a J. All other officers with J numbers do not contribute to a pension, so it was quite an understandable action on the part of the pay clerks involved. Even you should be able to see that." He pursed his lips. "Besides, you're living quite well. You live in barracks, you eat in the mess—all you're missing is a little pocket money."

"My God," I pleaded, "I'm on operations. I may get killed. Before I do, I want a few pounds to enjoy myself—to have a beer or two, to go out on the town, to spend foolishly. For all I know I may only have a week to live. Can't you at least take the money back over four months?"

He stiffened. "Your attitude is quite unsatisfactory. You only want the money to spend on drink and chasing women. And you may go missing. If you do, still owing us money, you'll put my staff to a great deal of unnecessary work. My pay clerks are overseas, living in London, being bombed, subject to all the dangers of frontline life. I have to consider their morale. They're entitled to consideration. There's nothing I can do for you."

"Good God!" I yelped. "I'm flying over Germany!! I'm in danger too? Gimme a break!"

"Sorry, but the matter is closed. There is nothing I can do." He walked away and left me gesticulating at a counter.

I was condemned to a month of high thinking and plain living.

The good people of Timmins, Ontario, came to my rescue. They had adopted No. 433 "Porcupine" Squadron, since the city is the centre of the Porcupine district of Ontario. They sent cigarettes to the brave boys on the squadron. I did not smoke. I used my fags for barter and got along.

The matter was not closed, however. After I had survived not only my temporary poverty but my operational tour, an appreciative government shipped me back to Canada. After a month's leave I was posted to Boundary Bay, near Vancouver. I made a pilgrimage to the accounts section to ensure that my pension deductions were being properly deducted. They weren't, I got it straightened out, and I went home happy—at least I thought I did.

Officers, however, had to pay income tax in Canada. I was assessed at the pay of my rank. A sharp accounting Flight Sergeant noticed that I had overpaid my income tax, because I had been charged tax on the extra amount of my pension dues, which were exempt. "I'll just skip the income-tax payment for the last month of the year," the helpful NCO said. That sounded quite all right to me

Two months later I checked my bank account. Nothing was in it. I hurried back to the accounts section, to seek my helpful friend the Flight Sergeant.

He was gone, having been transferred to greater things. His successor was a clever man. He had checked my pay account, and noticed that I was not apparently paying any income tax. He jumped to the conclusion that I had not paid any since I had come back from overseas. He then charged my pay account for the whole six month's worth of income tax he thought I had not paid since I returned to Canada. I jumped up and down in rage, but the only thing the accounts officer could suggest was that I apply for an income tax refund. I did.

For the next month I lived again in grinding poverty, as did my wife and our baby. I wrote begging letters to the income tax department. They ignored them. However, in their own good time they did send my refund.

Unfortunately by that time the cost of living had gone up by more than two dollars a bottle.

CHAPTER NINETEEN

Halifax aircraft of F/L Pierce's crew, Skipton-on-Swale, 1944.

When we returned from our first operational leave, we found we were back on the battle order at once. In seven days we flew five times, which made us one of the senior crews on the squadron. We were always available; none of us went sick, or turned up late from leave, or had any excuse for not flying. We had always pressed on, despite things going wrong. Nobody consulted us, of course. They just put us on the battle order and sent us out, and out we went.

We were not unhappy about it. The accepted wisdom was that if you kept in flying practice you had a better chance of survival. Besides that, the short nights during the summer meant shorter trips, which were automatically less dangerous. The high command was busy smashing up the French railway network, and doing it with heavy bombers. Short nights suited that business very well.

Our first trip was to drop mines in the Kattegat, the strait between Norway and Sweden. We had to go a long way to do this 'gardening' as it was called. On the way out I got off track, but we saw no flak or fighters, and dropped our mines from 15000 feet. On the way back I stayed on track, and the fates rewarded us for my good work by arranging for us to be picked up by predicted heavy flak at Ringkobing on the Danish coast. Linklater threw the Halifax into wicked evasive action, and we escaped with half a dozen holes. The flak hitting the fuselage sounded as if a giant were pounding on it with a sledgehammer, but the fighters left us alone. We were pretty blasé about flak, or at least I was, since in my secluded cubicle I did not see it, but fighters were a worry. The cry from the gunners, "Corkscrew starboard—GO!" was guaranteed to catch my attention and make me pay attention to something besides my navigation. This was never followed by the savage jabber of machine guns, nor the acrid stench of cordite in the aircraft; all through our tour the gunners never fired their guns except for test bursts over the Channel to make sure they worked. Our job was to drop bombs and get back, not to shoot down Jerry fighters. The received wisdom was that it was better to evade the fighters than to fight back; if you fired, another fighter would see the tracers and join the fray, and one of them would shoot you down. So time after time we were attacked by fighters, but except for one instance we always evaded them.

Actually, when a gunner searched the sky, his eyes tended to focus on a spot ten feet ahead of him, leaving the rest of the sky unguarded. The dice were loaded in favour of the fighter; he had a hundred miles an hour more speed, he could pick the time and place of engagement, and his cannon far outranged the .303-caliber guns we carried in our turrets. The bomber, especially when it was carrying its bomb load, was sluggish and slow, and was carrying a heavy load of gasoline, which would blow up when it was torched by an incendiary shell.

Furthermore, our gunners were looking in the wrong direction. We had a mid-upper turret well-placed to detect aircraft coming from above, and a rear turret whose gunner had a good view behind. The German, however, had developed a method of attack they called 'Jazz Music,' in which the fighter would fly underneath the bomber and fire at it with guns set in the plane's roof, firing upward at an angle of 45 degrees. Most of the German fighters who shot down night bombers reported that their victims never fired back. Most of them, indeed, never saw their killers. The best place to keep a look-out would have been a mid-under turret, or simply a hatch in the floor through which a gunner could keep watch. The space, however, was taken up by the H2S blister and its scanner. The brass at Bomber Command Headquarters scoffed at reports that bombers were being shot down from underneath and did not warn the crews soon enough. If they had, the pilots could have tipped the aircraft up on one wing at intervals, and spotted the prowling fighters underneath, but the secret was well kept.

The planners of Bomber Command were in a double bind. It was H2S alone which made night bombing accurate enough to be a reasonable method of making war. Before radar came on the scene, bombers had the same difficulties I had had when our H2S packed up on the way to Mannheim, and on many trips the bombs were simply dumped on Estimated Time of Arrival, usually simply plowing some farmer's field. With radar bombing accuracy improved tremendously, especially when the better navigation of the Main Force was combined with Pathfinder Force's placing of markers in the right places. However, the German Lichtenstein fighter radar homed in on the H2S. After we finished our tour the crews were advised to use H2S as little as possible, but this was generally not desirable, since it was the only effective navigation aid we had; all the others were being jammed by the Germans once we crossed the Dutch coast.

Most of the crew did not seem to worry. We stayed reasonably normal, although we noticed that Linklater was getting thinner and thinner. My own equanimity was helped, of course, by the fact that I did not look out. On one occasion over the target, just after we had dropped the bombs, I was passing the next course up to the pilot to head home. "Fly two-eight five," I said, "two eighty-five." There was no response, and the aircraft did not turn. "Damn it Link!" I said testily into my microphone, "turn onto two-eight-five!" There was no response again. "Hey, Link—" I began again, and then Bob Bamford reached over and switched off my microphone. "We're coned! Shut up!" I looked around me, to see the whole interior of the aircraft lit up in a silver glow from the searchlights which had us pinned like an insect against the clouds above us. Link threw the aircraft around like a Tiger Moth, and we dived out of the cone and headed home, with Link flying my course at last.

On only one occasion did it appear we were about to be shot down. A fighter surprised us and put a row of holes in the starboard wing. We shook him off, but the aircraft was doing strange things, and Link feared he would be unable to control it. His voice came over the intercom: "Prepare to jump! Prepare to jump!" I stood up, slapped my folding navigation table, maps and computer and pencils and all, against the wall, reached for my parachute, slapped it onto the clips on my harness, and bent over the trap door in the floor, ready to jump. Then Link and Ron got the plane under control. "Okay gang," Link said a minute later, "We got it—holding all right now—mid-upper—can you see anything of the starboard wing?"

"Looks all right," Adams answered. Link put the aircraft into a gentle turn and then into a dive, pulled out, nosed up again. The Halifax behaved reasonably well. "Guess we'll make it," he said at length, "what was that course, navigator?" I told him, and then went down on my hands and knees, picked up my scattered navigation tools, and went back to work. Needless to say, for that brief moment before Link regained control of the plane, I had been terrified. What impressed me, in retrospect, was that I had felt absolutely no hesitation in bailing out, once the command "Jump! Jump!" had come from Link; I was so anxious to get out of an aircraft which might be bursting into flame that I would have welcomed throwing myself out of that black hole in the bottom of the fuselage under my feet. It was indeed true that big worries drive out smaller ones.

One symptom of our reaction to the strain of operations was that we became increasingly unwilling to change anything. We had to urinate on the tail wheel in exactly the same order before every flight, file into the aircraft in the same way, go through the same airborne ritual every time in exactly the same way. Link and Ron Ashelford went through their pre-takeoff checks in the same way, like priests readying themselves for an airborne mass, with every word and every motion ritually correct.

After we had twenty trips in, Linklater was asked to volunteer for service on a Pathfinder squadron. We talked it over, and unanimously turned it down. We did not want to do anything that might change our luck.

And once, after I had climbed aboard the aircraft and settled down, with my maps thumb-tacked to the navigation table, Linklater called up to say, "What do you always say just before you get into the kite?"

"Once more unto the breach, dear friends."

"Well, damn it, this time you didn't say it. Get out there and say it and then get back aboard again."

I complied. After all, for all I knew it was that magic phrase that so far had kept us reasonably safe from harm.

In one other way I fell victim to superstition. I had always had a facility for writing verse, which at times had made me popular with young ladies. But I harked back to poets like Rupert Brooke and Wilfred Owen who had died young in the First World War, and felt that the military gods did not like poetry, and would punish those who were addicted to it. I was careful not to write a line of verse as long as I was on operations.

CHAPTER TWENTY

Soldiers I met always told me that compared to them an airman led a sheltered life. While the soldier has to carry his home on his back, sleep under hedges, and cook meals over campfires, the airman flies out in a comfortable aircraft and comes back to clean sheets and a well-cooked meal. This was true enough. There was another factor which made our life more bearable. The airman practically never sees death at close quarters, never is required to advance over dead bodies, and seldom sees his comrades killed beside him. A military airman sees planes go down, sees them explode in mid-air, sees them crash, but they look just like pieces of metal, and the thought that human beings are dying is hidden or dismissed from his mind. Those who drop bombs never think of the death and destruction they dealing to those below.

On operational squadrons the air force was careful to keep losses from becoming obvious. Empty beds were filled as quickly as possible by replacements. Empty seats at the dinner table were not particularly noticeable, because crews went on leave, were out on the town they were not flying, took off for practice cross-countries, and perhaps even vanished because they were screened from a tour after surviving it. Aircrew returning from a raid did not linger in the crew-room to see who did not come back; they were always dead-tired from the tension, and after drinking a mug of coffee laced with rum they hurried through their bacon and eggs and went off to bed.

Flags were never brought down to half-mast because of missing crews, nor was there any official notification of them to the rest of us. Losses—80% of them deaths—came to light in casual conversations. At my station there were two navigators whose names happened to be May and Amy. They maintained low-key competition as to who was flying the more operational trips. One day, seeing one of them in the mess, I asked him how the race was going.

He shrugged. "Amy went for a Burton over Brest," he said. "Tough," I answered, and changed the subject. On another occasion over a beer in a pub I mentioned a red-headed sergeant pilot who had passed through Heavy Conversion Unit at the same time we did, and whom we had seen greeted by his very beautiful newly-married English wife, who made all our heads turn. "Oh, he cracked up a week later," one of those at the table said. "Dead." We nodded and went back to our beer.

Appleton's crew, Skipt-on-Swale, 1944.

*Harrison crew, Skipton-onSwale, 1944. F'O Harrison, Sgt.
Denis Whitebread killed in flying accident 1944.*

When a bomber crew was lost, it was unlikely that a member of another crew would know everybody in it. The various aircrew trades tended to stick together, with pilots spending their time in the pilot's crew-room, navigators checking logs and discussing navigation problems in the navigation crew-room, and gunners, engineers and wireless operators talking over common problems. Thus, although I might have been friendly with a navigator who did not return, I would have only an idea of who his pilot was, and would not know his gunners or his flight engineer at all.

The rank structure also kept men apart. Pilots and navigators tended to be largely officers; the bomb-aimers were often officers; and the gunners, flight engineers and wireless operators were usually sergeants, who lived in different quarters, ate in different messes, and tended to seek entertainment with their peers. At intervals our crew would join for a night at a pub, more because it was expected of us than for any other reason. But none of us went on leave together. When I went on leave I would visit my relatives, or go to some vacation spot such as the Isle of Man with another navigator. Thus we seldom knew our fellow crew-men well enough to miss them deeply if they were lost.

I once saw the body of a man killed in battle. One summer

afternoon in 1944 the squadron sent a daylight raid against German army targets. The Germans threw up a curtain of light flak. One of the shells smashed into a squadron aircraft, and a piece of flak sliced through the bomb-aimer's aorta. He bled to death in his position in the nose of the aircraft.

I happened to be standing at the edge of the runway when the aircraft landed. There was a flurry of activity, with an ambulance, the padre, the squadron commander, the engineering officer and several others moving around it. Then I saw the dead man lifted out of the trap-door underneath the navigator's position in the nose. His heavy wool sweater was soaked with blood, and when I looked inside the aircraft the floor was puddled with blood which had caked into dark-brown mud.

I took one look, gagged, and hurried to a water fountain, where I choked down a couple of mouthfuls. I walked back visualizing the body of the man as he was lifted down, his arms flapping, his big flying boots bloodied, his face chalk-white. At the officers' mess I busied myself with a magazine. I knew I was flying the next day, and I wanted to forget it. None of the men around me mentioned it. It was the luck of the crew, the luck of the draw.

As the war went on more men I had known met their deaths. Like all sinners, I confess that I felt a brief euphoria that they had died and I had not. I always felt ashamed of myself, but the feeling was there, for me and for all the other aircrew, although most of them were reluctant to admit it.

Once or twice I heard a voice and felt a hand stretch out from the past. When I was stationed at Claresholm, Alberta, I became friendly with an American student pilot who had come north to join the RCAF before Pearl Harbour. His name was Patrick Neff Templeton, of Wellington, Texas, and he carefully explained that he had been named after a Texas lawmaker named Pat Neff. He was rather miffed when I admitted I had never heard the great name. Soon, he said, he would be flying Wellington aircraft named after his home town. In due course he gained his wings at Claresholm and was sent overseas.

I followed him to England a year and a half later. As I was reading a Canadian paper, my eyes came upon his name in a casualty list—"Missing, presumed dead." I put the newspaper away and went on to a classroom where I was taking an indoctrination course. I sat down at a desk. Carved into the desktop were the words *Pat. N. Templeton—Wellington Texas.*

The world I was living in came home to me with a jolt one day halfway through our tour. A raid was launched against Kiel, the north German seaport on the Kiel Canal which joins the North Sea to the Baltic. My crew did not fly that night, and the bomb-aimer, Bob Bamford, and Jim Linklater, who lived in the same twelve-man dormitory that I did, had gone out for the night while I stayed at home. The other beds in the room were occupied by members of three other crews. I went off to sleep, expecting to be awakened in the middle of the night as the men returned.

When I woke I was alone in the room, except for a service police-man sitting on the bed next to me. All the members of the three other crews had been shot down the night before, with the conventional 80% of them killed. The service policeman was there to protect their belongings until they were gathered up and sent to the next-of-kin. One of the missing men was a navigator called George Gill who had accompanied me on a holiday on the Isle of Man a couple of weeks before. (He survived the war.) The incident shook me a lot worse than the sight of the dead man had.

There was a conviction among aircrew that a man who began to act strangely was on the 'chop list.' One of the lost pilots, who had just returned from as flight commander's course and had been promoted to Flight Lieutenant, had begun to snap and snarl at the other members of the dormitory. In his case, it was right.

One of those who mourned him most was a WAAF with whom he was carrying on a torrid love affair. She did not know, and nobody ever told her, that he had a wife in Canada. The incident reaffirmed my determination to stay faithful to my own wife. I wondered if the happening might have been a warning from God.

The night was expensive in terms of our squadron's celebrities. One of the wireless operators, a splendid-looking man with a herculanean physique, who had formerly been a disciplinarian, had taken part in the making of the movie *Captains of the Clouds* by ordering James Cagney off an air station. One of the gunners was Les Marchildon, who had pitched for the Philadelphia Phillies before the war. (He survived as a prisoner of war.) A third was a navigator named Clerc (pronounced 'Clare') who was a PhD from a Swiss university, and was renowned for his habit of treating group captains as his inferiors and getting away with it. We missed them.

CHAPTER TWENTY-ONE

Second sight, as our fathers called it, or extra-sensory perception, as 'the intelligentsia' terms it now, is seldom met. In wartime, it is a good thing, it is not. If aircrew, for instance, had an actual premonition of death before they took off it is doubtful if the crews would have pressed on the way they did. A glance around a briefing room before an operation showed a group of young men, some percentage of them doomed to die in the next few hours, all of whom seemed confident that the axe would fall on somebody else.

Nevertheless, people did have premonitions. I had one myself once, before a night operation over Germany. I was depressed and downcast, and after I had prepared my map and worked out my flight plan in the special navigators' briefing that took place in the afternoon, a few hours before the rest of the crew was briefed, I looked so down in the mouth that a flying control officer with whom I was friendly asked me outright if I felt a premonition. "Forget it," he told me. "The things you worry about never happen." His words did not cheer me. He did not have to face the flak himself.

I dragged my way out to the aircraft, climbed into it after having urinated on the tail-wheel and made my ritual misquoting of Shakespeare, and made my pre-flight checks. I said nothing to the rest of the crew. Such a thing was simply not done.

We took off. I sat chewing my lip in the rest position until it was time for me to crawl down into my place in the nose and go to work. Once involved in my navigation things were easier. I had a job to do, so I did it.

We plowed on through the night sky, the gunners looking for fighters, Linklater keeping an eye on the sky ahead and checking periodically to make sure the gunners were awake and alert, the wireless operator listening out for German transmissions and jamming them with engine noise, and the flight engineer babying his engines. I worked away in conjunction with the bomb-aimer who was giving me fixes. We approached the target along our dog-legging track. Linklater told me when he saw the target ahead. We flew to it. Bob Bamford fused the bombs and climbed into the nose. I snapped my parachute onto my harness. Link opened the bomb doors. We dropped the bombs, closed the bomb doors, and turned for home.

We flew back over the North Sea and crossed the friendly coast. The landing was routine. We were never coned by searchlights. No fighters attacked us. We were not hit by flak; the shell bursts were not even close. The engines worked perfectly. There was no icing. The meteorological winds were fairly good. The radar worked. Nothing happened at all. For all the excitement it might as well have been a cross-country.

I never had any more faith in premonitions. I never had another one either.

A month or so later I climbed into the aircraft with confidence. We had been briefed to attack a German fighter airfield at Soesterberg in Holland. We would fly over enemy territory for hardly more than a few minutes, since the Allied armies were not far away. The sky was full of our fighters, and no German fighters could live in it. We looked on it as a pretty easy trip.

Meanwhile, my wife was living in Winnipeg She worked at a Royal Canadian Air Force equipment depot, keeping up the family connection with the storekeeping trade. That morning she felt herself distraught as she prepared herself to ride to work on the streetcar down Notre Dame Avenue. At her desk she felt worse. A chill seemed to have risen within her that gradually spread to her entire body. She tried to bury herself in her work, but it was no use, and each time she looked at my photograph on her desk she felt worse. Her friends tried to cheer her up, without avail. Finally her supervisor, seeing her condition, told her to take the rest of the day off, but she was dedicated to her job, and she stayed.

Then, as the day wore on, she felt better. The depression lifted. The paralyzing sense of foreboding slowly vanished. At the end of the day she was her normal self again. She went to work the next morning in her usual good spirits, although she was still wondering what ice had clasped itself around her heart.

Over Holland our Halifax was flying toward the German airbase that was our target. We had been briefed to take a photographic mosaic of the airfield, which required flying straight and level. Linklater settled down on the proper course as the airfield came in

**Photo—mosaic of bombing run over Soesterberg,
Holland, by Linklater's crew. August 15, 1944**

sight, and the other aircraft in our gaggle, our squadron mates,
jinked back and forth with their bomb bays open, waiting for the
field to come up into the bomb-aimers' field of view. I was looking
out. There was flak around, but it was not in front of us, and I was
looking to the front.

I bent over to make an entry in log, peering at the Air Position
Indicator in front of me with my head lowered to read its dials.
Suddenly there was an ear-splitting crash, and the aircraft lurched
and staggered. A piece of flak has smashed through the fuselage
just above my head. If I had had my head raised it would have
killed me.

The burst threw Linklater off his stride a little, but he recovered
and Bamford dropped the bomb load among German fighters in
their dispersals. We destroyed quite a few of them. Our job done,
our photographic mosaic taken, we flew home without further
trouble. There was a new window for me to look through, courtesy
of the Luftwaffe flak service, but nobody had been hurt. Link wrote
"DCO" (Duty Carried Out) in the flight authorization sheet.

When I returned to Canada my wife told me of her experience.
We checked the date and the time. Her time of fear and worry had
come on the day when I had come within a few inches of death,
and when we allowed for the seven-hour difference in time between Winnipeg and Britain, the hours coincided perfectly.

Her Irish ancestors must have bequeathed her, on that day at
least, the gift of second sight.

129

CHAPTER TWENTY-TWO

The administrative staffs at Bomber Command stations were efficient. One of their grim skills lay in processing the affairs and gathering up the belongings of missing men. They had a lot of practice at it. Some 9913 or 9980 Canadians lost their lives serving with Bomber Command (depending on which set of records you take your figures from.) As soon as the operations officer tallied up the results of a mission and found out who had not come back, the process went into high gear.

Our crew found out all about it one day in the summer of 1944. Bomber Command was sent periodically to bomb targets in France in support of the army. France was an ally (if a difficult one) and the high command was reluctant to drop any more bombs on France than we had to. As a result after we had been briefed to fly V-Victor on a daylight mission to a French target, our wireless operator Frank Russell copied an order for us to return to base without bombing the target. The army had advanced faster than had been expected. We were not particularly happy about it—the trip promised to be a fairly easy one, but it would have counted toward the completion of our tour, and we had gone through all the preliminaries, including the sweating it out before the take-off.

The drill called for us to fly back to Skipton-on-Swale, report to the control tower, and then fly out to sea to jettison our bombs. We were ordered not to land with bombs on, since a bad landing could result in the aircraft blowing up and killing the crew, and what was worse, putting the airfield out of action.

We flew back to the station, dutifully reported to the flying controller in the control tower, and then flew by Flamborough Head, the promontory north-east of York over which we had set course many a time for Germany. We flew past the fishing boats bobbing about on the North Sea, and over deep water. Bob the bomb-aimer selected a whitecap, got it into his bomb-sight, and pressed the bomb toggle. The bombs splashed into the North Sea, the aircraft jumped upwards as it always did when the load was released, and we turned back for the Yorkshire coast. Linklater had been trained for coastal command where low flying was *de rigeur*, and he skimmed the wave-tops as he had near Patricia Bay just after we first met. We had to climb to cross the coast. We played around a little as we flew back over the Yorkshire dales, the same country that James Herriott, the famed veterinarian author, has celebrated in his books such as *All Creatures Great and Small.* We flew over the ruins of Rivaux Abbey and admired the spires and buttresses. Link held the Halifax straight and level until a gradually-rising side-hill brought our height over terrain down to about fifty feet, and then pulled back the stick and climbed to a height more in keeping with Bomber Command customs. We flew over Ilkley Moor, the locality of the famed 'Yorkshire National Anthem,' the song *On Ilkley Moor Ba Tat.* It was a splendid afternoon, and we enjoyed ourselves, knowing that there would be no German intruder fighters around, and that we has no specified time to return to base.

We flew back to base, called up the control tower, and landed normally. I closed out my log and headed back to my quarters. There was no debriefing, since we had dropped no bombs.

My palatial quarters were waiting for me as I had left them; a Nissen hut with twenty beds, a stove, and water-pipes running around the walls upon which we could hang our clothes on coat-hangers, there being no lockers or cupboards. Nobody complained about it. The army had things a whole lot worse.

I entered the empty hut, walked over to my bed, and reached up to take something out of the pocket of my uniform jacket. The room, however, was not as empty as I thought. Just as I did so a heavy hand fell on my shoulder. "Just what do you think you're doing, sir?" a gruff voice said. I turned to look into the cold and disapproving eye of a service policeman, in full regalia—SP armband, web belt, and revolver.

"Uh?" I said in surprise. "What do you mean?"

"You, sir," said the policeman, glowering at me and using the word "sir" without meaning it, "are interfering with the personal effect of an aircrew member who has gone missing. This is forbidden by air force law."

"Who—me?" I sputtered.

"Yes. These effects are the property of Flying Officer Emmott, who failed to return from operations this afternoon."

"Hell," I said, "I'm Flying Officer Emmott. I'm here. I didn't go missing."

"My orders are clear," the SP said, his voice as cold as ever. "Nobody is to touch the effects of any missing aircrew until they are inventoried by the Committee of Adjustment."

"But I am F/O Emmott! I'm here! I didn't go missing!" I pointed to the name tag sewed to the battle-dress jacket I was wearing. "I'm him! I'm not dead! These are my clothes!"

"You having any trouble, corporal?" a second service policeman, who appeared from the vicinity of the bed belonging to my pilot, said ominously as he walked over to back up his colleague. He looked at me, his lips a hard line. "We've had trouble with people stealing the effects of missing airmen. It causes great distress to the next of kin. We don't intend to have any more of it." He took my arm, his other hand on the butt of his revolver holster. "You'll have to come to the guard room with me." The two men marched me out, their faces wooden, their ears deaf to my protests.

At the guard room the provost officer was called in. The service policemen stated their case. It was open and shut. One of them presented a paper bearing my name; I was unequivocally missing. I had been caught red-handed interfering with the property of a missing officer. The provost officer was stern. "This is a very serious charge, Flying Officer. I will have to take a formal statement. You are not required to say anything or make any statement, but anything you do say will be taken down in writing and may be used as evidence against you at your trial."

"Holy cats! I'm not missing!"

This obviously was a mere technicality. I was not charged with being missing; I was charged with stealing clothes from someone who was officially missing. The provost officer unbent a little.

"We'll just check on that." He lifted the phone.

"Operations confirm that aircraft V-Victor of 433 Squadron, pilot F/O Linklater, navigator F/O Emmott, is missing," he told me after a brief telephone conversation.

"What have you to say to that?"

"Here, lemme talk to the controller."

I reached for the phone. "Hey, get out your binoculars and look at V-Victor's dispersal. The kite's there! We ain't missing!"

There was a brief pause.

"Well, I'll be damned! Then who is missing?" came the voice over the phone.

Further investigation revealed that when we had reported back over the station before we dropped our bombs, V-Victor of our companion squadron, No. 424, had called up at exactly the same time. The controller, in confusion, had checked in only one V-Victor. We had not reported; therefore we must be missing. The wheels were set into motion. Service policemen were sent to guard my effects. It was reassuring, in a way. If I had been missing, nobody would have been allowed to steal any of my belongings.

There were more conversations over the telephone. I showed the provost officer my paybook with my photograph in it. Finally he was convinced. He nodded unsmilingly and let me go, with the unspoken comment that he was letting me off this time but I was not to do it again. The two policemen were obviously disappointed. Their open-and-shut case with its promise of a juicy court-martial had evaporated; moreover, it was a court-martial of an officer. Nothing pleases an airman more than seeing an officer in trouble, as I knew well from my own service as an airman.

"Orders are orders, I guess," I said to the provost. The two corporals saluted me as I left, rather unwillingly. A fine fish had jumped out of their net.

"This calls for a beer to celebrate," I said when I reached the officers' mess. "I'm back from the dead!" The squadron adjutant congratulated me and my pilot, who had joined me. "You're the first complete crew that ever came back to the station after being posted as missing."

"It didn't last long," I said.

"Lucky for me. If you actually had been missing I would have had to write a letter to your next-of-kin, and I don't know anything good to say about you."

CHAPTER TWENTY-THREE

An important job done by Bomber Command was the laying of sea-mines. In the shipping lanes of the Baltic Sea and from the Skagerrak south along the Frisian Islands and coasts of northern Germany and then France to the Bay of Biscay, Halifax and Lancaster aircraft delivered most of the more than forty thousand mines laid during the war. Eight hundred German or German-controlled ships were sunk by them.

Our crew was selected to lay mines on May 21, 1944. Mining trips were much preferred by the crews over bombing missions. There were only six aircraft or so on such a job, which reduced the risk of collision. The route to the target would usually be over water, away from flak, and although fighters were always a threat, mining trips usually took place at the same time as bombing missions, and the night fighters would be vectored toward the bombers, which posed the greater threat.

At briefing we were told that cameras would be mounted above the H2S indicators to show the ground picture appearing on the screen, which encouraged the bomb-aimer to get things right. If we were not sure of our position we were to bring the mines back, since mines dropped at random posed a threat to our ships too. A landing with mines aboard was not something we looked forward to! The intelligence officer told us not to get closer than twenty miles to Heligoland and its companion island Wangerooge, which guard the entrance to the Kiel Canal fifty miles to the south, because they were crammed with flak guns manned by naval personnel. He also warned us of the presence of sperrbrechers, German naval vessels bristling with anti-aircraft guns. Because they sailed around, he could not tell us where to expect them. We had been told about sperrbrechers in our previous incarnation as torpedo bomber crews, so we felt at home with them, although it seemed a bit unfair to have to face them again now that we were in Bomber Command.

When the lorry carried us out to V-Victor we saw that the four mines, wrapped in green canvas, were too bulky to permit the bomb doors to close, and the armourers had had to pump up the doors manually until they touched the big cylinders. Link looked at them with concern, wondering how much extra drag they would cause. The aircraft was overloaded as it was, and Link always considered the take-off as the shakiest part of the trip.

Once aboard the aircraft we carried out checks—to find that the distant-reading compass was not working. We had a simpler but much less accurate compass aboard the aircraft, and Linklater elected to press on without it. It was to cause considerable trouble for me, since it fed the Air Position Indicator, and also stabilized the radar picture so that north was always at the top of the screen. Without the Air Position Indicator I would have to work a lot harder to plot the aircraft's position, and when the radar was in use Bob Bamford and I would have to make mental calculations to swivel the radar picture around so that it made sense, because now the top of the picture would always be where the nose of the aircraft was pointing. I thought I would be able to cope, however, and I was just as anxious as anybody else to make a trip which was considerably safer than one over Germany.

The ground crew wheeled up the 'trolley ac' (short for "accumulator," the English word for battery) which was a gasoline engine driving a generator which provided the power to start the engines. As soon as an umbilical cord was connected at the port inner engine Link said, "Goose her, Ron," and Ron hit a button. First a whine, and then the radial Hercules engine roared, followed by the other three. With power, the gunners tested their turrets.

At the head of the runway Link turned and set the brakes. We heard him and Bob go into their litany:

"Trim tabs?"—"Elevator at 2 , rudder and aileron neutral."

Mixture control?"—"Down."

"Propellor speed?"—"Fully up."

"Flaps?"—"Thirty."

And so on throughout the rest of the check.

Link called control. "Rosecream Victor to Layboy, ready for take off." Brakes were released. The Halifax began to roll ahead. The tail wheel caused some vibration, and the aircraft was a quarter of the way down the runway before it lifted off. Link's voice came, "Flippin' clot of an aircraft!" as he struggled to pull V-Victor off. We rocked as the main wheels skipped over small depressions in the macadam. Seconds before we reached the end of the runway we were doing less than the safety speed for take-off. Then V-Victor lifted off, but it still would not climb. Link pushed the control column ahead a little to gain flying speed. Hedgerows and elms came closer. Then we bounced up a few feet, and Link said, "Wheels! Brakes!" and in a calmer voice to control, "Victor clear Layboy." With the extra drag caused by the mines overcome, we thought the worst part of the trip was over.

As we orbited Skipton we saw Oboe, Queen, Baker, Able and Nan take off and struggle up to prescribed height, and then we set course for Flamborough Head. We turned to head for Heligoland. Russ, the wireless operator, logged a no-message signal, which did not require an acknowledgement. A wireless operator's greatest fear was to miss a signal which might be a recall or an order to divert to another station on return.

At the turning point for our last outward leg I reported that it was only twenty minutes to our target area, and Link told Bob to turn on the H2S. Over water it could tell us nothing, since there was no topography to bounce radar echoes back to us. We were into the Heligoland Bight now, and fixes from H2S would take the place of Gee fixes which were now unobtainable.

Then Bob told Link, "All we can get on the H2S are horizontal green lines." I looked at it, but neither of us could find anything wrong with the settings. "Come on back to the junction box with me, Russ," Bob said. They looked at the box, to find four leads from the blister, and also the power supply, lying unplugged and dancing in the aircraft's vibration. Neither of them knew which plug related to which socket. Russ knew that the engines were putting 4500 amperes into the power system, and that putting the wrong plug in a socket might disable the lights, the instruments and the turrets, and he hesitated slightly. Bob, with the valour of ignorance, grabbed the largest metal plug and rammed it home. Sparks flew, but no howls of dead turrets or instruments followed. Bob scrambled back to his H2S set and reported a clear picture.

Suddenly multiple bursts of heavy flak jarred us. Adams called, "Searchlights all around!" Link's voice came, "Norm, where's all this stuff coming from?" I was too busy to answer him, and he calls again, his voice strained and belligerent.

"We must be over the islands," I answer. With the inaccurate compass I had had to use, and without an Air Position Indicator, my dead reckoning position was enough in error to put us inside flak range. "Gimme a fix, Bob," I said, and he answered. When I plotted the fix it made no sense, and I looked at the H2S screen to say, "The DR compass is dead—north isn't at the top of the display any more—gimme a relative bearing of the island." Bob responded, and I worked frantically to find our correct position and compute what heading we must fly to get us out of danger, performing mental gymnastics to correct for the skewed radar picture, whose orientation kept changing with every turn the aircraft made. Meanwhile Link had shoved on full boost and plunged into a cork-screw, chanting "20 degrees starboard, 500 down," a pause—"40 port, 1000 up," as he did it. The naval gunners kept changing their fuze settings, happy to have one aircraft over them and no bombs coming down at them. Link had heard my words to Bob, and said, "Jesus, can't you figure something out? What a useless bloody crew I got!" Every few seconds we were bracketed by four boxes of two or four red or white explosions. A searchlight flicked by the wingtip, but it lost us. Then the sky went black again—we were out of range. I continued my work for a few frantic seconds and then said, "Go onto one ninety-three—one-nine-three—speed 175, drop point in five and a half minutes, Bob." He checked the H2S picture, climbed into the nose. "Bomb doors open!"

On our run-in towards Cuxhaven flak came up from coastal guns or a flak ship, and in the slewing aircraft Bob was not sure he had not overshot his aiming point. "We'll have to go round again." The flak guns got an even better crack at us but Linklater held V-Victor steady, our mines went down where they we supposed to, and we dipped a wing to turn away as we headed for home. Ron Ashelford removed the metal plates above the bomb-bay and reported that the mines had indeed gone. The gunners reported no prowling night-fighters, and we relaxed a little. Bob turned off the H2S set and climbed up to the jump-seat beside the pilot, to fly the aircraft for a while as Link rested his arms. I continued working, keeping referring to the Gee set until at last, outside the range of German jamming, I got a useful signal. After that it was a reasonably routine flight back, even if I had to do routine plotting that previously the air position indicator had done for me. Link muttered again about a crew that can't even answer a simple question. Bob and I said nothing. Neither of us could deny that we had let ourselves fly over Heligoland which we had been so carefully briefed to avoid.

Our aircraft was the last home that night; the ground crew was happy to see us. When we trundled back to our dispersal pan we looked the aircraft over, to find only a couple of small holes in the port wing and the tail plane. Russ patted the fuselage and said, "Vicky, you're a good old girl," and we all agreed with him.

In the crew room the debriefing officers and the squadron commanding officer were waiting for us. Nobody criticized us for getting off course, but commended us for pressing on despite two equipment problems. Lesser crews, they insinuated, would have aborted the flight. We were too tired even to feel elation—simply relief at being back in one piece.

We took off our flying gear and headed for the mess for post-operational 'spam' and eggs. There I told the crew that I never heard anything on the intercom until I recognized my name, and that the unanswered question had never entered my consciousness. I did tell Link that he was on the right course but that a change in wind drift had shoved us over the island. Bob went on to say, "I didn't know we were off course until the flak hit and then you were pasting me to the wall one minute and floating me to the ceiling the next while the compass went around in circles." Link rebutted by saying, "The needle was pointing to magnetic north, wasn't it?" Again we had no answer.

(I did not tell them that all I remembered was the faulty radar and the fact that when we got over Heligoland I was relieved because now I knew where we were; we had a fix, and I could work out a new wind and a new course to steer, and that my navigation was once again under control. Of the flak, the searchlights, the cork-screwing and the pilot's desperate litany I had only the faintest memory. Bob and Russ had to tell me about it the next day.)

We had a mining mission later which was less memorable. We had been briefed to drop mines in the seaway leading to a harbour on the Dutch coast. Only a couple of hours, and we would not have had to fly over enemy territory. Nevertheless, the trip would have counted as a sortie leading to the completion of our tour. When we got out to the aircraft the engines would not start, and we had to cancel the trip and return, disgruntled, to the locker room to take off our flying clothing, knowing we would have to replace the easy trip with a dangerous one.

CHAPTER TWENTY-FOUR

We shared our air station at Skipton on Swale with our companion squadron, No. 424, the Tiger Squadron. We seldom referred to our squadrons by their names; 424 or 433 was identification enough. We shared the same messes and the same facilities, although our crew rooms and our sleeping accommodation were separate.

We took each other for granted. There was little inter-squadron competition among the aircrew, largely because so many of us were not on either squadron long enough to develop any deep feeling for it, and possibly because *Der Luftwaffe* provided enough competition for anybody. Aircrew were always in a state of flux, with the average crew, in the grim days at least, lasting for only fourteen trips, which meant that half of them were always fairly new replacements for those who had failed to return, or for those lucky men who had finished their tours and been screened. The ground crews stayed around longer, but maintenance was centralized, with men working for whichever squadron needed work done, and they gave their allegiance to the station, not a particular squadron. Squadron sports days were few and far between, because if the weather was good, as it needed to be to hold a field day, the squadron would be flying, and since, like burglars, we worked at night, we would be sleeping during the day.

424 was a more prestigious squadron than 433. 433 was the fourteenth and last Canadian bomber squadron to be formed overseas, while 424, the sixth such squadron, had seniority dating back to 1942, and had flown Wellingtons in North Africa.

Those who had bombed Rommel's troops in Africa were long gone by the spring of 1944, and nobody had any tales to tell of fabric-covered Wellingtons over the desert. We did have a leaven of men on their second tours, but few returned to their original squadrons, having been shipped to whatever squadron needed replacements when their instructional tours were up. In any case they mostly talked among themselves, the telling of war stories being looked upon as 'shooting a line,' while we sprog veterans-to-be gravitated to our fellows.

I never heard boasting by members of either squadron. American aircrew tended to blazon the names of the German cities they had bombed on their leather jackets, but we, in the British tradition, played things down. Army regiments carried their battle honours on their flags, but our battles were too recent to be memorialized. We were all members in common of the RCAF, and as aircrew our loyalties tended to go to our trades—mine was to the 'navigators' union.'

We saw little of our commanders, except during briefing, or during debriefings when the squadron OC or the group captain commanding the station would wait to see how many of us would come home. The officers who controlled us were the leaders of the various trades—the navigation leader, the bombing leader, the gunnery leader, the wireless leader, and the flight engineer leader. The pilots worked with their flight commanders.

There was only one officers' mess, but there were two sergeants' messes. Officers were predominantly aircrew, who had always been at the top of the pecking order, with the groundcrew officers giving them pride of place.

Among the sergeants it was different. The sergeants' mess was the heart of the groundcrew empire. As in every other military organization, it was the sergeants who made the Air Force run. Ruled as a fief by the senior sergeant-major (the Air Force, to keep things complicated, insisted on referring to a sergeant-major as a Warrant Officer, although the airmen usually called him Major) and was presided over by the flight sergeants (their rank was equivalent to staff-sergeant in the army, and they were not necessarily sergeant-pilots). The sergeants' mess was prestigious, an institution feared and revered by the airmen. The sergeants ran the crews that serviced the aircraft, adjusted the compasses, kept the stores, handled the pay accounts, and ran the messes. Groundcrew officers there were in plenty, but it was the sergeants who made sure that the real work was done.

Sergeants, up to 1939, had travelled a rocky road to their rank and their stripes. They had suffered through all the tribulations to which aircraftsmen are heir—drafty barracks, kit inspections, cleaning officers' boots, standing on parade when the slightest imperfection in turn-out meant confinement to barracks, constant lack of privacy, and the petty tyrannizing of NCOs. They had maintained aircraft in rain and in desert heat, in such far reaches of the Empire as Mesopotamia or India, where their skill at improvising had kept the aircraft flying. They had slogged through years as corporals, the meat in the sandwich, too low in rank to enjoy any special privileges but too high to be friendly with airmen any more, and forever being saddled with jobs like canteen corporal or corporal in charge of a barrack room, where the criticism landed on their shoulders but none of the praise, the target for airmen's complaints and the butt of sergeants' tempers.

They were a highly capable group. Some of them admittedly had an unquenchable thirst for beer, but they knew their jobs, they knew their drill, they knew how to look after (and terrorize) their men, they knew how to keep their officers out of trouble, and they usually served as role models, with their shoes brilliant, their uniforms pressed, and their buttons gleaming. Now, finally having made sergeant, they could luxuriate in their longed-for eminence, able to relax in the company of their peers in the sergeants' mess, where the food was best on the station—the sergeant cooks saw to that—secure in the knowledge that they made the Air Force run.

Then, in 1939, this happy world was brutally invaded. The Royal Air Force, finding that the aircraftsmen gunners and wireless operators would have a rough time if they were taken prisoner, decided that all aircrew would be given at least the rank of sergeant. They flooded into the sergeants' mess, where they had every right to be; they wore sergeants' stripes, and they were risking their lives for the privilege.

Friction began immediately. A man who had to wait two decades to put up sergeants' stripes resented seeing those same three hooks on the sleeve of an eighteen-year-old who had been a schoolboy a year before. The behaviour, discipline and deportment of these newly minted sergeants left much to be desired. Their uniforms tended to be scruffy and unpressed, their hair was too long, their boots were unshined, and they walked around with their hands in their pockets. After a trip over Germany where they had seen their comrades die, they took unkindly to the reproofs of a groundling, no matter how senior. If the wanted to take off their jackets while they played ping-pong, they did; if they wanted do loll around the mess in the middle of the day, just because they had been flying the night before, they lolled. These same sins were committed by the officers, but sergeants had always had to pretend not to see them. They did see the shortcomings of the sergeant aircrew, and were outraged by them.

Worst of all, the aircrew received higher pay. The groundcrew grudgingly admitted that the aircrew risked their lives, but that was only fair—they got paid for it, didn't they? Flying pay in the RCAF for airmen was a full 75 cents a day.

It was not unheard of for an airman who had suffered under a sergeant to remuster to aircrew, gain his wings, and then be promoted to flight sergeant for some feat of arms. If he met his former tormentor, now a rank lower, the erstwhile tyrant was in for a rough time.

Efforts by the groundcrew sergeants to keep these upstarts in their places were sabotaged by the senior officers. A crew could not be left without a radio operator, a pilot or a navigator because he was undergoing punishment for some petty crime.

The aircrew saw the other side of the coin. They had put their lives on the line; they objected to being harassed by groundlings, who were often petty tyrants. Their lives, they realized with chilling clarity when they arrived at the squadrons, were likely to be short, and therefore should be merry; they took unkindly to militaristic restrictions.

There were squabbles and fights, and parades of erring aircrew before adjutants and squadron commanders, who were in the cleft stick of having to maintain discipline while they sympathized with a man who might just have come back from Essen with a dead crewmate, and who very likely had only weeks to live himself. At last the Royal Air Force, with he RCAF following in its path, bit the sour apple and formed aircrew NCO messes specifically for the aircrew sergeants. That separated the two warring groups, and comparative peace returned.

But not always. One summer evening a Halifax belonging to 424 Squadron, following a 433 aircraft on a taxi-strip, ran into the aircraft ahead of it. One of the propellers sliced into the rear turret and cut off the rear gunner's head.

Shortly afterward the accident was being discussed in the aircrew mess. Someone from 433 made some uncomplimentary remarks about 424 pilots, and of 424 aircrew in general. The 424 men took offense, and soon a full-scale donnybrook was in progress. By the time the service police arrived every window was broken, all the furniture was in pieces, the carpet was in shreds, there were holes in the walls where heads had been shoved through, the bottles in the bar had been used as bludgeons, and the mugs and glasses as missiles. Walking wounded filled the sick bay. The mess members lived in squalor while repairs were made.

The station commander was enraged. He ordered an inquiry and fined every member of the erring mess ten pounds—a lot of money when five pounds would pay for a weekend in London. The regular NCOs shook their heads in disgust, agreeing that nothing more could have been expected from sergeants who had never gone through the cleansing process of being corporals. The combatants looked on it as a wonderful fight, and all were good friends the next day. Those who survived it and the war looked back on it with nostalgia.

Not all the fighting was done in the mess, of course. 424 enjoyed the distinction of having the most famed team of air gunners in Bomber Command. Sergeant Peter Engbrecht and Sergeant G.C. Gillanders, mid-upper and rear gunner respectively of Halifax D-Dog, were attacked fourteen times on the night of May 27, and Engbrecht shot down two aircraft. On June 10, again in D-Dog, they did it again, and four nights later they drove off a fighter which was seen to be on fire as it disappeared. During the whole war 424 Squadron claimed nine victories, and the two ace gunners got six of them.

Engbrecht was awarded the Conspicuous Gallantry Medal, the equivalent of the Distinguished Service Order, and a near miss for the Victoria Cross, and Gillanders was awarded the Distinguished Flying Medal. Engbrecht came from a family of conscientious objectors and he was of pure Germanic descent. Both of them, with their crew, survived the war.

Shortly thereafter the rumour gained credence that some gunners (not necessarily the two aces) had taken to turning on flashlights in their rear turrets to attract enemy fighters so that they could shoot them down. It was never proved, of course, and probably it was not true. Gunners carried flashlights in their flying boots—a handy place to find them in a hurry—if they had to clear a stoppage. Some pilots muttered darkly about it, however, swearing they would never fly with anyone who did such a thing. How they could find out was a mystery, since the rear gunner was isolated at the back of the aircraft where nobody could see him.

424 had another unfortunate distinction. It was led by unlucky Wing Commanders.

On 21 January 1944 Wing Commander A.N. Martin was killed in action. He was succeeded by Wing Commander J.D. Blane.

Blane was a permanent force officer who had spent his time in training command until he took over 424 Squadron. Inevitably, as one of the few experienced officers the RCAF had when the war broke out, and the service was expanding at mind-boggling rate, he had spent much of his time administering and otherwise flying a desk. He was sent overseas very likely at his own request, since it was easy and far from unknown for a permanent force officer of fairly high rank to dodge combat service if he wanted to.

He reached the squadron expecting to be welcomed with the same respect, almost awe, that he was used to on his Canadian stations. Instead, he was greeted with something approaching suspicious hostility. The battle-hardened aircrew wanted as their commander someone who had faced the flak and the fighters, not somebody they dismissed as a sprog. When Don Blane, innocent of combat experience, took over the squadron he found himself addressed with formal politeness but his comments downgraded and his orders questioned, dismissed by mere flying officers as uninformed and possibly dangerous. Indeed, one very junior officer in the bar once told him to "get some time in." His image was not helped by efforts to enforce some of the spit and polish discipline he was used to.

The situation irritated and depressed him. He could demand but not command respect until he had faced the same dangers into which he was ordering his subordinates. Unfortunately, Bomber Command forbade its squadron commanders from flying too often, because of the administrative chaos caused if they went missing, and he knew that his men, ignoring this, condemned him for sitting on the ground.

Thus it was that on 28 July 1944, when the squadron was briefed to attack Hamburg, that he flew himself. Very likely he decided to do so because he knew the target was far more danger-ous than the French railway yards that No. 6 Group had been concentrating on for the last couple of months. No OC had a crew of his own, so he chose an experienced crew whose pilot happened to be out of action that day. Blane attended the briefing with his new crew, donned his flying clothing, drew a parachute, handed in his personal belongings like his wallet as everybody else did, and climbed into a lorry to ride to the dispersal where their aircraft was standing. The crew climbed aboard. Blane taxied out to the end of the runway, received the signal from the green winking eye of the Aldis lamp, and took off.

They were never heard from again.

The captain of the crew, who with his men had been two or three sorties from finishing his operational tour, wandered to the crew room the next day. He was shocked, outraged and furious to find they were missing.

He stormed into the office of the station commander, a group captain, elbowing aside the adjutant who tried to stop him, deaf to the words of the orderly room sergeant. Stamping up to the group captain's desk, he launched a tirade of abuse at him.

"God damn it, what in hell d'you mean letting that bloody sprog Blane take my crew and get them killed? Jesus, three more trips and we would 'a' had our tour finished—and now they're dead. That goddam Blane didn't know his ass from a hole in the ground about ops, he didn't know a god damn thing about how to handle a kite over a place like Hamburg, and he had the goddam nerve to take my crew with him and get them killed! He was a goddam murderer, and you're one for letting him! He had no business taking my crew, and you had no bloody business letting him! My crew! My goddam crew, and they're all dead!"

The group captain stood up. The adjutant, who had just shouted to the orderly room sergeant, "Call the service police!" stood behind the door, shocked into immobility. Nothing like this had ever happened during his whole service. "This is a court martial offence!" he told the pilot. "You can't talk to a group captain like that!"

"Group captain be fucked!" the pilot shouted, "he killed my whole bloody crew!" The group captain's eyes bulged. And then the pilot dropped into a chair, covered his face with his hands, and burst into tears. "My crew!! My crew!" he muttered brokenly.

"You are under arrest—" the adjutant began, but the group captain waved him to silence. "There's something about a band of brothers," he said. "A crew is like that." Indeed, a bomber crew had more claim to the title than the fighter pilots of the Battle of Britain, each of whom flew alone. These men had faced deadly danger together, depended utterly on one another, saved each others' lives, and lived, argued and celebrated together.

The group captain himself had never made an operational flight over Germany. He felt himself at even more of the same disadvantage as Blane before this man who had proved himself, despite his much higher rank. He turned to the adjutant. "Get one of the flight commanders to take him somewhere and get him a drink."

A few moments later, when the pilot had been escorted from the office, the group captain called in the adjutant. "Screen him," he ordered. "Give him credit for a completed operational tour. And get him off the station today."

The man disappeared. No formal action was taken. The affair was a nine-day's wonder, until the pressing events of the war drove it from people's minds.

Wing Commander G.A. Roy, DFC, who had commanded the squadron before when it had been flying tropicalized Wellingtons in North Africa, took Blane's place. He lasted eight weeks. In October he was shot down and lost a leg.

His successor was Wing Commander C.C.W. Marshall. In January it was decided to replace him by another wing commander named Williams, whom it was desired to give the experience of command before the war ended. He arrived on the squadron and busied himself getting familiar with the men and the machines. Then one day he took off in a Lancaster. Just after the aircraft became airborne it blew up, with all aboard killed. Marshall resumed command of the squadron until March.

He and his successor survived the war.

CHAPTER TWENTY-FIVE

A navigator's life is forever bound up with time. The easiest check on the skill with which he works is to see how accurately he computes his Estimated Time of Arrival at his destination. Navigators are always checking their watches. In England two or three times a day a time signal in the form of a series of pips would come over the BBC radio, and it was easy to see who were the navigators because every one of them would stop what he was doing to look at his watch and fiddle with the stem. The navigators kept such constant track of the time that the ritual—dear to American airmen and featured religiously in movies, of crying, "Three—Two—One—Hack!" was unnecessary in Bomber Command.

In coastal command navigators used celestial navigation, where precise timing was extremely important, since an error of four seconds would put a celestial observation in error by as much as a mile. Bomber command did not use celestial navigation except on rare occasions, but we did have to reach turning points and targets on time, and we were sharply criticized if we did not.

We were drilled to twist the knobs our Gee sets, record the readings, plot them on a special map, transfer the fix to our plotting charts, draw vectors from our air position to the fix, find a wind, and alter course to the next turning point, all in six minutes. It took a lot of doing, and the six minutes never seemed long enough. We recorded the time to the closest tenth of a minute, sub-dividing the watch-face into ten parts mentally. A tenth of a minute was not very long.

Sometimes, however, a tenth of a minute could be very long indeed, particularly if an engine happened to be on fire.

Earlier in the war the great bomber pilot, Leonard Cheshire, noticed that very few Halifax aircraft managed to make it home on three engines. When he took one up to find out why, he discovered that if a Halifax stalled after losing an engine it went into an uncontrollable spin. After a terrifying minute he managed to get the plane under control and land. He reported the problem, which he was convinced was caused by a faulty rudder design.

Handley-Page, the manufacturers, refused to interrupt production to cure the fault, and it was not until a Polish test pilot was killed while making further tests that the change was made. However, the incident left the Air Force with the legacy of requiring crews to bail out quickly if they lost an engine in flight under certain circumstances.

Our squadron's ruling was that if an engine caught fire over England, and if the fire could not be put out in twenty seconds, the crew should abandon the aircraft. Thus it was that on a cross country flight one day when one engine caught fire that Linklater called to me over the intercom "Navigator! Start counting! Tell me when it's twenty seconds! If the fire isn't out then we're jumping!"

I held my arm out below my eyes, concentrating on the hands of my watch. The sweep second hand was making its steady circle of the face. Meanwhile Link and Ron Ashelford, our flight engineer, were pushing buttons and pulling switches, feathering the engine, cutting off the fuel, and smothering the fire with the extinguisher in the engine nacelle. My watch-hand kept up its inexorable travel a third of the way around the clock-face. Smoke and flames streamed out behind the faulty engine, and then the flames died and it was jutting smoke, and then the smoke whirled away. Finally Linklater's voice came "Okay, we got it out. We're sticking with the kite." Then his voice sharpened. "Navigator! What the hell were you doing? I told you to tell me when twenty seconds were up! We shoulda bailed out—we were just lucky we got the fire out. What the hell were you doing— were you asleep?"

"Keep your shirt on, Link," I replied. "When you told us that the fire was out exactly eighteen seconds had elapsed."

"Eighteen seconds? You're crazy! It musta been two or three minutes!"

"Eighteen seconds, "I said. "Navigators can tell time, you know."

"Jeez! I never woulda believed it!"

"Time passes fast when you're having fun," I said.

"It sure passes slow when you're not," Bob Bamford put in. "I should put a couple of extra hours in my log book." We went back to work and completed the training flight.

Flying time itself was important to everyone. By present-day standards, all of us were woefully inexperienced. Pilots had more time in than the other crew members, but many of those on operations were commanding crews with only three or four hundred hours under their belts. That many hours would not qualify a commercial pilot to hold a co-pilot's job today. Linklater, because he had been a staff pilot at an Air Observer School, and then had gone through two OTUs, reached the eight-hundred mark halfway through our tour, and we were convinced that his extra experience had meant the difference between life and death many times. He was joking one night that statistics showed that accidents had a habit of occurring to pilots with eight hundred hours of flying time, and that his could come any time. He fooled statistics—we never had one.

F/O D.J. Linklater, F/O N.W. Emmott,
Skipton-on-Swale, Yorkshire, 1944.

I kept my obsession with timing right up until it was time for us to make our final trip. We were relieved to find that it was a mining trip all by ourselves, to do our 'gardening' in the estuary of a river that led to a port frequented by submarines. We were to fly out to sea west of the Brittany peninsula, stooge along well out of reach of enemy anti-aircraft guns or flak ships, and then drive straight in to the French coast south of the hot spots such as Brest and St. Nazaire where the Germans objected strongly to

Allied aircraft. There would not be much danger. Later I wondered if the flight commander had purposely put on an easy trip because it was our last trip before we were screened, although at the time I thought it was just the luck of the draw.

It being my last trip, I was determined to make it as navigationally perfect as possible. We had to dog-leg around a bit, but the trip was laid out fairly straightforwardly, and we would even be in Gee coverage most of the time. I carefully calculated the time to set course so that we would arrive over the harbour at the right time, using the latest meteorological winds. We climbed into the aircraft and took off.

The actual winds were completely different from the forecast winds. This did not bother me much, although it did, however, mean that we were continually getting ahead of time. The result was that I had to tell Link to dog-leg—alter course sixty degrees left, hold the heading for three minutes, and then alter back a hundred and twenty degrees the other way for three minutes, and then resume the original course. The maneuver would waste three minutes, and correct our timing.

We flew down to the tip of England, headed out over the Atlantic, and entered the Bay of Biscay, dog-legging every twenty minutes or so to lose time. Linklater moaned and cursed every time I called up the unwelcome order to alter course that sixty degrees. Like everybody else in the aircraft he wanted to get the trip over with, to fly back to Skipton-on-Swale and turn in our parachutes and not have to fly over Germany any more. Stretching out the flight by wasting time over the Bay of Biscay seemed madness. But we were under order, and we obeyed them, and I navigated to drop the mines at the right time.

At last we turned east and headed for the coast. Bob Bamford picked up the coastline on radar, now that we were no longer so far out to sea that there was nothing on the radar screen but blackness. Our position was right, our timing was correct within seconds. Bamford crawled into the nose. "Bomb doors open!" he called to Linklater. The bomb doors unfolded. "Bombs armed!" he said. Linklater repeated it. I looked at my watch. We were three seconds early—a perfect navigational trip. Bob could see the headland he had been briefed to recognize. He pressed the switch. "Bombs gone!"

The aircraft did not lurch upward as it always did when the bomb load fell away. "Go look at the bomb-bay, Ron," Linklater said. Ashelford took his flashlight (in keeping with English practice, he always called it a 'torch') and peered into the bay. "Blast!" he reported. "They didn't go! They hung up!"

"Damn it!" Linklater cursed. "We gotta go round again! Gimme a course out and a course back!" I went back to my chart and computed the courses to fly. We flew west and then swung around to the original final course, with Ron checking the circuits. Everything seemed correct. "We'll try it again, said Linklater. We returned to the same point in the harbour. Bamford pressed the bomb-tit. This time the mines fell free, and the aircraft jumped with joy as it should have.

There was still no flak. The gunners, if there were any (we had been briefed to expect flak) perhaps had been caught napping the first time, and did not expect us to return. We were not shot at. After two or three minutes over enemy-occupied territory we were back over the friendly sea again, out of reach of anti-aircraft shells. We headed back west, putting distance between us and any German fighters. In any case we never saw any that night; they were probably farther north, protecting the *Reich*, not France.

When we turned north again, however, the tail wind we had coming down strengthened and turned into a fairly strong headwind. It was a long slog back to base, and the sky was lighting up with the dawn when we got back. The crew complained. There was nothing I could do: I did not invent the wind!

We climbed down, overjoyed to be on the ground again, our tour completed. When we turned in our parachutes, in keeping with ancient custom, I pulled the ripcord of mine in honour of completing the tour. One of the parachute riggers rushed over to extract the ten-shilling fine appropriate to such a deed in ordinary times, but I proudly pointed out that in my cases it was legal, and the only chance I would get on the squadron to pull a ripcord, since I had missed my chance while bailing out over Germany.

Thus it was that I completed my operational tour with a mine-drop that was five minutes late. My perfect navigational trip was recorded as a mediocre one. Of course the crew knew that it had been some obscure fault in the electrical circuits, but it left me with a bad tastes in my mouth. I had wanted that last trip to be my masterpiece.

CHAPTER TWENTY-SIX

After we landed from our last trip, our thirty-sixth as a crew (Link had done one more as second pilot, for experience), we had a party in the mess to celebrate our screening, and followed that up with a gathering in a local pub which included the ground crew. We were all elated. It was something like having a death-sentence repealed. The dangers which we had dismissed from our words but not from our minds while we were on ops could now be looked in the face. They appalled us.

I had written to my wife every day since I had been overseas—sometimes just a postcard, concealing the fact that I was in danger, and trying to imply that I was still undergoing training. Now, with my tour over, I told her I had been on operations. Later, she told me she had suspected it all along.

We were given leave. I went up to Scotland to visit relatives and see the Scottish sights. One night, in a hotel bedroom, I relived one of my trips, and woke up soaking with sweat and livid with terror. All the dangers of the nights when we had flown over enemy territory with flak and fighters and enemy radar stations and German cannon conspiring to do us to death, crowded in upon me, and I sat bolt-upright in bed, clutching the blankets to me. I sat shivering with fright for half an hour, and then went back to sleep. The monster was exorcised; I never had such a nightmare again.

When we returned to the air station we were taken to Allerton Park, where the headquarters of No. 6 RCAF Bomber Group was situated, to meet Air Vice Marshal C.M. "Black Mike" McEwen, the commander. He liked to meet screened crews, perhaps to persuade himself that some of the men he commanded could actually survive operations. Except for this visit, we never met any of our high commanders, the highest-ranking officer who ever saw us being our station commander, Group Captain F.R. Miller (who went on to become the Chief of the Air Staff of the RCAF after the war, and who impressed me as being a decent chap). Black Mike greeted us warmly, leaving us a little nonplussed by his lack of formality, and telling us he would have us shown around the headquarters by one of his 'boys.' The 'boy' turned out to be a squadron leader with the DSO.

I expected to be sent to an Operational Training Unit as an instructor, as my pilot and Frank Russell, my wireless operator, were. By the time I completed my operations, however, England was awash with aircrew, since the British Commonwealth Air Training Plan had reached its zenith and was turning out aircrew by the thousands. A beneficent RCAF decided that I was not required in Britain, and sent me back to Canada.

I returned on the Queen Mary, which was lightly loaded, most of its passengers being headed the other way in October 1944. There were a number of returning American aircrew on the ship, although we Canadians tended to keep to ourselves. One of them was a young officer who was being led around the deck by an attendant; it was obvious that he had been blinded. I felt pretty lucky when I saw that. The Americans wore leather jackets with the names of the cities they had attacked emblazoned on the back. We Canadians agreed that this was blatant self-advertisement, but still wished we could do it ourselves. We did not have leather bomber jackets, of course; the RAF flying overalls we had worn on ops had been returned to stores before we left the squadron, and they were scarcely the things we would have worn anywhere but in an aircraft anyway.

We were met off the coast of the United States by a blimp, and later by a destroyer, which sniffed around us like a dog around a cow. Then we sailed past the Statue of Liberty and were unloaded onto a dock, where magnificent women of the American Red Cross met us with coffee and doughnuts, obviously mistaking us for some of their own boys. We were all herded aboard a New York Central train to take us to Ottawa. We even had berths, and the next morning we had breakfast in the dining car. That kind of luxury amazed us, and we realized that at last we were far from the theatre of war.

When we reached Ottawa we were met by an official delegation which welcomed us, again to our surprise. There was even a small band there; we had not seen one since we left the Initial Training School where our aircrew training started. In all honesty we had not missed them much. We were given billets and told to report to a hall where we would be properly documented and presented with things like operational wings, little badges to advertise to the world that we had served in combat and completed a tour. None of us could prove we had actually flown against the enemy, so we were told that the gadgets would be mailed to us later.

Before reporting to the hall, a number of the returnees had visited beer parlors. Used to English beer, which was far less alcoholic, they arrived in a state of riotous intoxication, walking up and down the hall shouting and making indecorous suggestions to the women officers who were trying to brief them as to what they were to do in Canada. The same thing had happened with every returning draft, so the ladies and their male comrades were tolerant.

We were all given a month's leave. I was ordered to report to RCAF Station Boundary Bay near Vancouver, to serve as a stores officer. That was the best the Air Force would do for me, since battle-experienced aircrew were ten a penny in Canada, and we did not have battles to fight out of the West Coast. I did not care, since my objective was to get back to the beautiful woman whose photograph I had carried with me on every operational flight.

My wife met me at the train in Winnipeg, and we had some glorious days together. Her father had served in World War I, and in our conversations we found ourselves comrades in arms, if a generation removed. The gap had closed since I had gone overseas; after all, I had spent three years over Stuttgart one night.

We travelled west to Nelson, my home town, where my father made sure that his friends made much of us, and where I was even invited to read the lesson at St. Saviour's Pro-Cathedral, the beautiful Anglican church in which I had been confirmed. I was overshadowed by the presence of one of my school-mates, who had won the Distinguished Service Medal for gallantry in Italy. I rationalized my own medalless state by reflecting that I had never done anything particularly brave.

In due course I reported to RCAF Station Boundary Bay. The stores officer there (he was now called the Equipment Officer, doubtless to improve efficiency) welcomed me with restrained resignation. There were a good many tour-expired aircrew in odd jobs at the station, and the professionals put up with them because they had to. Most of them knew nothing about their ground jobs and cared less, and my middle-aged squadron leader boss expected nothing of me. With my five years of experience behind me, however, I was soon able to give him help. We became good friends. I also found a sergeant who had been an AC2 working for me when I had been a sergeant at Ucluelet, and we spent a good deal of time yarning about shared experiences. The time-warp affected us both; he called me Sarge, as he had done in 1940, and I called him Miff. The airmen listening to us wondered what was happening.

I had to find my wife as place to live, and we searched out a room in a big old house in nearby Ladner occupied by a widow in her late seventies. Her late husband had been a mighty hunter, and had owned two dogs, one called Shot and one called Bang. Occasionally I had to call Bang, the survivor, which required me to stand on the back porch and yell "Bang! Bang! Bang!" This no doubt caused any listeners to wonder what kind of cretins the RCAF had elevated to commissioned rank in those slack days.

We managed to convert Bang to Anglicanism from Roman Catholicism. His mistress went to her church by taxi, which Bang wanted to follow but was too elderly to keep up with. The Anglican church was much closer, however, and he followed us there and walked in, his tail supersonic with joy, to join us. When the sides-man rushed up to throw him out, he gave vent to a series of heart-broken wails that made it seem he was being tortured to death. The fact that he had just rolled in a dead fish did not make him any more popular. We wished he had stayed a Catholic.

Nobody in Vancouver ever gave servicemen any discounts on anything, but this rule did not hold good in the United States. When my wife and I visited Seattle, we decided to go to a movie. The attendant looked at my light-blue air force uniform and said. "Go on in—I've got a son in the Navy too." After the show, we stopped into a coffee shop. The cashier looked at me as I stepped up to pay my bill and said, "Forget it. I've got a son in the Army, just like you." Later, at a doughnut shop, the cashier recognized my uniform instantly as she said, "No man in the uniform of the United States Marines has to pay for a doughnut in my shop!" I did not enlighten any of them.

There were some pleasant surprises too. One day in the mess I was sitting glancing at a copy of the *Victoria Colonist* when I saw a headline, on page 13, reading, "Local Man Awarded Decoration." Datelined Sidney, British Columbia, (the closest community to

Patricia Bay) it reported that one Flying Officer N.W. Emmott, of Sidney, had been awarded the Distinguished Flying Cross. I sat bolt upright. "Holy smoke! That's me!" Then I remembered that my last address in Canada before I went overseas had been at Sidney, where my wife and I stayed while I was at the Operational Training Unit. I was flabbergasted. I had thought that escaping with my life was the only decoration I could hope for, especially since I had escaped any sort of official notice during my operational tour. I was a little curious as to why I should have to rely on a newspaper to find out about it, but then I considered that I was not very important. Later I was pleased to hear that Linklater and Bob Bamford had both been given the same distinction. I decided then that I had belonged to a pretty good crew.

My opinion of my importance was confirmed a few weeks later when I decided to request that I should be put back on flying duties instead of continuing as a stores officer. This called for an interview with one Group Captain Robert Turnbull, who had a distinguished combat record. He asked me when I had flown in Bomber Command, and when I told him he snorted, "Did an easy tour, didn't you?" I had to admit he was right. I resigned myself to going back to work as a stores officer. A few weeks later, however, I was notified that I was returned to flying duties and was transferred to Patricia Bay.

Just before I left Boundary Bay, a parade was broken up by a spectacular display of flying. The details deserve a chapter to themselves.

CHAPTER TWENTY-SEVEN

For over three quarters of a century spectacular displays of aerial acrobatics have been made at air shows and exhibitions, usually by single-engined fighters or trainers performing over airfields or lake-fronts, and seldom lasting more than half an hour or so. They are never performed over the main streets of cities in two countries, continued for five hours, or made with big, heavy multi-seat aircraft. All these taboos were broken on December 8, 1944, when the most spectacular flying display that any of the spectators were ever to see was made by Sergeant Don Palmer Scratch, Royal Canadian Air Force.

Don Scratch was born on July 7 1919, the son of a country doctor in rural Saskatchewan. His mother separated from his father when Don was a child and moved with her son to Ashmont, Alberta, a village near Edmonton. When the war broke out he welcomed it because it gave him a chance to fly. On July 20, 1940, he joined the Air Force, in Edmonton. He had applied long before, but it took the Air Force, swamped with applications for enlistment, months to get around to his file.

R60973 Aircraftsman Second Class Scratch D.P. followed the trail that so many thousands of his compatriots took during those years. He went to No. 1 Manning Depot in Toronto, where he lived in quarters which once had housed sheep and pigs and goats, at the grounds of the Canadian National Exhibition. He stood in line to receive inoculations and his pay and his meals. He took intelligence tests, learned how to drill and clean his buttons and slope arms. A month of this, and he was sent off on guard duty. The RCAF, swamped by volunteers, could not train them as fast as they enlisted, and as it waited for aircraft to be rolled off assembly lines, for airports to be built, and for instructors to learn their trade, it kept its embryo aircrew busy carrying rifles around the perimeters of air stations. Scratch was sent to No. 119 Bomber Reconnaissance Squadron at Yarmouth, Nova Scotia, as a security guard, where he looked at Northrop Delta seaplanes bobbing about on floats in the harbour and wished he was flying one of them. Two months of this, and he was sent back to Toronto to No. 1 Initial Training School, where he was subjected to a crash course in mathematics and basic aeronautical knowledge that lasted for six weeks.

His next move was to No. 2 Elementary Flying Training School at Fort William, at the head of Lake Superior, where he was introduced to deHavilland Tiger Moths. Little single-engined biplanes with plastic coupe tops, they were members of a line of aircraft called 'Moths'—Puss Moths and Cirrus Moths and Gypsy Moths—which the RCAF had been flying since 1924. Fabric-covered and seemingly fragile, they were actually tough and serviceable two-seaters, maneuverable as gulls, which were just a little hard to fly. The RCAF's Training Command liked them that way—it made the students better pilots.

Leading Aircraftsman Scratch—who had been reclassified when he went to ITS, and had a white flash in his cap to tell the world he was Aircrew Under Training—found himself immediately at home. When he put his hands on the crude stick of a 'Tigerschmitt' it was as if craft and man melded into one personality. He passed his flight checks, was assessed by his flight commander as an outstanding student, keen to fly, conscientious, with the right attitude, reliable and hard-working. It took him six weeks to learn how to handle a Tiger Moth, including how to lose height by putting it into an intentional spin, and how to throw it around the sky in standard aerobatics which formed part of every tyro pilot's training. He liked that.

From Tiger Moths he graduated to No. 1 Service Flying Training School at Camp Borden, north of Toronto. Here he learned to fly Harvards, single-engine monoplane two-seaters with all the modern improvements like retractable undercarriages. Harvards trained most of the Allied fighter pilots who fought the Hitler War. LAC Scratch flew the exercises that were to make him a battle-worthy pilot; circuits and bumps, formation flying, navigation exercises, night flying, precautionary landings, bombing missions with 6-pound practice bombs, and gunnery missions. He graduated with little difficulty, gaining glowing remarks from his instructors. At the end of April he stood stiffly at attention to have his wings pinned on his chest, and he traded the white flash in his cap for his sergeant's stripes. He was now a qualified pilot.

He was sent to No. 118 Fighter Squadron, based at Rockcliffe, near Ottawa, to guard the nation's capital. He stayed there only six weeks, but he was checked out on the Grumman Goblin (the US Navy's FF1) a single-engined biplane which had been a first-line fighter in the Thirties, but was hopelessly obsolete now.

His next step was to go to the East Coast, where there was at least a threat. On June 18, 1941, he found himself back as a pilot at the same squadron he had served as a security guard the year before—No. 119 BR Squadron at Yarmouth. It was equipped with Bolingbrokes, Canadian-built versions of the British Bristol Blenheim aircraft. The Bolingbroke was a four-place twin-engined monoplane with a mid-upper gun turret, a single forward-firing machine gun, and two Wasp Junior engines, weighing rather less than 10,000 pounds empty and 14,000 pounds loaded. The Blenheim, touted at the beginning of the war as Britain's best bomber, had turned out to be perilously close to a death-trap when it met German fighters, but despite a terrible record for unserviceability it was good enough for patrols in the peaceful skies over the Atlantic off Nova Scotia.

Scratch was not enthusiastic about his job. The Bolingbrokes were only stopgaps; with their range of only 300 miles, their patrols could succeed only in keeping German submarines a little further from the coast than they might otherwise venture, and the most sophisticated detection aid they carried was the human eye-ball. The patrols were boring, uneventful and for all that Scratch could tell, useless. His disenchantment was obvious to his flight commander, who rated his skill at his job of anti-submarine patrol as moderate, which meant pretty poor. Maybe it was good for a man who wanted to be a fighter pilot.

For seven months he flew out of Yarmouth, and then went with his squadron to Sydney, Nova Scotia, at the north tip of Cape Breton Island where it juts into the Gulf of Saint Lawrence. He arrived there in mid-January 1942 and went back to patrolling. It made more sense, however, since the Bolingbrokes with their short ranges could still fly a tight blockade against the submarines who were cruising the St. Lawrence river itself. Perhaps he was getting reconciled to his job. It was uneventful for two months. Then the unreliable Bolingbroke caught up with him.

On March 16 1942, just after take-off, his starboard Wasp

Junior cut out in a climbing right-hand turn. Turning into a dead engine is shaky at the best of times, and the aircraft had barely enough flying speed. It stalled. Scratch lost control, and the plane crashed into the tree-tops. The navigator was killed, the wireless operator and the gunner were both badly injured, and Scratch was pulled from the wreck more dead than alive. He had multiple cuts and bruises, and both ankles were shattered. His doctors expected him to be crippled for life. The accident investigation absolved him, attributing the crash to defective spark plugs.

Undiscouraged by the doctors prognostications, Scratch fought to regain his health. As he worked at the exercises the physical therapist prescribed for him, he kept his mind fixed on his chief objective—to get back into the cockpit. He graduated from his bed to a wheel chair, to crutches, to a cane. Discharged from hospital, he went home on convalescent leave. He returned to his squadron, and when the medical officer pronounced him fit for duty again, he seated himself behind the control column of an aircraft and took off. Despite the crash, he had not lost his touch, and he went back to duty with 119 Squadron.

On April 24 1943 he was promoted to commissioned rank. Two weeks later he was transferred to 119 BR's detachment at Mont Joli, on the south shore of the St. Lawrence river. Hudson patrol bombers (Lockheed's military version of their Lodestar transports) flew from the field, but Scratch did not stay with them long. A month later, on June 5 1943 he was transferred to RCAF Station, Gander, Newfoundland.

Gander was the hub of the highest-priority venture on the East Coast. German submarines had all but succeeded in cutting off the flow and men and munitions to Britain by concentrating on the famous gap in the middle of the Atlantic, out of range of most of the aircraft based either in the British Isles or Newfoundland. Liberators—big four-engined B24's—had started flying from St. Eval in Cornwall to close the gap, and the US Navy had a squadron of them in Argentia in Newfoundland, but the RCAF had none.

Then, in May 1943, Wing Commander Clare L. Annis, the RCAF's most experienced anti-submarine commander, made a trip to Washington where he met an old friend of his, a lieutenant colonel in the USAAF named Hobson, who had joined the RCAF at the outbreak of the war and then had transferred back to the USAAF after Pearl Harbor. He opened doors for Annis, who pleaded his case so

160

effectively that the USAAF made some B24's available to Canada. No. 10 BR Squadron was equipped with them and made their first operational flight in June, just as Scratch arrived at Gander.

Scratch was posted to 10 BR on October 16 1943, and soon was flying on long patrols over the bleak and cold North Atlantic, escorting convoys and hunting submarines. With his experience, he expected to be made an aircraft commander, considering it nothing less than his due. He was however given a co-pilot's job, important but not as prestigious as that of a plane commander, and usually reserved for new pilots just out of training school. As a man who had joined the RCAF as soon as he could, Scratch found his position a rankling one. He wanted to be a captain. He knew he was a good pilot, and he had commanded his own Boling-broke—even if the smaller plane had not carried a co-pilot.

The answer given was that his broken legs had not healed completely enough to ensure that he could take the strain of controlling a heavy Liberator should he lose an engine on take-off. Furthermore, should a submarine fight back with its deck-gun during an attack and shoot out an engine, the pilot had to be able to retain control no matter how viciously the aircraft bucked and twisted. The man at the controls had to be strong enough to do the job, no matter how arduous the circumstances.

Liberators, five times as heavy as Bolingbrokes, and jammed with brand new and recently-developed radar and anti-submarine equipment, worth a million great big 1943 dollars, and by far the most effective anti-submarine weapon the RCAF had, were far too precious to have any chances taken with them at all. The crash of one of them in which the entire crew was lost would affect the lives of 200 people.

The crews were all very highly trained, and only a few men in the whole Royal Canadian Air Force were capable of operating the equipment, interpreting the results of what they saw, and then making an attack on a submarine. The Battle of the Atlantic was reaching a climax, and the contribution of the Liberators was vital. To trust one of these mighty weapons to a man whose legs might buckle at a crucial moment did not make sense.

Scratch did not believe it. He protested, but to no avail. One mark against him was that he did not look robust. He was slight, almost skinny, about five feet nine and no more than 135 pounds, with fair hair that was becoming thin on top. He showed the scars of his brush with death and the month he had spent in hospital, and he lacked the forceful personality that might have made his superiors discount his appearance. He was moody and rather unpredictable, but not a heavy drinker; not the type of a good drinking man that would have made him worthy of comradely trust. Mild, not wild, he caused no disturbances in the officers' mess; he was just another pilot whom everybody called "D.P."

Some of those who knew him say that the broken legs would not have been enough to keep him out of the left hand seat. His superiors just did not consider him captain material, they say, and used the physical argument as an excuse. No matter what the reason, Scratch wasn't having any. He could fly better than 90% of those who had been designated as aircraft commanders, and his legs were as strong, he was convinced, as they had ever been.

The Newfoundland summer, with Scratch flying twenty-hour patrols over the Atlantic, found him growing more moody and withdrawn. He saw other men, with less service and less experience, made aircraft commanders and promoted to the rank of flight lieutenant. The worst part was that nobody could prove his legs were weak; it was only a medical opinion.

On the night of August 7 1944 Scratch was sitting in the officers' mess at a party at which beer flowed freely. He drank his share. Through the fumes of alcohol the discrimination he felt he was subjected to took on ever greater dimensions. The mess emptied. He looked outside into the darkness.

If his superiors considered his legs were too weak to ensure that he could control a Liberator under all circumstances, then it was up to him to prove otherwise. He considered that he could fly a Liberator, at 60,000 pounds all-up weight, its four engine, its long Davis wing with the big Fowler flaps, its twin tails and its bombbay, all by himself. Ordinarily it was unthinkable to fly it without at least three men—a pilot, a co-pilot and a flight engineer. There were four engines to control, to synchronize, to adjust the revolutions, the mixture and the manifold pressure, and four propellors whose pitches had to be set. It was no mean job, especially since the aircraft had appeared on the scene only a year before and still elicited a great deal of awe from the men who flew them.

Lit by determination and alcohol, he walked to the hangar line. Some of the Liberators were under cover in the hangars, but there was not room for all of them. Scratch looked several over and selected one that looked ready to go. He climbed into it through the bomb-bay doors, usually left open, and settled himself in the pilot's seat. Nobody had looked at him as he walked down the hangar-line; nobody questioned him. After all, he was an officer and a pilot, whom everybody expected to have legitimate business in the aircraft he flew. Nobody turned a hair when he closed the bomb-bay doors, turned the fuel on, turned on the master switch, and pressed the starter button for one of the big engines.It coughed and sputtered and then burst into full-throated life.

He went through the pre-flight drill, the cockpit check, carefully and thoroughly like the first-class pilot he was. One by one he started the engines. There should have been a ground crewman standing by with a fire extinguisher in case a blow-back resulted in an engine fire, but he could not be in two places at once and he didn't want company. He did not need one; all four engines started normally. Scratch had taken the chocks away from the wheels before he started, holding the aircraft steady with the brakes. When he pushed the throttles forward and released the brakes the aircraft rolled away from the hard-stand. He squeezed the microphone button on his control-column and called the control tower.

"Taxi clearance!"

"Cleared to taxi," came the reply.

Night take-offs were routine, and operational aircraft never filed flight plans. Nobody in the tower thought anything of it. Scratch increased power, turned onto the taxi-strip leading to the end of the runway, and pulled the throttles back a little as his speed built up.

"Take-off clearance."

"Cleared for take-off."

He lined the Liberator up with the runway, checked magnetos, made sure that the mixture was full rich, the propellor pitch full fine, the carburetor heat full cold, and the flaps fully up. He pushed the throttles forward and the engines snarled as the aircraft gathered speed. He pulled the stick back gently and the aircraft left the runway. He leaned over, pulled the undercarriage control lever to retract the wheels, and waited until he had a couple of hundred feet of altitude before he levelled out to allow his airspeed to build up. He pulled the throttles back from take-off to climbing power. The air station fell behind him.

Now that he was in the air, he had proved that he could take off and fly a Liberator single-handed. But what was he to do next? There would be one feat which would prove incontrovertibly that he could handle a Liberator under any circumstances. He would fly the aircraft to Europe, by way of the Azores. He headed out over the coast and kept on southeast over the Atlantic. During his regular patrols he had flown to the Azores many times, and he knew the general course to fly. He settled down on the right heading and engaged the automatic pilot, and made sure that it was holding the right airspeed and the right altitude.

Scratch checked around the aircraft to make sure that everything was in order, and returned to the left-hand seat to look out through the wide side windows over the grey Atlantic, with the white-caps flecking the dull water. For some three hours he flew along. Then, as he went through his routine checks, he found that his intention to go to the Azores could not be achieved. There was not enough fuel.

When he took off the aircraft had been only partly refuelled. The long thick wing of the Liberator contained the fuel tanks, and the maintenance dogma of the day dictated that the load in them when the aircraft was on the ground should be kept low. At the same time the asphalt hard-standings on which the aircraft were parked were suspected of being fragile, and the word was to keep the aircraft light. As a result, aircraft were refuelled before take-off.

Scratch, of course, had not had the plane topped up before he took it off all by himself. Regretfully he realized that he would have to swing the nose around and head back to Newfoundland.

Although he could not reach the Azores, he could still prove his point that he was completely capable of controlling a Liberator all by himself. As the fumes of alcohol cleared from his brain he may have settled on what seemed to him a rational course of action, or he may have considered that all was lost anyway, and that he might as well be hanged for a sheep as a lamb. In any case, when he flew over the coast of Newfoundland he found the US Navy base of Argentia ahead of him.

Argentia was one of the bases which had been traded to the United States by Britain in exchange for fifty overage four-stack destroyers four years before. Newfoundland at the time was not part of Canada, but a crown colony directly administered by Britain. Now Argentia was staffed by American sailors who themselves flew Liberators on anti-submarine patrols.

The base erupted like an ant-hill poked with a stick when a Liberator, with the red-white-and-blue roundels of the Royal Canadian Air Force, roared down out of the blue and commenced a spectacular 'shoot-up.' (Airmen of the day called it a shoot-up, although no bullets were fired.) Scratch flew between the hangars, stirred up dust on the parade ground while the flag whipped in his slipstream, blew pebbles from the tarred roofs of the hangars, and rattled the windows of the messes and barracks. He tore over the camp, engines snarling at full power, climbed out, whipped around in a tight circle and made another pass. The Americans, Pearl Harbor fresh in their minds, stood to their guns, but there were no bombs and no bullets, and even the Americans were not averse to a little shoot-up of a rival establishment now and then if they thought they could get away with it.

To the commanding officer of the base it was not that simple. A plane, even with RCAF roundels on it, could be a danger.

"What the hell's that crazy bastard doing anyway?" he demanded of his aides, and when he saw that they knew no more about it than he did, he got on his hot line to Washington. Maybe there was some international significance in what the strange aircraft was doing; Canadians, generally pretty well disciplined, were slow to commit such flagrant violations of flying regulations. Washington knew nothing about it, of course, and the Navy man who received the Argentia commander's query immediately called Ottawa.

RCAF Headquarters was as flabbergasted as Washington had been. The officer taking the call made excuses and immediately called the commanding officer of RCAF Station Gander, Wing Commander H.B. "Brandy" Godwin. The call came as a shock to him. Of all the problems that afflict a station commander, that one of his pilots should steal an aircraft and beat up a base belonging to another country was the one which had never crossed his mind. He stood open-mouthed for a moment before he promised to investigate and call back, and then fired a barrage of questions at his aides, none of whom knew more than he did. A stolen car, a break-in at the sergeants' mess, an attempt by a prisoner in the guard room to escape, had all been foreseen and guarded against, but to steal an aircraft single-handed—? Nobody had even thought that one man, unaided, could take a Liberator off. There were just too many taps and instruments and switches and controls for one man to handle.

The officers at Gander—the Chief Administrative Officer, the Chief Technical Officer, the officer in charge of the service police, and especially Wing Commander Max Martyn—the officer commanding No.10 BR Squadron—were all in frantic action, but outside of confirming that one of the treasured Liberators was missing, there was little they could do. Pilots of a fighter squadron could be sent to shoot the aircraft down, but there was no point in that. Nobody had been hurt, and Liberators were too valuable to take chances with. As they were debating their next moves, the Liberator, with Flying Officer Scratch alone at the controls, appeared over the horizon and headed straight for the station.

Engines roaring, the big plane screamed between two of the hangars, its high twin-tail the only thing visible as it disappeared behind the building and then flashed out again to pull up over the hospital. That outraged Godwin most since the building shook, test-tubes broke, as the Liberator missed the roof by inches. Scratch pulled the plane up at the edge of the field, turned, and roared back to fly between two more hangars. Once more gravel streamed from hangar roofs as the slipstream from four engines tore it free; once more men streamed into the open to watch the display, standing open-mouthed with their eyes skyward, and scattering or dropping flat as the plane hurtled toward them. The aircraft flew back and forth, across the parade ground, across the runways, pulling up again over the hospital, blasting the headquarters building with the CO's office in it with the ear-shattering crescendo from his engines. Helplessly Godwin stood shaking his fist at his errant pilot flying one of his precious aircraft. The display was even more dazzling than the one which had been made at Argentia, the maneuvers more breathtaking, with Scratch throwing the patrol-bomber around as if it were a fighter. Martyn climbed up onto the platform running around the top of the control tower, and Scratch drove him off it with a breathtakingly close pass. Furious voices screamed into microphones, telling Scratch to stop his beat-up, to come down, to land. He paid no attention to them for a while, until he tired of his sport or decided that the inevitable could not be postponed any longer. He climbed up a thousand feet or so, put the plane into level flight, engaged the autopilot, and let down the undercarriage. In a Liberator it was routine to check the position of the nose wheel to ensure that it was fully down by having the flight engineer look at it through a small window in the front of the aircraft. Scratch left the pilot's seat, clambered down into the nose, checked the nose-wheel, and then regained his seat. He switched the autopilot out and prepared for the landing.

Landing a Liberator was a complicated business. There were four engines whose revolutions and manifold pressure and mixture had to be adjusted, whose carburetor heat controls had to be set full cold, whose fuel supplies had to be changed over for the landing, and whose propellors had to be set into fully fine pitch. He had to set the flaps and the trim. It took him a while to complete the check-list There was too much work for one man, but Scratch did it all. He circled the field, approached the runway, babying the throttles to keep the right airspeed, touching the control column and the trim controls to keep the right path of descent, and flared out. The aircraft settled down as the wings lost lift and the wheels kissed the runway. It was a beautiful landing.

He taxied along the runway and turned off at an intersection. He trundled back to the hangar apron, swung into a parking place, and cut the engines. To the cluster of jeeps and cars surrounding him he waved, and then he opened the bomb-bay doors and climbed down through them. Wing Commander Martyn stood in front of him, turning purple. Scratch looked at him, thought back to his approach, with his hands flashing everywhere in the cockpit, doing all the things a co-pilot normally would do for him as well as controlling the aircraft, and shook his head.

"Christ, have I been busy!" he said.

"You're under arrest," Martyn barked.

The service policemen beside Martyn and Godwin converged on Scratch. Within minutes he was on his way to his room in the officers' quarters, where he was held in close arrest while the Commanding Officer convened a court of inquiry, and then called back to Ottawa, trying to explain the unexplainable.

Scratch was court-martialled. The facts were incontrovertible, the conclusion foregone. He was found guilty of "whilst on active service, flying an aircraft at an altitude below 1000 feet while not in an authorized low-flying area," and "making a flight which was not duly authorized." He was sentenced to be dismissed from the service, equivalent to the old-fashioned punishment of cashiering. The court gave him his due; the findings stated that he had handled the aircraft during his escapade "correctly and with considerable skill." Everybody admitted that he had certainly proved that despite his broken legs he had the strength to fly a Liberator.

His dismissal was dated September 2, 1944. Scratch, however, still hankered after aircraft, still yearned for the feel of the control-column in his hands, the force that pressed him back in the seat when he opened the throttles, the roar of engines in his ears, the smell of oil and gasoline. He checked with RCAF recruiters. After all, he had 800 flying hours, he was highly qualified, and it was a shame to waste his skill. The recruiting sergeant looked into the fine print and found that Scratch could enlist in the RCAF for flying duties, but not as an officer. He would be entitled to a sergeant's three stripes, but that was all. Scratch did not hesitate. He rejoined the Air Force less than two weeks after he had left it.

It was late 1944, and the RCAF was readying a force of Liberators to bomb Japan from Burmese bases. Scratch was an obvious candidate. He had to fly as a co-pilot, not as a captain. There was no hope of his leading his own crew, whose other pilot, navigator, and probably wireless operator were all officers. Scratch shrugged. He would fly against Japan in the right-hand seat, doing what the captain told him. Once in a while he would shoot a landing, and that would be his reward.

He was sent to No. 5 Operational Training Unit at Boundary Bay, just over the border from Washington state. The OTU was set up to convert pilots who had been trained on other aircraft onto the Liberator, and then to train the crews in the skills they must have to stay alive while they blasted the Nipponese Empire. Most of the aircraft of the RCAF had conventional undercarriages, with a tail-wheel, but the Liberator had a tricycle landing gear. To introduce pilots to it gently, they were trained on tricycle-gear Mitchell (B-25) light bombers. The OTU was equipped with both types of aircraft, Mitchells and Liberators.

Scratch joined his crew and took the conversion training. He didn't really need it, but he was in no position to argue. He did the circuits and bumps the curriculum called for in the Mitchell, and then went through the motions of learning to fly the Liberator. His instructors had no argument that he already knew how to fly it. They said he was probably the best pilot Boundary Bay had seen.

Scratch knew how good he was. He didn't pay much attention during his ground classes, but he did not make an issue of it.

168

Nevertheless he was bored and unhappy. After the day's work, in which he sat through lectures he could have given better than the instructor, and flown around the circuit in the right-hand seat while the pilot flew inexpertly in the left-hand one, he left his officer crew-mates and accompanied the air gunners and flight engineers, most of them fresh-face kids with gleaming new sergeants' stripes, to the sergeants' mess. He would eat his supper and then head for the bar. The sergeants' mess did not serve hard liquor, and he had to content himself with beer. Scratch made out with the beer, looking back regretfully to the days when, as an officer, if he wanted a scotch and water he could get it.

Longingly he looked at the left-hand seat of the aircraft every time he flew. Who should be the captain? The best pilot, and he was the best pilot, the most experienced. Returning to the bar, he would brood some more.

On the night of December 5 1944 he was brooding a little more than usual, and he was drunker than usual. Things hadn't gone well that day, and he needed the beer he was putting down. Midnight came, with his mood still black. The night outside was black also, but not blacker than his future looked. He went back to his room and dozed. He could not sleep. At about four in the morning he could not stand his bare barrack-room any longer. He went outside into the raw night, damp with the threat of rain. It did not snow in Boundary Bay, but it was cold with a chill that bit into his bones. He would have preferred the sharp cold of Newfoundland or his Alberta home.

He walked up to the hangar lines, where the Liberators and Mitchells were lined up waiting for the next day's flying. Like magnets they drew Scratch toward them. He walked up to one of the Liberators and peered through the open bomb-bay. He climbed into the fuselage almost by reflex action, and clambered into the cockpit. He slipped behind the control column; not the right-hand one, but the pilot's. Reaching forward, he checked the familiar switches and controls. His fingers cracked a throttle, flicked an ignition switch.

He pushed a starter button and an engine burst into life, with white smoke pouring from the exhaust stacks until the engine suddenly caught and the slipstream blew the smoke in shreds past the tail. A second engine, and then a third; and then all four were going. Scratch settled into the seat, snapped on the seat-belt and shoulder-harness, and shoved the throttles forward. The aircraft lurched ahead. Scratch turned it toward the runway, and steered it past the other aircraft where they stood, bulky in the dark. He adjusted the throat microphone and squeezed the button on his control wheel.

"Ground control—taxi clearance."

He was cleared to taxi to the runway.

But the taxi-strip was narrow, and Scratch's head was fuzzy. The big Liberator veered toward the side. Scratch kicked at a brake but could not stop the swing until a fraction of a second too late. A big tire rolled into the soft shoulder, muddy from a week of rain. The plane lurched as the wheel dug in. A main wheel and the nose wheel slewed into the ditch at the side of the strip. Scratch gunned an engine to try to pull it back onto the concrete, but it was too late. The nose wheel collapsed backwards and broke. The plane pitched forward, and two propellors dug into the earth and sheered off. Scratch slapped the ignition switches, cut the throttles, and sat still for a few moments as he absorbed the extent of his disaster. Then he unbuckled his seat-belt, climbed down from the pilot's seat, left by the rear door, and stood for a moment on the wet taxi-strip. The aircraft would not fly again that day.

He left the stranded Liberator and walked back toward the parked aircraft. Liberators seemed jinxed. He'd try a Mitchell. Picking one that bore the serial number HG343, he released the ladder that swung down between the main wheels and climbed aboard. Once again he was in the pilot's seat. It was still dark, just before five in the morning. He started the engines, taxied out, rolled down another taxi-strip from the one on which sat the bogged Liberator, and jockeyed engines and brakes to make sure that he did not make the same mistake twice.

He asked for clearance, got it, and took off into the darkness. The thunderous snarl of two engines—the twin-engined Mitchell made much more noise than the four-engined Liberator— faded into the night. Off to one side he could see the glow of Vancouver. The street lights of the sleeping villages of Ladner and Boundary Bay were underneath him. He climbed until he was just underneath the cloud deck, and headed south toward Seattle. It was about 110 miles away, a thirty-minute flight for a Mitchell, one of the fastest of the Second World War light bombers.

The Mitchell was a splendid aircraft. Scratch felt the power under his fingers, the agility at his control, and exulted. He'd show them what a real pilot could do.

He'd start by waking up Seattle, the beautiful city that devoted so much of its effort to building such Boeing planes as the B17 Flying Fortress. Lining up his aircraft with one of the main streets, he hurtled down out of the sky and tore along lower than the roof tops. Through the stone-and-concrete canyons he flew twisting and turning, rocking his wings, blasting scraps of paper along the streets with his slipstream, waking up everybody, bringing thousands out to see what was the source of this hellish noise that had invaded their early-morning calm.

He climbed above the building tops and did barrel-rolls and rolls off the top and Immelmans and loops, all of them aerobatic stunts that a Spitfire pilot would have had trouble in performing. He spotted knots of spectators and scattered them by diving at them. He held his dives until it seemed certain he would crash, and then pulled out with his tail all but touching the ground. For half an hour he kept up his show until he was tired of Seattle He decided to see what Vancouver could offer. As he headed back over the Canadian border he throttled the engines back to sedate cruising power. He gave Vancouver the same spectacular show that he had already given Seattle. He flew down quiet suburban streets, the snarl of his engines rattling windows. The citizens rushed out of their houses, as little less sleepily than the ones in Seattle, since it was nearer time to get up. They stood gesticulating, and now and then Scratch scattered them too.

Telephone lines were burning up with complaints, and senior officers in two countries were standing in their pyjamas, yelling questions and orders. Air Vice Marshal F.V. Heakes, Air Officer Commanding Western Air Command, was told of a Mitchell in Canadian colours that was terrorizing Seattle and Vancouver, and ordered Kittyhawk fighters aloft to intercept it and drive it down. That was easier said than done. As long as the plane stayed over populated territory where it could fall into a crowded street it could not be shot down. In any case it would run out of fuel sooner or later, and the pilot would have to land it.

Meanwhile at Boundary Bay things were still normal. The Commanding Officer, Group D.A.R. Bradshaw (his subordinates, though not to his gruff and uncondescending face, called him

"Darby") had ordered a full-scale ceremonial parade, as he did once every week. Wednesday was a good day to hold it, and unless rain was pelting down in torrents it always came off, with a band playing, while Group Captain Bradshaw walked up and down the ranks where men and women stood rigidly to attention. He knew about the stolen Mitchell and the damaged Liberator, and he knew that Kittyhawks from Patricia Bay, where they had been stationed for four years without firing a shot in anger, had been sent up to intercept it. But that was something he could do nothing about, except to rehearse a few words he would say to the pilot—it was thought it might be Sergeant Scratch, but nobody could be sure—after he landed. He put on his gold-braided hat and his greatcoat and got into his staff car, which drove him at eight o'clock to the parade ground where the squadrons waited.

Sergeants stood behind each flight, with the flight commander in front and the supernumerary officers at the back. The airwomen stood in their own squadron, with their own officers. The station Adjutant called the parade to attention to hand it over to the Commanding Officer. Eyes turned as the sound of an aircraft broke the early-morning silence. "Ole Darby'll raise hell about that," an airman spoke out of the side of his mouth, and the man beside him nodded slightly, knowing that Darby's wrath was not to be taken lightly.

Then the orderly, carefully-dressed ranks scattered in wild confusion as a Mitchell plunged out of the sky straight at them. Nobody knows if a formal "Dismiss!" was ever uttered, but men and women threw themselves flat o the tarmac, ran for shelter into the hangars, or even dived into holes that had been dug for telephone poles. The men crouching in them in uniforms that a moment before had been spic and span never noticed that the holes were half-full of cold water. They were too absorbed in watching the spectacular flying display that Sergeant Scratch was putting on just above their heads, now that he had an audience that would appreciate his virtuosity.

Bradshaw dashed to the control tower, where he climbed to the platform from which he could see the Mitchell. He picked up a microphone to call the erring pilot, ordering him, then exhorting, and then begging him to come down and stop this idiotic if brilliant demonstration of flying skill that was attracting attention over half the west coast, and could scarcely have been more embarrassing to the brass of the RCAF.

172

Scratch answered by diving straight at the control tower, missing the wooden railing round the platform by inches, his wing-tip scything through the air and forcing the burly Bradshaw to the floor. Deaf to his furious orders, his aides literally manhandled Bradshaw to a lower floor out of harm's way. He found another microphone. "You will be treated sympathetically," he promised. Scratch did not say if he believed him.

Some airmen, entranced by the display, had climbed to the roof of a hangar to watch the fun. Scratch saw them, and swept over the hangar, blowing pebbles over the hangar eaves and onto the parade square. As one man the over-eager spectators fell flat on their faces and then scrambled for ladders. The roof emptied as if by magic, and the climbers stood on the roads, avoiding one another's eyes.

Orders went to the fighters—"Drive the Mitchell out to sea and shoot it into the water," but Scratch was in an aircraft not much slower than the Kittyhawks, and he kept low, where the fighters were restricted in their maneuvers—where his antics terrorized spectators more. Time and again he made fools of the fighter pilots, once or twice even making an approach to the airfield, lowering his undercarriage, and flaring out for a landing; and then as the Kittyhawk flashed past him, he raised his undercarriage, whipped into a tight turn, and was off and away, miles from the furious fighters. Again and again he tricked them, heading out to sea, waiting until he was almost far enough out over the water to allow a shot at him, and then whipping into an Immelman or a stall turn and heading back again over land. He teased and foiled and humiliated the fighters for another three hours, never allowing them to get him into a position from which he could not escape. The Kittykawks were hampered by the fact that they were under orders not to shoot him down over land.

By ten o'clock he had been in the air for five hours, demonstrating to the watching pilots, as one of them who had flown Mitchells in combat in Europe said, "He's a better pilot than any of us." He went on, "After five hour of an ordinary flight I'd be wringing wet with sweat, and I'd be dog-tired; I don't know how he could whip that plane around as long as he has." Just after he had eluded another determined attempt to force him down—he had already outlasted one flight which had had to return to its base to refuel—he found himself over a small island about six miles from

Boundary Bay. He flew straight and level for a brief moment, and then put the aircraft over on its back and peeled off in the best Hollywood fashion in a vertical dive. The Mitchell screamed downward, its motors blasting with every ounce of power. The watchers in the fighters expected him to pull out at the very last moment as he had done so many times before. But instead he kept on straight down, plowed into he rocky surface of Tilbury Island, and exploded in a burst of flame that immediately turned into a great pillar of greasy black smoke. The fighters flew over the island, blasting the smoke of Sergeant Scratch's funeral pyre with the slipstreams of their own Allison engines. They called up Boundary Bay to tell what had happened and flew home.

Nothing was left of the plane but a few scraps of charred metal. Some shreds of human flesh were collected and sent back to his next-of-kin, formal identification being made from a laundry mark on a shirt—his old officer's serial number. They were buried in Saint Paul, Alberta, a small town near Edmonton. He died in the twenty-sixth year of his life.

But in those last five hours he had put on the most spectacular display of aerial gymnastics that any Canadian, and very probably any man alive, has ever made in a plane—certainly a twin-engined plane. Perhaps he lost control in the last seconds, perhaps he saw his future bleak before him and purposefully put an end to his life. As a fighter pilot, rather than a coastal patrol airman, he might well have made himself as famous as his illustrious contemporary, the brilliant and unstable Buzz Beurling, Canada's top ace in the Hitler War. The fates decided otherwise. The attention he drew to himself led first to disgrace and then to death. But pilots who fly over Tilbury Island now look down, and those who remember say, "That's where D.P. Scratch went in."

CHAPTER TWENTY-EIGHT

In April 1945 I reported to Patricia Bay for the third time in my career. I was looking forward to the posting, since it involved living in the most pleasant climate in Canada, close to Victoria, amid the beautiful Vancouver Island scenery. I would be making flights over the Pacific where I could practice the overwater navigation I had learned at Summerside and while I was going through Torpedo Bomber OTU, in what, compared to the shell-torn skies over Europe, was perfect safety.

After I joined a coastal patrol squadron, flying Lockheed Ventura aircraft, I found myself welcomed rather less than warmly by the other aircrew, only a handful of whom had overseas service, and I did not make myself more popular when I referred to the "heavy flak over Cape Flattery" (the headland jutting out from the northwest corner of the state of Washington.) However, the officer commanding solved his problem with me by sending me to a "leper colony" of a crew all of whom had seen combat, thus keeping me out of the hair of the other aircrew.

In any case I had scarcely reached my new squadron when the European war ended. I managed two patrols, both completely uneventful, although I did have some fun firing a machine gun out of the mid-under position at whitecaps. An economical RCAF, mindful of the fact that during the whole war only one hostile submarine had ever been seen off the West Coast, disbanded the squadron.

I wangled a transfer to No. 122 Squadron, a composite outfit formed to do 'joe jobs' like flying target-towing lines for the coastal artillery to shoot at. It had a Search and Rescue flight, which to my dismay was stationed at the north tip of Vancouver Island at Port Hardy, deep in the bush. Me being a navigator, that was the place for me, and I duly flew up to the crude and isolated station in the rain forest. When I got there I put thoughts of being a warrior on the back burner and turned my mind to housing.

I had had enough when I was overseas of having to make do with a photograph I carried in my battle dress pocket, I was thoroughly enjoying married life, and I did not think much of the prospect of living monastically in Port Hardy. When I first arrived at Patricia Bay, I had found a furnished room for us in Oak Bay, one of the silk-stocking suburbs of Victoria, and I had thought I was all set.

Our landlady in Oak Bay was a dragon who would have put Saint George to flight. Her late husband had been a member of the cabinet of the British Columbia government at the time of the First World War, and she never let anybody forget it. Her standards were high. One of her neighbours, she told us, had been trying to insinuate himself into the social whirl of the district, but she was having none of it, and periodically felt compelled to put him in his place. He was a retired Army officer who had lived in the area for twenty-five years.

She was even more severe with lesser lights. A Chinese gardener had looked after her grounds for thirty years. She had never allowed him inside the house.

The inside of the house displayed some confusing details. They were explained by the fact that one of the rooms had been used to contain the coffin of her husband before his funeral. She had simply had the room closed off, feeling that any lesser use for it would be *lese majeste*.

Her membership in the upper crust was testified to by her grasp of economics. On one occasion we wanted a fire in the fireplace in our room, the weather having turned unseasonably cold. She supplied a few sticks of wood— and charged extra for them.

She also demanded absolute silence at all times, and we were properly reprimanded for all sounds. My wife unfortunately had a squeaky fountain pen. With the shortage of accommodation in Victoria at the time, however, we were in no position to argue, and we didn't. What I did so, once I had been sent to Port Hardy, was to look for a place to live there.

It sounded harder than it was. Indeed, five years before, when I had been stationed at Ucluelet, I had helped to build some impromptu married quarters.

When the war broke out, the Department of National Defence had strung air bases along the west coast of Vancouver Island, on the Queen Charlotte Islands, and along the fjord-indented coast between them. Some of them, like Ucluelet at the south end of Vancouver Island and Coal Harbour at the north end, Alliford Bay on the Queen Charlottes, and Bella Bella on the mainland, were all bases for seaplanes and flying boats. Later, runways were hacked out of the bush at places like Comox, Tofino and Port Hardy, and Sandspit in the Queen Charlotte Islands.

The stations were surprisingly big, and staffed exclusively with men. War is always fought largely by boys, but a lot of the ground-crew were older men who had plied dozens of trades in civvy street. Most of these mature men were married, and they missed their families. Furthermore, the young regulars seemed to have as the foremost idea in their heads that they wanted to get married too. And here they were, perched on the rim of the world with nothing to do but their duty and nowhere to go but a movie once week in the drill hall.

There were no nearby villages to bring their wives to. If the men wanted their wives with them, they would have to build houses for themselves. They set to work.

The houses were not elaborate—mere cabins, without such modern cossetings as running water, electric power, or indoor plumbing. The war would not go on forever, and after the last shots were fired the air stations would go back to the bush. Furthermore, airmen were frequently transferred. What the situation called for was a cabin, not a house, that could be abandoned without a qualm.

With surprising speed tiny towns sprang up near the air stations. A location near one of the roads leading to the base, reasonably open, would be chosen and cleared. Lots would be picked out. There were always men would had built houses before, and would know how much lumber to order, and how much hardware. Arrangements would be made to buy the lumber at a mill, which could be fifty or sixty miles away, and to transport it on a barge or fishing boat. Prices were reasonable; in 1940 at Ucluelet first grade lumber could be bought for $20 a thousand board feet. A couple of decades later two boards would cost that much.

The men would then hurry out to their selected site and set to work building their cabins as soon as they finished supper every night. Most of them were handy with tools, and the skilled carpenters would advise them. The cabins came out summer cottage style, with perhaps two rooms; a bedroom and another room for everything else. At the rear there would be an outhouse, and water could be carried from a convenient spring; in the west-coast rainforest there was always a spring available. There would be a woodstove to provide heat and to cook on, sometimes aided by a Coleman kerosene stove, and kerosene or gasolene lamps for lighting. The beds were generally built in, with bed springs and mattresses resting on wooden frames (sometimes the springs were omitted, and the mattresses rested on the boards.) Tables and chairs were often home made, and bathtubs were generally the old-fashioned round galvanized iron tubs hung on a nail at the back of the house when not in use.

Three hundred dollars could build a cabin in those palmy days (of course, a month's wages for a Leading Aircraftsman with marriage allowance would only be about $120 a month.) When he was transferred the owner could sell it to his successor. The land cost nothing, since the people were actually squatters on crown land. Out in the bush nobody bothered with building permits or titles.

Conditions seemed primitive, but the people were young and strong, and not many of them had been used to luxury. Born in the depression, they considered that a steady job and money to spend made up for a great deal. Besides, the average length of stay at a bush station was only a year or so. The climate was mild enough to make spartan living conditions bearable; indeed, it was like living in a summer cottage.

The young wives were quite happy with their lot. The community was close-knit, with somebody nearby to help if emergencies arose. The facilities of an air base—the snack bar, the recreation hall, the gymnasium, the hospital, and the various messes at certain times—were open to them, even if on a *sub-rosa* basis. The air stations installed washing machines for the use of the men, which the women could use, and they were welcome to watch the movies and attend the shows put on by touring entertainment groups. Best of all, the wives could go to the air base to take showers. A good many children were born, and as long as they were pre-school age there was no problem.

As time went on the instant married quarters became organized. The men got together and built sidewalks, while sometimes Air Force bulldozers and graders would mysteriously appear and scratch out roads. A "mayor" would be elected, and a "town council." The residents all took turns, according to a roster compiled by the mayor, in doing jobs like collecting garbage and keeping sidewalks in repair.

The Commanding Officers of the air bases either turned a blind eye to the villages or encouraged them. A married man living with his wife got into no trouble in the wet canteen, nor did he gamble in the barracks, and he did not get into brawls over women at fish canneries and Indian reserves. Besides, the married men were always the most skilled and reliable tradesmen.

I experienced the situation twice. In 1940 I was stationed at Ucluelet while it was still being hacked out of the bush. Still single at the time, I had no interest in setting up housekeeping, but I did lend a hand to one of my friends who was building a cabin for his new wife.

Then in 1945 I was posted to Port Hardy. Port Hardy had a well-established married patch which rejoiced in the name of "Joker-ville." Originally built by airmen, it was expanded by employees of Pan American Airways, who serviced a staging point for aircraft flying shuttle service between Seattle and Alaska. The Americans thought big; they piped in running water, and installed an electric generator. Unfortunately by the time I got there Pan American had put larger aircraft into service and eliminated the staging stop. They pulled out their men and their diesel generator as well. The lights went out, but the water kept coming. The "mayor" organized a roster to patrol the pipe leading to the spring which supplied the water to make sure there were no leaks or breaks caused by trees falling across it.

One of the cabins in Jokerville was available, since its occupant had just been transferred away. I bought it for $300. It was a two room affair, with a wooden platform eighteen inches high jutting out into the building from one wall. A partition divided it in two; the side jutting into the kitchen became a couch, while the other side became the bed.

The house had one great luxury—there was a water-heating coil in the wood stove which fed a shower installed in a little tin-sided stall built into the corner of the ktichen. There was also a sink in the kitchen, a luxury by no means to be discounted. The stove had another benefit; we could dry the washing in the kitchen, since it was generally foggy and clothes in the open took days to dry.

After I had bought the cabin, I wrote to my wife, who was staying in Vancouver, asking her to come up to Port Hardy and to bring along a mattress and some bedding. She brought it up in a single-engined Norseman floatplane which landed at the nearby Indian village, Fort Rupert. An Indian boy in a rowboat saw the plane taxiing back and forth uncertainly in the harbour, and brought her to shore, where I was waiting for her in a jeep. I took her proudly back to her new house, and if she was dismayed she hid it very well. Actually it compared favourably with the gardener's cottage in which we had begun our married life in Sidney before I went overseas. It was bigger and had more facilities!

Setting up housekeeping was easy. Our predecessors had left their furniture (a kitchen table and two chairs) and a few cooking utensils. We put our mattress on the wooden bed, without benefit of a spring, and covered it with the sheets my wife had brought and blankets and pillows I had borrowed from the air station.

An axe went with the cabin, and the surrounding forest was full of firewood. I noticed, however, that I seemed to be the only person doing much chopping. One of my neighbours enlightened me.

"Just get some coal from George," he counselled.

The air base furnaces burnt coal, which was freighted in from Nanaimo on a barge. The barge was moored at a pier at the end of road which went through Jokerville. Residents helped themselves to enough fuel for their stoves, and the RCAF never mssed it. Neither did King George, who strictly speaking owned it.

With ample supplies of coal, my wife soon became the social leader of the community. Our house was the only one with hot water and a shower, and furthermore we had a battery-powered radio, which was rare in those low-technology days. The other ladies would gather each morning, bringing goodies and taking turns having showers, while the rest listened to the news on the radio, drank coffee and discussed the state of the world. After the coffee-and-shower was over, however, social leadership reverted to a wife of a sergeant, in her forties, who had lived on a Saskatchewan farm on the edge of civilization and knew exactly how to do everything required in a frontier environment.

Like all self-respecting villages, Jokerville had its dogs and cats. The commanding officer of the station, who had brought his wife to Jokerville, found out all about them one day when he, a pious fisherman, had caught a salmon whose magnificence astounded all who saw it. He brought it proudly back to his cabin and hung it on a nail while he went inside to get his camera. He was briefly

180

delayed inside the house; when he reappeared with his camera he found nothing left of the fish except the skeleton, while a number of neighbours's cats sat about, cleaning their whiskers. Cats take orders from nobody, not even the commanding officer.

Our cabin was close enough to the air base to allow me to walk to work, which I did every morning at eight-thirty, just like any good civil servant. At intervals I would be on standby to navigate an aircraft on searches if an aircraft were lost, and when this happened I slept at the air station. If not on standby, I simply went home, to have supper with my beautiful redhead and enjoy the delights of married life.

My wife fed me well. A Canadian Pacific coastal steamer called at Port Hardy every ten days, to deliver provision for the port and for the general store at the Indian reserve at Fort Rupert, between the village and the airfield about a mile or so from Jokerville. When it docked, the women from Jokerville would gather at the store, which was managed by a twenty-year-old Kwakiutl who had succeeded to the leadership of his numerous family. When he arrived with his truck they would follow him into the store, where he would set about carving up the side of beef he regularly received. His method pricing was simple; stewing beef was twenty cents a pound, steaks were forty cents, and roasts were sixty cents. After as few weeks my wife found herself helping to carve the beef, which helped her to obtain some of the better cuts. With her expert carving, we ate well every ten days.

Choice of the staples was limited but adequate. Fresh vegetables were scarce, but cans solved many problems. We could also obtain fresh fish, and we could gather clams on the beach. We were advised to leave them in pails of sea water laced with oatmeal. The clams would absorb the oatmeal and spit out the sand in their systems. It sounded weird, but it worked.

The quality of the meals depended on the skill of the wives, of course. One young wife, brought up in a wealthy home where cooking was done by servants, had a rough time. One day she came to my wife in tears, stricken because her cake had fallen.

"Make it into a pudding," my wife advised. "Your husband will never know."

At intervals we could take our wives to dinner at the air station, which had salads and other delicacies flown up from Vancouver by the twice-weekly scheduled flight—the "sked." The sergeants had the best meals, of course; the sergeant cooks made sure of that, but even the officers' mess was pretty good.

Social life in Jokerville was surprisingly active. Impromptu parties were always going on in one cabin or another. The single men on the base were starved for feminine companionship, and were glad to be invited to join us. Sometimes they did not wait for an invitation. It was not uncommon for a jeep to stop outside our cabin unannounced, and for several men, bearing such gifts as a bottle, to invite themselves in to talk, play games, and drink coffee. On one occasion a group of them appeared with some freshly-caught salmon and a pound of butter (rationed in those days, but obtained from the officers' mess.) One of them turned out to be an expert salmon filleter, and another was an expert salmon cook. It was one of the best meals we ever had, served by a man who had owned a restaurant in Denmark before he escaped by fishing boat to join the RCAF. One of the men had sworn he would never eat fish; when he tasted the fillets he stuffed himself.

Some days were enlivened by visits to the village of Port Hardy. There were two eating-places, one of them the conventional Chinese restaurant always found in every British Columbia small town, and the other a coffee-shop. At both places every spoon had its handle twisted into a spiral by loggers who had been there before us, showing off the strength of their fingers. Port Hardy, most of the time a fishing village, occasionally served as a place where loggers could let off steam. They were Homeric figures, two axe-handles across the shoulders, of whom it was truly said, "Even the stink from their socks was terrific." In the days before chain saws felling and bucking had to be done by hand, and only the mighty could handle the job. Once or twice airmen from the base would take one of them on of a Saturday night. After the airmen recovered consciousness they avoided doing it again.

The doyen of the nearby Indian village, Fort Rupert, was a cultured, well-educated widow in her sixties, the daughter of a Scottish Hudsons's Bay factor and an Alaskan Indian woman. She lived in a small, well-kept dwelling which was a treasure-house of West Coast memorabilia. She had chests filled with robes with linings made of ptarmigan down and robes made of cedar bark, baskets made of porcupine quills by Indian women of Alberta, and ceremonial face-masks. The great American anthropologist Franz Boaz had been a friend of hers, and had recorded many of the

182

stories of coastal life that she told me and my wife. She had reached the stage where mere possessions meant little to her. When my wife first called upon her, in keeping with the standards of any well-bred Canadian girl, she brought her a gift of a package of English biscuits. During their conversation my wife admired a set of beautiful linen napkins. Mrs. Wilson immediately gave them to her—the whole set. My wife was afraid to admire anything after that.

My life in the bush station that the single men considered a term in purgatory, but that we married men thoroughly enjoyed, rolled along pleasantly for a couple of months, until a dark cloud to which I had deliberately closed my eyes came along. The war with Germany had been won, but there was still Japan to take care of. As I lazed contentedly in my backwater, I was willing to let somebody else do it.

Then the call came for volunteers for the "Tiger Force," composed of battle-experienced aircrew, flying new bigger, longer-range Lincoln aircraft, to help the Americans bomb the Japanese into submission. I avoided the issue for a while, since I had done thirty-six trips over German territory and thought that I had used up my luck, besides which there were many around me who had spent their war far from the sound of the guns. Then of all people, a medical officer who would never have to face the flak himself pointed out to me that I was a regular and that it was my duty to volunteer. I did. Then I went back to my pleasant bucolic life, trying to put the matter out of my mind.

Meanwhile, the Air Force had to ensure that its aircrew knew their business. One day an Aircrew Assessment Team came to Port Hardy to test the crews, and had to guide an Anson aircraft around a many-sided course. I was lucky enough to make a perfect navigational trip, which left me looking forward to the report on the trip, feeling it could be nothing but congratulatory.

Then one noon my wife told me that she had heard President Truman speak on the radio, telling of a new bomb which had been dropped on Japan, with the force of 20,000 tons of TNT. I explained to her condescendingly that she must have misunderstood, since it must have been 20,000 pounds that President Truman mentioned. She was properly grateful for my correction, and respectful of my specialist knowledge on the subject. This was not the last time that she was right and I was wrong.

A few days later my wife, having heard a report on the radio, banged on a pot to alert the other wives of important news. "The war's over!" she cried. The women had brief celebration, and then another news flash came—the first report had been false. She banged on the pot again. "The war's not over!" "We know—we know!" they chorused. Then a third report came, with the official ending of the Far Eastern war. Once again she banged on the pot. By this time everybody was thoroughly confused, but after several more conferences the truth was established, and the celebrations which included everybody on the base began.

Everybody rejoiced, especially me. I did not have to go overseas again, to face the flak and the fighters, with both of which I was only too familiar. I was mightily relieved. There was only one minor fly in my ointment. The Aircrew Assessment Team was disbanded, and they never bothered to mark my wonderful navigation trip.

Things did not change much at the air station. We still had to stand by for search and rescue duty, and transient aircraft still landed for refuelling and maintenance. Some were American.

Thus it was that one night when I was orderly officer it was my duty to escort a visiting American pilot to his room in the officers' quarters for his overnight stay. As I led him along the corridor we passed the room reserved for the officers' servants (we actually had one) to polish shoes and press trousers. It was labelled, in the British tradition, with the word "Batman."

The American looked at the sign on the door and turned to me. "Do you keep a room for Superman too?" he asked.

CHAPTER TWENTY-NINE

With the war over, the Royal Canadian Air Force decided to shut down the coastal patrol stations on the West Coast, including Port Hardy. The personnel were posted to RCAF Station Sea Island, at Vancouver. There was, of course, no market for our cabin in Jokerville, and I had to wave goodbye to my $300 investment, although we did manage to sell our mattress to an Indian woman. My wife and I packed our few household goods, got a jeep ride into Port Hardy, and checked into the hotel there to wait for the Canadian Pacific coastal steamer that was to take us to Vancouver the next day.

The hotel had been one of a chain of cat-houses along the islands in the heyday of the logging industry, and sounds that shook the corridors that night, plus the sight of drunken loggers lurching along them, led us to believe that it had not changed much. The room was also infested with bedbugs. We were glad when morning came. We waited to eat breakfast on the steamer. At least the spoons did not have their stems bent into spirals.

We reclaimed our room in Ladner, and I reported to RCAF Station Sea Island. The RCAF was busy slimming itself down from some 250,000 people to about 12,000, a cut of some 95%. Everything else was strictly in a holding pattern, with the aircrew flying around on infrequent training trips and more frequent joyrides. Vancouver was going to remain a permanent station, and it began to fill up with regulars who would stay in the Air Force. I found myself surrounded by old friends.

We blended back into the general society at once. Wearing a uniform at all times, a must in wartime, was no longer compulsory, and after working hours nobody could be seen in uniform at all. Working hours were the conventional eight to four-thirty, which made us just another group of commuters. There was no point in trying to put on the dog, since there were too many recently-discharged airmen around who knew the truth about the

Air Force to be able to pretend to any distinction we did not possess.

For the twelve thousand positions in the 'interim Air Force' there was heavy competition. Several thousand aircrew officers, who had joined the air force right out of high school, had been used to the pay and perquisites of life as an officer, and they knew they had few qualifications for jobs other than as aircrew. They strove desperately to stay in, and many of them were desolated when they were not selected. A good many wartime wireless operators reverted to the ranks as ground wireless operators, and others simply applied to stay in any ground-crew trade that was open as ordinary airmen.

I was lucky. There were few regulars who were trained navigators, and I did have a decoration. I had resigned myself to going back to the ranks, hoping I would be offered at least a sergeant's stripes, and then had decided to leave the force and go to college. Then I was offered a permanent commission, which solved all my problems. My objective in getting a degree was to get a permanent commission, and now it was offered to me. I skipped the college course. It turned out to be a grave mistake.

But while I was in Vancouver I was in clover. I was making $360 a month, which was big money in those days—lots of lawyers made less. We had half a duplex to live in on Lulu Island. We had a new baby, a beautiful little girl named Elizabeth Jean. We even had an icebox—refrigerators were impossible to get. Best of all, I had a 1930 Model A Ford. We enjoyed ourselves.

But everything has to come to an end. The RCAF decided to increase the professional qualifications of its aircrew, and I was selected for cross-training as a radio operator. In the fall of 1946 I was sent to Clinton Ontario, where radarmen had been trained during the war. My daughter was introduced to air travel at the age of four months, when she and her mother flew to Winnipeg on a Trans-Canada Airways Lodestar. She had to hold an oxygen mask to the baby's face all the way across the Rockies.

In Clinton we rented a house owned by a couple who were taking an extended vacation in Florida. They were rock-ribbed born-again Christians, who were dead set against drinking and smoking. We did not smoke, and pretended we did not drink, and were allowed in. When the good couple returned from their vacation, their grown-up daughter visited them from Toronto. Going down to the cellar to stoke the furnace, I found her sitting in front of it blowing smoke up the chimney. The son, who had recently left the air force after serving as a radar officer in Iceland and later in France, came out to the officers' mess one day. In deference to his parents' shunning of alcohol, I offered him a coke. He accepted, found an excuse to leave me, and headed for the bar. He turned out to be the best two-handed drinker I have ever met in my life.

The radio course was interesting, and gave us a solid grounding in both radio and radar. It also required us to learn Morse code. Like some fellow students, I had trouble with dots and dashes. Thus it was that when the wife of a colleague said to my wife, "I hear our husbands are both in the dumb Morse class," that she flared up as she rushed to my defence. "I'll have you know," she said, "that my husband is in the smart part of the dumb morse class."

Dakotas of the No.435 transport Squadron, Edmonton, ALTA, 1948.

We were graduated as qualified radio operators, which made us radio navigators, and with two others I was posted to No. 435 Transport Squadron in Edmonton. There I found myself the victim of a disease that I had contracted when I remustered to aircrew—

at each new station I was a rookie again. There were a number of experienced radio officers on the squadron, all of them with four or five years of practical experience gained in such places as the Western Desert, and all of them far more competent than we graduates of a basic course. We were relegated to an unofficial ghetto for a while, until the other aircrew got used to us.

All the radio navigators, however, were basically navigators, not radiomen, and as soon as we could we got back to our basic trade. I returned to the navigation business by flying equipment into the bases in the Arctic where the Dew Line (Distant Early Warning) was being built. It was good training for us. The country was still largely unmapped, and it was so close to the magnetic pole that the magnetic compasses were unreliable and direction had to be controlled by air-driven gyroscopes checked by celestial observations, and there were practically no radio-navigation aids like radio ranges, common though they were in the more densely-populated parts of the country. It was sink or swim, but we soon learned, and we became proud of our ability to navigate planes in the arctic with the very minimum of navigational equipment.

The United States Air Force sent C-82 Flying Boxcars to Edmonton in 1948 to freight equipment to the Dew Line sites, but omitted to send navigators or radio operators with them. Canadian radio-navigators were pressed into service. I made a number of trips, mostly at night, to places like Sawmill Bay on Great Bear Lake, navigating the aircraft and working the radio.

On one trip fifty miles after we had taken off from Edmonton we were all by ourselves in the winter air, in flying conditions that were as smooth as glass. The pilot climbed up to five thousand feet and put the plane on automatic pilot. The flight engineer climbed into the rest position at the rear of the crew cockpit and went to sleep. The co-pilot need not worry about radio range navigation, since there were no radio ranges—I was doing the navigation, and went to sleep. The pilot dozed off too. Soon I was the only man awake aboard the aircraft as we flew through the cold air.

There was no danger, since we were the only aircraft for fifty miles and we were not going to bump into anybody. There were no mountains on the way to bump into either. In the navigation position I sat, beavering away. I checked the heading on a star, took a sight on a star with my sextant, worked out a fix, calculated the aircraft's position, decided if I needed to alter heading or not, and

**F/Lt N.W. Emmott sighting with sextant
in a Dakota, Arctic, 1948.**

noted all the details down in my navigation log. Then I moved to
the radio position, tuned up the radio, called up Edmonton, trans-
mitted a message in morse telling control where we were and when
we expected to get to Sawmill Bay, asked for the weather at
destination, and copied down the message I received in morse
code. By this time it would be time to go back to being a navigator.
Whenever we would cross some identifiable feature such as a river
or an island in a lake, I would spread out my topographical map,
peer over the sleeping pilot's shoulder, and mark down our position. When I had to alter heading I would wake the pilot and have
him adjust the automatic pilot. I tried to make the adjustment myself once, but it took a little practice to do it right, so I had to keep
waking the pilot up.

When we neared Sawmill Bay I woke up the pilot to make the
landing, and he in turn woke up the co-pilot, who woke up the
flight engineer. They landed the aircraft and taxied up to the
refuelling point.

This consisted of a number of 45-gallon drums of gasoline, with
a hand-operated toggle pump. The flight engineer took his screw-

driver and absented himself to do his flight engineer duties; the pilot went off to check the weather, and the co-pilot went with him to help him do it: and I went underneath the wing to help the one airman at the refuelling point pump 1000 gallons of gasoline into the aircraft's tanks. I would have had some help, but the aircraft was loaded with a tractor and a half-tracked vehicle called a 'weasel.' An airman drove out the tractor and left it idling outside in the twenty-below weather as he went back to drive out the weasel. As soon as he got the weasel outside the tractor decided it did not like the weather, and stopped. It was decided to restart it by pushing it with the weasel. This was done, and the tractor started but the weasel stopped. Then the tractor pushed the weasel and started it, but in so doing the tractor stopped. This went on a couple more times, until somebody drove up with a four by four truck, which pushed whichever of the two vehicles was silent at the moment, and the three vehicles drove off in triumph to a heated hangar. All the time, of course there was nobody to help me pump gasoline. I was a busy boy.

The pilot returned. We climbed aboard the aircraft. I gave the pilot a heading to fly. He climbed to cruising altitude, set the head-

F/Lt Emmott navigating in the Arctic, 1948

ing, and turned on the automatic pilot. The flight engineer climbed into the bunk and went to sleep. The co-pilot went to sleep. The pilot went to sleep. I thumbed through the Air Almanac, checked the heading on the stars, calculated celestial position lines, worked out fixes, determined the wind velocity, figured out our position, altered heading if I had to, tuned the radio, copied morse, sent messages, completed my navigator's and my radio operator's log.

When we reached Edmonton the American pilot said to the American co-pilot, "Let's go downtown and check out a few bars." He turned to me. "You come too."

"No thanks," I answered. "I'm tired. I'm going home to bed."

He shook his head. "I don't see why. It seemed like a pretty easy trip to me."

Whenever I flew with an American aircraft I filled up the pockets of my parka with cans of ration food. There were always cases of rations aboard the aircraft, which I was naturally entitled to eat, since I was a member of the crew, and the most hard-working one. One of the cans contained cookies and candies. I never ate them, but always took a few of them home for my eighteen-month-old daughter Elizabeth. I would open the can for her as she watched.

One day Elizabeth came toddling up to me holding out one of the little brown cans, making it clear that she expected me to open it and give her the cookies and candy. Unfortunately, that particular can was one that I had brought home by mistake. Its contents were clearly labelled "Pork and Beans."

I took the can from Elizabeth and tried to explain to her that there was no candy inside. It was rather difficult, since she spoke little English. At last I did the only thing I could think of; I opened the can and let her taste the contents. She looked at me sadly, shook her head, and went off on her baby pursuits. At the age of a year and a half she had learned that she could not even trust her own father.

CHAPTER THIRTY

The Air Force sent me back into the navigation world after two years at Edmonton by shipping me down to Summerside, Prince Edward Island, to take the Specialist Navigation Course. Moving was not so easy now, since we had acquired two more daughters, Barbara Kirsten and Shelagh Deirdre. For the first month after our arrival in Summerside we lived in a hotel room, where my wife had to do the washing for two babies in the bathtub. We had left Barbara with her grandmother in Winnipeg, which made things a little easier, but it was still a strain on her. We had to spend the time in the hotel while we waited for a cottage, which we had bought, to be improved by the addition of a new kitchen and a bathroom.

We had shopped around to find a contractor to do the job, and had been given a high price by one of the entrepreneurs in the town of Summerside. Then we asked the advice of the man who lived across the road from us. He turned out to be one of nature's geniuses, who could estimate the amount of material needed to build an extra room with a glance. He quoted a price half the other man's. We engaged him, and he did a wonderful job.

When we bought the little house from its Newfoundland owner we also bought a Model A Ford car and six chickens. The car ran well and the chickens got fat. When my wife remarked to the farmer next door, with whom she was on good terms, that the chickens were doing well, he answered, "So they should be. I see them heading for my barley field every morning."

The month that it took to build the addition to our little house caused no extra trouble, since we had not received our furniture, shipped by the Canadian National Railways apparently by way of Greenland. The moving company in Edmonton, MacCosham's, was every bit as efficient as the railway; when we received our dining room table we found that the crate surrounding it had been nailed to the top of the table. Registered letters to the company complaining about this were unanswered. We ruefully recognized the truth of the Air Force maxim "Three moves is a good as a fire."

The house was small; I proudly told my colleagues that there was in fact room for a chair in the kitchen between the washing machine and the refrigerator. There was a master bedroom which was quite large enough to contain the bed and a dresser, provided that we did not want to open a bureau drawer and close the door at the same time. We also had an oil-fired space heater which worked pretty well, except that we felt compelled to get up in the middle of the night to make sure it was not over-heating, as space heaters tended to do from time to time. Nevertheless our little home was an improvement over the rented rooms which other students on the course had to put up with.

We had a telephone, a three-person party line. When the phone rang we listened for our call, two shorts and a long. One of the other householders on the line had a friend who at intervals was determined to get through, come what may. In the middle of the night—usually a Saturday—he would call and let the phone ring thirty or forty times. He was wroth, not to mention drunk, when we lifted the phone to tell there was probably nobody home. He would curse us and then call for another forty rings.

Prince Edward Island was run by legislators who did not believe in drinking unless you were sick, which meant that the only way to get a bottle of liquor was to get a prescription from a doctor. The doctors, needless to say, found a lot of ill-health on the island, especially on Saturdays. I felt sick myself on occasion, and once when I was leaving the liquor store a rubby-dub cast an approving eye at the bottle of Canadian sherry I was carrying. "There's a lot of good drinking in there for a dollar," he told me.

The island was famous for potatoes, but queerly enough it was hard to buy potatoes at the general store at the nearby village of St. Eleanor's, because it was taken for granted that everybody would grow their own. It was also famous for fur farms. We met evidence of the fur farm industry one day when our daughter came into the house telling us of the pretty kitty she had met outside, complaining that the kitty had not let her pet it. It was a real pretty kitty, she said, with a bushy tail and a broad white stripe running down its back. A farmer had tried ranching them since skunk fur is widely sold in the better shops under the name of "Alaska sable," but for some reason he had given up and then simply let his charges loose.

The skunks made themselves at home at the air station. They would take up residence under the Ground Instructional building, where I took my course and later had an office. One airman on the base was an expert at getting rid of skunks; nobody else could do it, but he could. Nobody else knew what to do, and he kept his knowledge a trade secret. He was always getting into trouble for something, but he kept his corporal's hooks because we could not do without him. His indiscretions were not confined to the military sphere; one day his parish priest gave him, as a penance for some grievous sin, the task of painting the parish church. An impossibly short time later, when he reported the job finished, the priest went to check on the work, to find it all done. It was the best job the priest had ever seen. The priest was torn between hoping that the pious but sinful corporal would see the evil of his ways and stay on the straight and narrow, and the thought that if he did stray there were other churches that needed painting.

Meanwhile I was immersed in the Specialist Navigation course. It called for continuous study, and the men who were taking it constituted a tough league. One of my friends, invited to have dinner with us one night in our luxurious cabin, told us that he knew only one way of easing the strain he was under. "I go into the washroom, turn on the taps to hide the noise, and stand there and scream."

It was on this course that I was introduced to the Lancaster aircraft, in which we took our training flights. It had been the most successful bomber of the war, and my own squadron, No. 433, had had its Halifax aircraft replaced by Lancasters after I left it. The Lancaster could carry a heavier load farther, and was therefore more cost-effective (not that anybody had invented that catch-phrase yet.)

The Lancaster was an aircraft that was built around a bomb-bay, and after the bombs had been accommodated whatever space was left over was given to the crew. There were obstacles all the way up the fuselage, such as the main spar that ran knee-high across the aircraft, and various bulkheads. Never once did I make my way from the door near the tail to the navigator's position facing sideways behind the pilot without cracking my head on something at least twice. I did not like it as much as the Halifax, partly because it was an aircraft that was hard to get out of. In the Halifax the navigator had a trap-door underneath his table to open and

Lancaster Aircraft

live through if the aircraft caught fire, but in the Lancaster he had
o climb up on the navigation table and try to escape through a
natch in the roof, which some wartime genius had reduced in
liameter in order to save money in production. In battle, during
such raids as the one on Nuremburg at the end of March 1944, a
slightly larger proportion of Halifaxes engaged were shot down
compared to Lancasters, but of those that were lost a higher
percentage of the crews escaped with their lives. Thus there was a
marginally better chance of surviving the war in a Halifax than in
a Lancaster. However, by the time I got on the Spec N course that
was ancient history, and the Lancaster was a safe enough aircraft
f nobody was shooting at it.

During the course we made visits by Lancaster to selected places
n Canada, in the USA, and in Britain. We visited military bases,
and the factories of companies that made navigational equipment.

One of the firms we visited during our trip to England was an
instruments company which had spent two decades making
sextants for the air forces. All of us had cut our teeth on their
Mark IX sextants, and had gone on to the Mark IXA, which was a

significant improvement. Those who had served on Coastal Command had used sextants on every flight, and even I, who had flown in Bomber Command during the war, had relied heavily on sextant observations when I had been navigating aircraft in the Arctic. We had been given a thorough grounding in celestial work during our course, and we all were as expert as any group in any air force. One of our tasks was to recommend a new sextant to replace our time-tested Mark Nine A.

As long as piston-engined aircraft ploughed their way through the skies at a dignified two hundred knots or so, sextants could be used with the navigator standing in an astrodome, a perspex bubble in the roof of the aircraft. With the advent of jet aircraft, storming along at Mach 0.85 at 40,000 feet with their interior pressurized, astrodomes were no longer practical. The answer was to use periscopic sextants, which had shafts a couple of inches across which were inserted in small, hermetically-sealed airlocks in the aircraft skin. The RCAF wanted to make sure it got the best of the several competing brands on the market.

During our course all the students wore the old-fashioned observer's wing, the single-wing "O" popularly called the 'flying areshole.' However, it had been decided that the wing would be changed to a double wing with a world-globe surmounted by a crown in the middle. It looked very much like the pilot's wing.

The course director, a navigator, was the first man in the RCAF to put up the new and much-welcomed wing. He wore it proudly as he visited the plant of the instrument company in England. We were shown all through the factory, watching workmen busy manufacturing sextant, seeing the intricate machinery, observing the delicate processing of the mirrors and the lenses.

Our host, who had been a Royal Air Force pilot during the war, told us how wonderful his new periscopic sextant was. It would do everything but talk. It would sight the faintest stars, give incredible accuracy in its readings, obtain bearing on landmarks, and improve the aircraft's aerodynamics. We listened attentively. There were a few things we didn't like about his sextants, but we all nodded sagely at his words.

Then, after the tour was over, the ex-RAF pilot relaxed with our course director over drinks in the company boardroom. He looked at our director's brand-new double wing, and jumped to the conclusion that our leader was not a navigator but a pilot.

196

"Everything I've told you about the sextant is true. It's a marvel-
ous beast. It will do everything I've said it will." He lifted his glass.
But tell me, old top—why are you so concerned? Isn't that kind of
slave labour done by that navigator bastard in the back?"

It is purely coincidental that for the next third of a century the
RCAF and its successor has used Kollsman periscopic sextants
from the United States.

CHAPTER THIRTY-ONE

It was while I was stationed at Summerside that I had my first experience of life in married quarters. I was to live in married quarters three times, in Summerside, in Greenwood Nova Scotia, and then in Winnipeg.

It has been the practice of military services for several thousand years to supply quarters for their married men to live in. I met them first at Trenton in 1937, where I was sent as an AC2 to polish an officer's floors, and in Vancouver as an AC1 when I sent to mow Flight Lieutenant Turner's grass. I did not, however, expect to enjoy occupation of one of them myself. The 12,000-man air force was not big enough to put much pressure on the housing market during the piping time of peace.

Then the Cold War started, and when the Korean War broke out Canada suddenly decided it would expand its air force explosively to 50,000 people. To flesh it out, a call was sent to the ex-servicemen who had worn Air Force blue during the Second World War to rejoin. These retreads represented a good bargains for the RCAF. They were all fully trained, and required only a refresher course to bring them up to speed. They had known the Air Force, and then the cold hard civilian world, and found they preferred the Air Force, which meant they would be amendable to discipline and willing to go along with the good old Air Force bull. There was one stumbling block in recruiting these battle-experienced, capable bemedalled men, and these clever, experienced technicians—they were all married. The Air Force decided to build married quarters to house these capable men who were ready and willing to tell such sabre-rattlers as Joseph Stalin where to head in.

The government of the day did not find the prospect unwelcome. Canada was under pressure from its NATO partners to increase its military expenditures, and money spent for a house in the married patch was just as much a military expenditure as that spent on a gun or an aircraft, and would last a lot longer. Besides, it was convenient do have men on an air station within arm's length. The reactivated air stations soon were loud with the sounds of hammers and saws.

The houses were well-built and well-planned, and comfortable to live in. In keeping with military practice, their size depended on the rank of the occupants. Airmen have modest houses; non-commissioned officers have slightly better ones; junior officers have houses a little larger; senior officers have large houses, and the biggest one of all is reserved for the station commander. This sometimes meant that the large houses were occupied by childless couples, while parents of large families had to make do with much smaller ones. But such has always been the way of the military, and rank has always had its privileges. Anyway, to a corporal with several children who otherwise would have had to pay high rent to a rapacious landlord, a married quarter was a godsend, especially since light and heat came with the house and the station Construction Engineering department looked after maintenance. There were no job jars for the men on an air station. Airmen in married quarters lived pleasant, secure and even dignified lives.

In those baby-boom years married quarters were soon inundated with children. Schools were set up for them. At Summerside and Greenwood the dependents' schools were more elaborate than the spartan wartime buildings in which the air force students took their training. None of the children had to cross a road to go to school. Teachers competed to get jobs on an air station, since among other reasons there were a large number of young men of marriageable age there, and we got the best. The children did not conform to their parents' ranks; the most brilliant boy in the Greenwood school was the son of a corporal, the slowest the son of a wing commander. Since the men of the RCAF have long been fa-mous for getting all the good-looking women, as well as the smart-est, the children of such unions tended to be remarkably good-looking and to go on to become doctors, lawyers, scientists and Rhodes Scholars.

The women in the married quarters were enormously competent, and had a social conscience. In Summerside they saw that the local hospital was ill-equipped, and determined to improve it. The fact that this would take potful of money did not deter them. They organized a fashion show, the first which Prince Edward Island had ever experienced. The Commanding Officer of the base, one of whose responsibilities was public relations, and who was clever enough to recognize just how smart his men's wives were, gave them everything they wanted.

The airmen's mess was pre-empted for the show, the construction engineers built a runway for the models to parade upon, and the flight sergeant cook, who had an international reputation, made the best ever *hors d'ouvres* the island had seen. The service police were given the task of making sure that all visitors had a place to park. The Commanding Officer appeared in full uniform accompanied by his wife in evening dress.

One of the wives had managed a fashion shop in Vancouver. She combined the knowledge of a French couturier with the commanding presence of a drillmaster in the Coldstream Guards. She knew exactly how the models should walk and pirouette and stand to show off the clothes, and she trained a corps of dressers to change a models's complete outfit and leave her without a hair out of place in about thirty seconds. Under her skilled but iron hand everything went like clockwork.

The show featured fox furs and mink coats from Prince Edward Island, all of them magnificent. The wives included a number of startlingly good-looking women who showed the clothing off at its best. There was even a children's portion of the show, in which my five-year-old daughter walked down the runway in pyjamas and a dressing gown. She didn't want to leave.

The fashion show was a huge success, with everybody that was anybody in all PEI attending. The profits outfitted a hospital room with all the most modern equipment. The stock of the Commanding Officer, who immediately became the darling of the city of Summerside, rose sky-high in Air Force eyes. It was a great tribute to the care with which airmen chose their wives.

At Greenwood the ladies organized the biggest and best Red Cross chapter in Nova Scotia, and held a blood-donor clinic which outdid the attendant local doctors' wildest dreams. The group raised money by putting on plays with first-class casts, and used the money by buying the local hospital an incubator. Life, especially infant life, was safer in the Annapolis Valley with the Air Force around.

There were Cub packs, Scout troops, and Brownie and Girl Guide organizations in full bloom, all with leaders who were experts in a dozen different fields. Sunday schools flourished. I was conscripted as a teacher, holding the job at every Air Force station I ever lived after I was married. It had its repercussions, however. One night, during a mess dinner a group of us were gathered around the piano singing air force songs. I knew all the words to the great ballad "Salome," few of which are printable. After the song was over one of the men looked at me and said, "My God, aren't you my kid's Sunday School teacher?"

Life in the married quarters was not always so serious. Greenwood is located in a backwoods section of Nova Scotia, not then noted for trendy thinking. Young and beautiful air force wives, it was rumoured, sat on their porches and in lawnchairs wearing shorts, low-necked blouses, and sometimes even bathing suits. On Sunday afternoons a parade of cars driven by the local citizens would be seen slowly circling the roads of the married quarters, which were open to the public. The wives were glad to be able to contribute to their pleasure.

Some of the sights must have confused them. One of the wives, busy making pickles, had to peel a basketful of onions. She sat on her porch wearing her husband's gas mask as she did it.

Canning vegetables became fashionable. One day a farmer appeared in the married quarters driving a truck full of vegetables. At the end his round he knocked on the door of one of the houses.. "I have some fine tomatoes here."

"I'm sorry," the lady said, "but I don't need any more."

"I'll give you a special deal," he said. "Half price."

"No, I'm sorry."

"Look lady, I'll give you the whole load for five dollars. I don't want to take them back home."

"Oh, all right then."

The farmer unloaded the tomatoes.

A neighbour, a lady of enormous capability and energy, walked over. The purchaser was a little concerned as to what she was going to do with all those tomatoes.

"We can make catsup," her energetic friend advised.

"What'll we put it in?"

"Beer bottles. There are always lots of beer bottles around. We'll have to scrub them out, and then sterilize them by boiling them for fifteen minutes."

The next day she had a catsup task force organized, with the lady of the house scrubbing out beer bottles, and the other women in the neighbouring houses on the lawn around Coleman stoves (all married airmen, devotees of camping, have Coleman stoves) with great pots of tomatoes and the appropriate spices bubbling away.

The lawn was cool and inviting, with the ladies sitting around the Coleman stoves discussing the affairs of the world, while the lady of the house had to sit inside, in a house that was hot and steamy, scrubbing away at a mountain of beer bottles. Those on the lawn filled the sterilized beer bottles with the aromatic catsup. There were more fillers outside the house than scrubbers inside, and soon the organizing lady began to call for more bottles. "Hurry up," she commanded. "You're getting behind."

The lady doing the scrubbing, bathed in sweat, her hair stringy, the room filled with steam, called back, "I'm going as fast as I can."

"It's not fast enough."

In desperation the scrubber gave the last dozen bottles a lick and a promise, plunged them into the boiling water for a minute or two, and took them outside to be filled. Then with a sigh of relief the ladies sat down to a cup of coffee before carrying the bottles to be stored in their basements.

A week later the lady of the house was having a bridge party with all guests dressed to the nines. Her husband served drinks. Suddenly an explosion resounded through the house. "What's that!" the guests exclaimed.

"It's in the basement!" the husband said, and rushed downstairs. There was another explosion, and another. He stumbled up the stairs, his face and his clothes dripping red. "My God, what happened? Are you hurt?" The man sputtered uncertainly, pawing at his face. Then someone burst out, "You smell like pickles!"

"It's that damned catsup—the bottles are exploding," he said, as more explosions shook the house. He closed the basement door firmly. "We'll just have to wait until the bombardment is over," he said, while his wife stood appalled, her hand to her mouth. The traces of yeast in the beer bottles, improperly washed out, had caused the catsup to ferment. The smell of fermented tomatoes pervaded the house—pungent, but not unpleasant.

"I'm going to have a bath," he said, and headed for the bathroom. The husband reappeared in casual clothes. "We'll clean it up tomorrow. Let's get back to the game." Everybody did, and the party which followed was the most successful of the year.

After the food-canning craze had run its course, the inhabitants of the married patch took to making beer. There was one bottle-capping machine which was carted around from one house to another, thereby advertising to all what the status of each persons's brew was. The beer produced was good, and nôbody objected to the fact that it left dregs in the bottles. It had other effects too. One Saturday afternoon a man and his wife repaired to the basement to bottle the latest brew. It was hot work, and they refreshed themselves with the odd bottle. One thing led to another. Some nine months later the lady presented her husband with a totally unplanned child.

The married quarters had lawns, but lawn furniture was scarce. During its wartime days the airmen's mess had been provided with tables with benches built into the sides, exactly in the fashion of the latest picnic tables. In the course of time the mess had been given conventional tables and chairs, and the benches taken to the dump.

Three of the ladies noticed them there, and one hitched up a utility trailer to the family car and drove to the dump, where the three loaded up a bench for each of them.

As they drove past the guardhouse an efficient service policeman who saw what appeared to be an organized raid on the air station, enquired what was going on. His manner changed, however, when he recognized the driver of the car. It was the Commanding Officer's wife.

The dump came in for attention on another occasion when the ladies held an impromptu party. The rule was that each lady was to appear in clothing made out something that somebody else had discarded. One woman appeared in a barrel. Another had a dress made out of old cardboard cartons. My wife outraged everybody by appearing in what appeared to be a beautiful white strapless evening gown. She was able to explain herself by pointing out that the gown was actually a discarded flare parachute, tastefully draped around her attractive frame to conceal a large burnt spot, which had caused the parachute to be abandoned on the dump. She had rescued it during the picnic table foray.

The ladies had their own names for people. In Greenwood the wife of the Recreation Officer was known simply as "Sport." The Dental Officer was known as "Officer Commanding The Drill Hall." The unkindest cut of all, however, was reserved for one of the squadron officers. There were two Squadron Leaders named Smith on the station, one of them the Accounts Officer, who was duly named "Accounts Smith." His namesake was correspondingly known as "No-Account Smith." He did not appreciate it.

It sounded an idyllic life, and in many ways it was, but the airborne gods demanded periodic sacrifices. One young officer, posted to a Greenwood squadron after having been graduated from the Operational Training Unit there, belonged to the crew of an aircraft which crashed with no survivors. His wife had moved into married quarters a month before the fatal flight. Within a period of less than a year she had been single, a bride, an air force wife, a mother and a widow.

CHAPTER THIRTY-TWO

Inhabitants of the married quarters led an active social life, and at their frequent parties it was customary to offer guests drinks. Since liquor prices in Canada have always been high, because governing authorities see drinking as sinful with a consequent necessity to levy high taxes on it, this caused a drain on the budget. Methods of obtaining liquors at lower prices were therefore explored.

The United States approached the matter from a different angle. US bases had "package stores," a code word which meant "liquor store," where prices were as great deal cheaper. Aircraft belonging to transport or coastal patrol squadrons landed at foreign bases as a matter of routine, and the crews would visit the package stores to stock up. The next problem was how to get the liquor home to a country infested by customs agents.

In the 1950s Canada's maritime patrol aircraft were Lancasters, which had big main wheels. The wheels retracted into wheel-wells behind the inboard engines. They did not take up all the space, however, leaving room for several cases of liquor to be secreted there. The aircraft would land back at base, the crew would dutifully report to the customs officer, and then the aircraft would be taxied to its position on the hangar apron. That night the crewmen would return to the craft, remove the cases, distribute the contents to the crewmen who had paid for it back at the foreign base, and go off happy in he knowledge that they had economized on this month's living expenses.

It was not always necessary to go to such lengths. At times aircraft could be landed at a time when the customs officers were off duty or otherwise engaged. Once an aircraft coming back from an exercise landed at Iceland, and the crew brought 24 cases of liquor, which they stacked in the rear of the fuselage. It was not even necessary to conceal it. If the customs officer did not levy duty on it, that was his fault.

Lancasters were equipped with automatic pilots, designed in

Britain during the war. They tended to be a little unreliable, since stray currents sometimes ran around their electronic insides, causing the aircraft to break into a sudden roll, pitch or turn. It was too dangerous to use them at low level, but when flying high where there was time and height to straighten out the plane they were safe enough. One aircraft flew home from Iceland at ten thousand feet, high enough to top the clouds so that the air was smooth, but low enough so that the crew did not have to use oxygen. All was serene. And then the aircraft bunted (made an outside loop). There was a moment of panic before the pilot slapped off the automatic pilot, straightened out the aircraft, and got back to straight and level flight. But in that mad moment twenty-four cases of liquors smashed against the top of the fuselage and every bottle was broken.

The Lancaster was awash in Beefeater's Gin and Bacardi's rum. Nobody was hurt, although every man in the crew had a broken heart to match the broken bottles.

There is no more repulsive sight in the Air Force than a drunken Lancaster.

This economical method of obtaining liquor lasted very well for about two years at Greenwood, with everything on a *sub rosa* basis. Then, in accordance with a corollary of Emmott's Law, "Whenever anybody has it good somebody always louses things up by being greedy," retribution struck. A corporal who was in on the deal started to sell some of the liquor in nearby Kentville. He was arrested and jailed, and the gravy train was off the tracks. The people in the married patch had to go back to homebrew, which was perfectly legal.

It must not be inferred that the people on the stations were drunkards. Aircrew cannot afford to drink too much, or to drink at all just before they go flying. The regulations say that eight hours of abstention must elapse before takeoff, and this was adhered to— after all, the pilots were in the aircraft too. Men doing highly technical work had to have their wits about them. As a matter of fact the only person at Greenwood who could really be described as a drunk was the wife of one of the senior officers. He had married money, and soon learned that any man who does so earns every penny he gets. While in her cups, she ran over the child of one of the airmen with her Cadillac, and it took a lot of finagling to hush matters up. The child was not badly hurt, but the wing commander was mightily embarrassed.

206

Booze was necessary for parties, but food was also required. The preferred food, of course, was lobster. Lobsters were plentiful in the Maritimes. When I first went to Summerside in 1943, a lobster could be bought at a streetside kiosk for twenty-five cents.

When we returned to the East Coast just as the Forties were turning into the Fifties, prices had gone up a bit, but lobsters were still cheap by Upper Canadian standards. Our officers' mess managers at Summerside and also at Greenwood were careful to organize lobster dinners on Saturday night, to which the wives were invited. A few of them were suspicious of these queer beasts, which did look something like insects, but as a rule it took only one bite for them to be converted. Bedeque oysters, the best in the world, were easy to come by also, and so were clams. One wife put the encomium on the Saturday night dinners when she said, "That's the only time that I ever had all the lobster I wanted." A lot of people from Saskatchewan became ardent seafood fans before they left the Maritimes.

Fishermen would cruise through the married quarters in trucks, from which they sold their catches. One of them, once sold my wife some splendid fish, which he assured her she would enjoy and remember for the rest of her life. His prediction came true when one of our friends, Maritime born and bred, saw what she was cooking. "Those are sea trout," the friend told my wife. "There's a close season on them, and if the Mounties catch you eating them they'll fine you a fortune."

Lobsters almost drove us afoul of the law later. After we had moved to Toronto, I drove my family to Hamilton to visit my wife's sister and her family. On the way we passed a truck selling lobster, and we paused to blow the budget on enough lobsters to feed our six and their five.

We had them for supper, and then were faced by a mountain of lobster shells. We put them in a garbage can and set the can outside the back door. Within fifteen minutes there was a caterwauling fit to raise the dead as every cat for a mile around homed on to the aromatic lobster shells.

"Put the garbage can down in the cellar," my sister-in-law commanded. We did so. A few minutes later her children came running to us in tears; they could not stand the smell of the lobsters. Statements that the cats thought it was just wonderful cut no ice with them at all.

"Take those lobster shells out and leave them at the dump," said my sister-in-law. My brother-in-law knew where the dump was, and we drove out in my car (he wouldn't let the shells into his) to the dump site, where we duly emptied the cans. Just as we were leaving we caught sight of a big sign. It read, "This dump is closed. Penalty for unauthorized dumping is $500."

We went white as we read it. I tramped on the gas, and we drove home, looking over our shoulders. All that night we lay in terror, waiting for a knock on the door and a heavy hand on our shoulder when the law caught up with us.

We got away with it that time. And we still love lobster. We only wish we could still afford it.

CHAPTER THIRTY-THREE

My next posting after Greenwood was to the RCAF Staff College at Toronto. I had to scrounge a trip to Toronto to spy out the land before my posting came due, and I thought I had everything arranged. I even bought a house so that my family, which now included four daughters—Mary Anne, born in Summerside—would have somewhere to stay as soon as we arrived. I drove my number three daughter, Shelagh, from Greenwood to Toronto in our little English car, while my wife took the other three girls, including baby Mary, to Toronto on the train.

Five-year-old Shelagh was a delightful companion on my trip, and she enjoyed having me all to herself. My wife's journey with the other three children would have been pleasant, were it not for the fact that Mary fell sick halfway there. When we got to Toronto Mary had to be rushed to the Sick Children's Hospital. We visited her there in her little crib. She looked up at us without crying, and then said, in her baby voice, "I'm going to have supper. I want milk and bread and meat and tatoes and jelly." Taped above her bed was a sign reading, "Nothing by mouth." She did not cry, but we did. We were terrified that she had contracted poliomyelitis, and the next two days, until we heard that she was out of danger, were the longest of our lives.

With the children well, I concentrated on the staff college course, which was extremely high pressure. I did get an unexpected break from it, however. The road allowance next to the house I had bought had a patch of very untidy weeds, which I set about chopping out, properly dressed in shorts. The patch turned out to be poison ivy. I missed a few days of school over that.

We had some pretty high-powered instructors, one of whom was a child psychologist named Doctor Blatz. He gave us one of the best pieces of advice I have ever received. It was, "Never give advice. If the advice is good, the recipient will take the credit himself, and if it is bad, he will blame you." He also told us that he had served on a board during the depression of the Dirty Thirties, and had found that a serious problem at the time was keeping people on relief entertained. Television, he said, would have been as godsend. It is heartening to know that now we have replaced the Roman formula of bread and circuses with welfare and TV. Nobody can says the world does not progress.

The course involved visits to the United States and England, as well as to selected bases in Canada. We flew around in the belly of a C119 transport plane, under rather spartan conditions, but really all we deserved. One or two of the trips to Canadian bases were by train, which I liked, since I have always been a train buff.

During our American visits we were always being entertained by somebody. At a Southern city we were invited to a cabaret in the top of a luxurious hotel. One of our students, who was of Scottish descent, enlivened the evening by appearing after the floor show in a kilt, playing the bagpipes. There was a thunderous reception by the others there, and he was the hit of the show. We were sent dozens of drinks by the other patrons. After that we encouraged him to bring his kilt and pipes everywhere we went.

During our American trip we visited Maxwell Air Force Base, the site of the American Air University. Maxwell is located in Montgomery, Alabama, which calls itself "The Heart of the Confederacy." We were carefully shown the brass plate set into the porch of the statehouse, which marks the spot where President Jefferson Davis stood to make the speech which brought the Confederate States of America into being. The citizens—all that we met, anyway—were unreconstructed rebels, who wanted to refight the Civil War, or at least to make it the best two out of three. Patriotic Americans though they were, they considered that the country would be much better run from Richmond than Washington, and they had their doubts, when they visited New York, about ever using the Lincoln tunnel.

A number of us were entertained at a hostelry one evening, and I was called upon to make a speech of thanks, which I did. I then took out of my pocket a Canadian dollar bill. "In 1867," I said, "a number of Canadian colonies joined one another to form the Dominion of Canada. This was achieved through the act of Confederation. Since Canada was brought into being by Confederation, we now qualify as Confederates. That is why we feel so much at home here in Montgomery, among our fellow Confederates." I waited for the cheering to stop, and then I waved the dollar aloft.

In those easy days, before Canada had hired highly skilled, well-educated, highly-paid economists to help the politicians govern, the Canadian dollar was worth $1.05 U.S. "This," I said, "is a Canadian dollar. As such it is Confederate money. And it is worth more than Yankee money." Needless to say, I did not have to buy another drink all night.

Not all my efforts were so successful. One of my tasks at the Staff College was to analyze the use of guided missiles, which were then just coming into use. I was required to come up with a recommendation for their deployment in the armed forces. After a lot of thought, I put out a closely-reasoned paper stating that the best course of action would be to amalgamate the three existing services into one unified service.

I was savagely marked down. My instructors told me that my recommendation was stupid, disloyal, and unworkable. They despaired of my future in the Air Force. There were enough red slashes on the paper to simulate a battle.

Twelve years later the three Canadian services were all amalgamated into a single service, the Canadian Armed Forces. It does not pay to be a prophet.

Two years later I wrote an article for the RCAF Staff College Journal, which drew the conclusion that despite the advances made in guided missiles, manned aircraft would be the predominant weapons in the skies for the next twenty years. The article was commented on favourably by the Toronto Globe and Mail Shortly thereafter the Avro Arrow, Canada's new fighter aircraft, was cancelled by the Diefenbaker government. My prophecy proved to be correct in Vietnam, various wars in which Israel was engaged, and then in the Gulf War. It did not pay to be a prophet then either.

I survived and was graduated, thus gaining the right to place the letters psac (all small letters) after my name. The p stands for passed, the s for staff college, the a for air force, and the c for Canada. Later I put the letters on my business cards to impress people in South America when I went there on marketing trips after I left the service. There is no record that it ever impressed anybody. In a sense the letters proved that I was a college graduate. I did not get a proper college degree until a decade and a half later. The trouble then was that I got it mostly at night school, which meant that I did not know anything in the daytime.

Being a trained staff officer, I was sent to Air Force Headquarters in Ottawa to be a staff officer. I thought that was only fair.

Air Force Headquarters was housed in a 'temporary' building, built during the war. It had been repaired several times, but what it really needed was a good fire. Nevertheless it lasted for a good thirty-five years, proving that the only thing more permanent than a temporary building was a temporary civil servant.

CHAPTER THIRTY-FOUR

I spent four years at Air Force Headquarters in Ottawa. My first job was in the training division, where there were two officers in the slot devoted to the training of navigators and radio officers. Two men had been needed when Canada, during the late Forties and early Fifties, had undertaken to train NATO aircrew from Italy, France and Germany. The scheme had been gradually phased out as the countries brought their air forces up to strength and did their own training. They were happy enough to obtain first-class Canadian training for pilots, who after a few years in the service would go on to fly commercial aircraft, especially if Canada picked up most of the tab. We did not object. We were good at training, having trained over 131,000 aircrew during the war, and we wanted to keep in practice. This was reinforced by the fact that people like to do things they are good at, whether they are useful or not.

The foreign countries, however, were unenthusiastic about training navigators or radio operators. Commercial planes with proper ground environments, unless they flew across oceans, did not need either. The number of trainee non-pilot aircrew fell off drastically. In any case, Training Command at Trenton was capable of running the entire training show, making all the decisions and handling all the logistics. As a result, for two staff officers at Ottawa there was very little to do.

I put up with my life of idleness for some months, and then went to my Group Captain, told him one radio-navigator could handle the whole job, and asked him to send me somewhere where I could be more useful. He was a notably open-minded unbureaucratic officer, who did not subscribe to the belief that every true office-holder should always strive to increase his staff and never give any of them up, and he moved me to another directorate. I flattered myself that for several years I saved the RCAF the pay and allowances of one squadron leader.

I was sent to assist a wing commander whose name I shall change to protect the innocent. Let us call him Wing Commander Wrong. He was the closest thing to a genius that I have ever met. He had the gift, which goes far beyond mere talent, of being able to see a concept without going through the intermediate steps of learning the lessons needed to get there. With only a Grade 12 education he was able to conceive and design intricate navigational computers which were the envy and despair of holders of masters and doctors degrees. He was always able to pierce immediately to the heart of a mechanical or scientific problem and come up with a novel and always successful solution. One of his favourite methods was to turn an established mechanism on its head; if the usual device had a cam driving a gear he would use it with the gear driving the cam, to solve problems others considered insoluble. He always had a clear idea of the operational problems he wanted the gadget to solve, how accurate it had to be and what tolerances he could allow. It was a great shame that he had not pursued his formal education. If he had, he would have ranked with scientists like Vanever Bush.

In the days when computers were mechanical and full of gears and electrical potentiometers and cams and wheels, like the old-fashioned arithmetical calculators that weighed fifty pounds and cost a fortune, he understood every "ingenious device" that made them work, and could see at once how he could get them to work better. Beginning with gadgets to solve immediate problems, which brought him to notice, he was soon foreseeing problems which would arise as new aircraft, which could reach new speeds and new altitudes, came into service to fly on new tasks. In particular, he knew exactly how to solve the navigation problem of the new CF-100 twin-engined jet fighter.

Like all creative people, however, his personality was not in tune with the Canadian peacetime military. All things were supposed to be done decently and in order, with all expenditures authorized before they were made, everything properly accounted for, and with no loose ends flapping in the breeze. That was not Wing Commander Wrong's method of operation.

Each year a budget was authorized for his directorate, with each task carefully plotted and priced milestones set up, and objectives delineated. As soon as the budget was authorized, Wing Commander Wrong dashed off on his own path. Funds allotted for one purpose were siphoned off for something he wanted more. He managed to overspend his pet projects, while holding back on some other project that one of the customers—the operational squadrons— wanted a good deal more.

One of the things that was not understood at the time was how expensive development was. The RCAF had always bought its instruments off the shelf, from Britain or the USA, after somebody else had paid for the development. The innocent airmen (including the Air Commodores in AFHQ) did not see why an instrument, which could be bought for about $5000 (although that was as much as a Cadillac cost in the Fifties) should cost a million dollars to develop. A figure like $50,000 seemed to make more sense, and this was what Wing Commander Wrong usually asked for. At first he himself considered that such a sum would cover the development he had in mind, and then, after the horrid truth had sunk in, he decided that sums like that were all that he had a chance of getting, and that was what he asked for.

In the internicene fighting for funds and resources which followed, in committee meetings he was inspired; convincing and credible, he was an expert at painting a picture of a Treasure City on the other side of a grassy plain, and having an expedition authorized to reach it. Soon the expedition found itself bogged in technological quicksands, beset by corporate brigands, running out of rations and money, but Wing Commander Wrong was always able to convince his superiors that it was not a matter of throwing good money after bad, that keeping on would result in some startling improvement to Air Force equipment. Then, at intervals, he would make good on his promises—he would produce impressive successes, gadgets that worked, that continued to work for decades, and that other air force clamoured to use. Our air marshals saw in him a star that could shine as brightly as those that glittered in American skies, of whom they were always jealous, and they tended to give him his head.

He had his detractors, of course, most of them lesser men. Some of them were simply jealous of him, while others resented the way he could get away with switching money around, thus fouling up their careful plans. At one time a wing commander was actually given the job of watching what he was doing, to make sure that he stayed within at least some of the guidelines.

Working for Wing Commander Wrong was a delight, an education, and nightmare. Keeping in constant motion as he did, the flak directed at him always missed, but it hit anybody in the vicinity who was not allowed to move so fast. It was like following the first attack plane over a target, who escaped unscathed but woke up all the gunners as the second plane came over. I always seemed to be navigating that second plane.

The first day I reported to him I missed my lunch. At lunch time I was in the cockpit of a CF-100 fighter, helping him to adjust a computer. He missed his lunch too, but such things never worried Wing Commander Wrong. Anyway, after that I always travelled around with a screwdriver in my pocket.

He was always prepared. He had a big black technician's bag with seventy-five pounds of tools, wires, batteries, and sometimes computers. "Carry this aboard the aircraft for me," he told me once as we were heading to the airport for a trip to New York. "Make it look light, so the stewardess won't complain about it." With my arm almost pulled from its socket, I walked nonchalantly up the steps to the plane, a fixed smile on my face. I got used to it, but my arms got longer.

Wing Commander Wrong was one of the best salesmen I ever met, provided that the stuff he was selling was his own. Coming back from New York City once on a New York Central train when trains still ran, he was sitting in a Pullman washroom explaining a computer he had invented and developed to an engineer he had met a few moments before. The train dashed through the dark countryside as Wing Commander Wrong said, "Let me show you how the vector addition system works." He dived into his briefcase. "I have one of the development models in my case, and it's hooked up to run on batteries." He set the gadget on the seat and turned it on. The counters spun briefly as they should have, and then stopped. Wrong looked at it, and immediately diagnosed the fault. "Just a loose wire," he said. Out of the briefcase he took an electric soldering iron. "I'll fix it—won't take a minute." He plugged the soldering iron into the socket for the electric razor. Every light in the train went out. Brakeshoes screamed as the train ground to a halt.

Wrong removed the soldering iron in the dark, wound it up, put it back in the case, put the computer in beside it, closed the case and shoved it into a corner, and continued his conversation with his new friend as if nothing had happened.

The conductor and the trainman, waving flashlights, stormed through the car, checking fuses. "If I find out who did this I'll kill

216

him!" the conductor snarled. Wrong paid absolutely no attention to him. A few minutes later the train jerked back into motion, and eventually arrived in Ottawa. Wrong was on the best of terms with his engineer by then, and later used him as a valuable contact.

The computers he designed were worth about $16000 each, which was about two years of my pay in those pre-inflationary times. He gave me the job of looking after his inventory, in honour of my storekeeping training, with the customary caution that if any of it got lost I was expected to pay for it.

I began my check. Three of the computers were missing.

I looked into every cranny. After one frenzied month I discovered that he had taken one to Fort Belvoir, Virginia, to see how well it would work in a tank. After another month I found he had left another with a boffin friend of his at the Royal Aeronautical Establishment in England. But there was still one missing. I searched for it frantically, but to no avail. Wrong shrugged. To my frantic enquiries he said, "It'll turn up." Such details could not have mattered less to him. He was already thinking of the next version of his computer.

One night he invited me to his house. "Come on down to see the model train I've set up for my son. I've fixed it so different power goes to different trains." I followed him down to the basement. Something caught my eye. "Hey, what's this?"

"Oh, it's one of the computers. I cut it in half with a hacksaw so that I could run the display end on hotshot batteries."

"Good God! That's what I've been looking for for three months!" I gasped. "How could you do a thing like this to me?"

He looked at me with resignation. Then he smiled. "I told you it'd turn up, didn't I? The books all balance now." I nodded numbly. He showed me how the train worked, and I had a good time playing with it.

He had a little English car which he could park in the most incredibly small places; one day he called me to see where he had put it in a spot only three inches longer than the car. It was just fine for running out to the aircraft at the military airport, since it could be shoe-horned into parking spots nobody else could use. But it had one fault. On a hot day it would get an airlock and the engine would stop.

It did so one afternoon when we were crossing the bridge from Hull to Ottawa during the rush hour. "Just an airlock," Wrong said. "It always clears up in a quarter of an hour. You stay here." He got out, walked to a shop at the end of the bridge, bought a copy of "Popular Science," and strolled back to the car, reading it. Meanwhile a tail of cars half a mile long stretched behind us. Drivers got out of their cars, berated me in English and French, and made all sorts of suggestions as to what I should do with myself. I stepped on the starter. The car refused to budge. I waited and tried again. The car ran a few feet and stalled. Wing Commander Wrong looked at his watch after a few minutes, got into the car, started it and drove off. It gave no more trouble that day.

Like all inventors, Wrong never wanted to freeze any design. He could always see a way to improve something in every gadget, and it was true that his improvements always worked. But the equipment, once built, had to be installed in aircraft, and that required stable blueprints of a frozen design. Every change meant three hundred blueprint corrections, which meant a delay, which snarled up schedules both at the instrument factory and at the aircraft factory. This infuriated the engineers, the schedulers, the planners, and the RCAF authorities who were confronted with additional bills.

As his assistant, I had to make many of the arrangements for the delivery to the aircraft company of the ingenious mechanisms he had invented. I worked out a schedule, had it approved by the wing commander, had it blessed by the instrument company, and presented it to the aircraft company.

The engineers around the conference table at the Montreal factory where the big anti-submarine aircraft were being built fixed me with their steely glances. They made it clear to we that my life and my fortune would be worth nothing if the schedule was delayed. I showed them Wing Commander Wrong's signature on the schedule. "We've seen his signature before'" muttered one of them. "You can't be sure of anything with him."

I stuck my guns, and emerged with everything signed.

The next Monday morning I received frantic calls from the aircraft factory. Nothing had arrived. I dashed out to the instrument factory.

"Whatever happened?" I cried.

The responsible engineer took me into a rework line. All the gadgets were in an orderly array, partly disassembled. "What's all this about? They were supposed to be shipped out to Montreal on Friday!"

The engineer shrugged. "Thursday afternoon Wing Commander

218

Wrong came in here and told us that the gadgets would run a lot better if the gyroscope turned around the other way."

I sat down. My mouth hung open. Everything would be delayed a week. My schedules were in ruins. The men at the aircraft factory would have my blood— and they did.

"Why didn't you tell him to get stuffed?" I screamed.

He looked at me. "You know how this company got started? To make those gadgets Wing Commander Wrong invented. Without him we'd still be in a shed repairing gyros. We've got a lot of good people working here— and they wouldn't be here if it weren't for Wing Commander Wrong.

"You know, you can't hire people to invent things—you can only find, usually by accident, people that can. You can't learn to invent, and you can't be taught, or take a course in inventing. You have to be touched by the finger of God. And Wing Commander Wrong is. If he tells us to make the gyros go round the other way we do it."

I lived through the next few weeks somehow. The gadgets were installed in the aircraft. As Wing Commander Wrong had foreseen, they worked a lot better with the gyros going round the other way.

Wing Commander Wrong was always polite and cheerful and wonderful to work for. I idolized him, even as I grew bent and scarred as the missiles aimed at him struck me. I learned a great deal about electronic devices and the way they were installed in aircraft from him, which stood me in good stead in later life. Watching him, I learned a lot about military intrigue as well, which also came in useful.

Just before he left his post, he took me to a meeting at another city. "I always take an unusual route to get to this next town," he said as we returned. "There's a restaurant there that serves the best Ukrainian food I've ever tasted. The way I go I avoid three lights, and a bridge." We ran up and down side streets, until finally we turned along a well-lit street and stopped in front of a restaurant. "That's how it's done," he smiled. We were going the wrong way on a one-way street.

Meanwhile my ordinary life continued, with me serving as a relief Sunday school teacher. One of my comrades in arms was Jewish, who one day was requested to give a talk on what we were doing in our directorate at his men's club of a Sunday morning. He asked me to come along to run the slide projector for him. The Saturday

219

before the presentation, one of my friends from my church called me up. "Will you take my Sunday School class for me, Norm?" he asked. "I want to go skiing."

"I'd like to," I replied, "But I have to go to the synagogue."

CHAPTER THIRTY-FIVE

My next posting after Ottawa was to Winnipeg, where I became staff officer at No. 14 Training Group. The Group had been formed in 1952 to control training on the prairies for the various nations who wanted aircrew training in Canada. For a while it was pretty busy, but when I got there most of the Danes, Germans, Italians and French had gone home, and there was very little to do. After my battles in Ottawa, as a flak-catcher for Wing Commander Wrong, I needed some peace and tranquillity, and I did not complain, as I had when I first reached Ottawa, that I had too little to do. I was disciplined regular, and if I was told not to do something, I didn't do it.

Winnipeg was a pleasant enough posting. My mother-in-law lived there, as well as two brothers-in-law, and we enjoyed visiting them. Our children loved to visit their grandmother, who indulged them as grandmothers do. They learned to travel to her house by bus and delighted in the adventure. In the summer we hooked up a utility trailer to our car and drove around from one campsite to another. One of these trips took us to Niagara Falls. Later we asked the children what they remembered about it. They thought for a moment, and then one of them said, "That's where we got the foot-long hot dogs."

Winnipeg is a fine place to live, except that it gets cold in the winter. Indeed, there are those who say that the people there spend all summer dreading the winter and all winter longing for the summer. Not everybody took that attitude, however. On one occasion when the temperature fell to thirty-five below zero, all the mothers in the married quarters drove their cars over to the school to bring their children home for lunch. When six-year-old Mary was having her lunch, my wife noticed she was wolfing her food.

"Why are you in such a hurry?" she asked.

Mary looked up and answered, "All the kids want to go out and play." Mary was allowed to walk back to school.

While I was serving as staff officer in charge of navigation and radio training at the Group Headquarters a valued friend of mine was posted to the Air Navigation School across the field from Group Headquarters. Being a trained Air Interception Officer, his job had been to operate the radar set in the back cockpit of a CF-100 night-fighter and direct the pilot to his target. He had been selected for cross-training as a radio officer, which meant learning the morse code up to twenty-two words a minute. He got up to eighteen words a minute—the speed I had had to pass out at when I took my radio course at Clinton a decade before—but try as he might he could not get up to twenty-two. He had to spend his hours in the radio training section, listening to recorded morse messages night after night. I felt for him. After all, I had been relegated to the dumb morse class once myself.

I could see him getting more and more depressed. Then one day in my official capacity I read a report that the International Committee for Air Organization had relaxed the morse requirements for trans-Atlantic aircraft from twenty-two to eighteen words a minute. I immediately wrote a letter to the Air Navigation School telling this, and authorizing the passing out of students with a morse speed of eighteen words a minute. I waited a few days, and then wrote a letter to Air Force Headquarters telling the brass what I had done.

Shortly after, as I expected, I received a furious blast from AFHQ screaming that the world-famous radio standards of the RCAF must not be lowered under any circumstances, and ordering me to revoke my previous instruction to the ANS immediately.

I was on good terms with the orderly room staff, and had made arrangements with them that such letters should be sent directly to me, bypassing my boss, the Senior Air Staff Officer. When I got the letter I closed the door to my office, ripped the letter up, piled the pieces into an ash tray, and set fire to them.

My friend duly passed his course, and went on to a happy and successful Air Force career. I knew that I was not prejudicing Air Force efficiency, because when I had been in Ottawa I had learned that a device called 'single sideband communication' which made voice messages as capable of driving through static as the old-fashioned dot-dashes of morse code were slated for installation in RCAF aircraft, while airborne teletypes were due to be installed in aircraft also. Sure enough, a few years later the Air Force trade of radio officer was abolished. I merely anticipated the inevitable.

Shortly thereafter I was transferred, and left before I had to reverse my previous directive to the school. After I reported to my new station my former boss, the Group Captain who had been SASO in Winnipeg, visited me. "A funny thing happened when you were in Winnipeg," he told me, his brow knitting. "A letter got lost."

I looked him straight in the eye. "I can't possibly imagine how a thing like that could happen in any such organization that you commanded," I said. "Everyone was careful about correspondence."

It was while I was at Winnipeg that the news came that the Arrow, Canada's new fighter aircraft, had been cancelled. Everyone in the RCAF had been looking forward to the arrival of the Arrow, being built by the Avro Company at Malton, Ontario. Conceived, designed and built in Canada, its flight tests had shown that it would be the fastest, most capable and most versatile fighter aircraft in the world; twenty-five years later aircraft like the CF-18 were matching but not surpassing it. Prime Minister John Diefenbaker, however, saw its price escalating, as such prices for military hardware always do, and wanted the money for his 'Northern Dream' in which great cities would spring up in the Northwest Territories. The story also goes that Crawford Gordon, the president of Avro, made an appointment to see Diefenbaker when his cause was *in extremis*. Diefenbaker had an appointment to speak to some school children for a quarter of an hour before he saw Gordon. Diefenbaker glowed in the adulation given him by the children and talked to them for an hour. Gordon used this interval to fortify himself with martinis. When he finally got see the Prime Minister he was somewhat under the influence. Diefenbaker was a teetotaller who despised drinkers. The upshot of the meeting was that the Arrow was cancelled, the design and production team was scattered to the four winds, and Crawford Gordon died, reportedly of a broken heart. The 'Northern Dream' also came to nothing.

The cancellation was a bitter blow to me. I had been working on the navigation system for the aircraft, finding myself in a bright new world. The aircraft flew so high that the length of a nautical mile increased, and so fast that it was necessary to invent a new airspeed meter. The job was challenging and fascinating, and I felt I had contributed something to it when I was in Ottawa. And now all that work had gone for nothing.

One of the factors in the cancellation was the existence of a number of high-ranking officers in the three services who were convinced that the day of the manned aircraft was over, with guided missiles taking over. The article I had written for the Staff College Journal had obviously not sunk in. I was right, but I might as well have been wrong.

Diefenbaker's slaughter of the Arrow did the Air Force almost as much harm as the big cut of 1932 (which was also imposed by a Conservative government.) It drove some 30,000 engineers, scientists and technicians out of the country, and set Canadian aerospace industries back thirty years. If the Arrow had been flying during the Vietnam war the USA would have bought hundreds of them.

The memory was still painful when one of my colleagues, a man who had joined the Air Force in 1928, came up for retirement. At his going-away party he told us what he had seen during his career.

"When I first joined up," he said, "I worked on aircraft with two wings tied together with streamline wires and struts, with hanging undercarriages, with big wooden propellors, and with rear cockpits where the gunner could stand up so you could see him. Then the designers got busy. They built wings that did not use streamline wires any more, and they got rid them and the struts. Next to go was the top wing. They built monoplanes instead. They brought in retractable undercarriages, so that in flight it seemed they had got rid of the wheels too. They invented turrets, so that you could not see the gunner any more. Then they brought in jet aircraft, and they got rid of the propellor. And then came the Arrow—and they got rid of the whole aircraft."

A roar of laughter went up, although we all felt like crying.

I stayed in the Arrowless Air Force, waiting for my next posting. To my complete surprise, it turned out to be as an exchange officer with the United States Air Force at Wright-Patterson Air Force Base at Dayton, Ohio. Such postings were considered plums, and I looked forward to my service in the United States . Before reporting to my new base, I was ordered to go to Ottawa to be briefed by the Personnel Directorate. I went happily, looking forward to being told what to look for, how to comport myself, who was who in the zoo at Wright Field, and other important information. I was determined to listen carefully and soak up every word.

When I got to Ottawa I was asked to sign a paper telling me that if the United States got into a war, I was to avoid combat service. Then they left me to my own devices.

224

CHAPTER THIRTY-SIX

Military forces like to send officers on exchange to one another. The techniques, methods and equipment used by foreign services are observed and reported upon. This was quite important for the RCAF, which tended to exist on the short end of the financial stick, and had to make do with fairly simple and often outdated equipment. Between the wars the service which had the most modern equipment, and where there was the most competition among RCAF officers to be sent, was the Royal Air Force; after the war it was the United States Air Force.

My own posting to Wright-Patterson Air Force Base was to the research and development center for manned aircraft. I was definitely an exchange officer, not a liaison officer, since my wife had given me clearly to understand that she would allow me no liaisons. I was to do the job a USAF officer would have done if I had not been there, and I was to be under the command of the USAF, although of course I had no power of command over anybody in the American services.

When I reported to WPAFB I was assigned to an electronic development section, where it soon became obvious that the USAF did not know what do with me. I was a highly-trained navigator, but the section was involved in technological innovations about which I knew practically nothing. After a couple of rather frustrating months I attended a brainstorming session on the subject, "How to Increase the Engineering Output of This Section." The next day I was transferred to another group. It was in another building, the quite-famous 'C and N' (Communications and Navigation) laboratory, where I should have gone in the first place.

The people in Building 22, the C and N Lab, had little idea what to do with me either. However, in an obscure corner of the field there existed a little tower built for some previous purpose which by now had been forgotten. In the tower was a digital computer and a star-tracker, together with an engineer. The device was supposed to have something to do with navigation, and I was a navigator, so I was turned loose on it. The star-tracker was an automatic sextant with a telescope which picked up the light from a star, the sun, the moon or a planet, and then read out the angle between the body and the horizon, just the way the hand-held sextants I had been using for years did. The associated digital computer was supposed to send the proper electrical signals through a maze of wires to make the sextant telescope point in the right direction to pick up the star, but nobody was sure how to set the right values into the computer to make it do it. Celestial navigation, including the spherical trigonometry on which it is based, had been stressed during my navigation courses. I was able to tell the engineer what values the star-tracker needed, and it dutifully locked onto the sun. We jumped up and down with joy.

The digital computer had been made by an organization I shall call the Computer Company. It was based in California, but it had an office in Dayton. Every aerospace company in the United States had representation in Dayton, because it was at Wright Field that all the decisions on what equipment would go into manned aircraft were made, at an expenditure of several billion dollars a year. The manager of the Computer Company's Dayton office was very unhappy.

Largely due to his efforts, a couple of years previously the Computer Company had sold the USAF on their new computer, which was indeed a startling advance in the state of the art. They had obtained a study contract, had built the prototype, and delivered it to Wright Field, where it was given some ground tests, and even had been installed briefly in an aircraft. The Computer Company had overrun their budget to develop the computer, (American companies always overspend study contracts) and the company was supplying field service engineers at its own expense to make sure the computer would run, supplying spare parts, and as well running up huge telephone bills for calls to California if anything went wrong. This was a reasonable gamble for a company which was aiming at finding a 'home' for its computer, (i.e. a new aircraft in which it would be installed as standard equipment.) The aircraft in mind was the C-141 jet transport, which was scheduled to come into production in a couple of years.

Then the base went through one of its periodic fits of reorganization, a disease which afflicts all bureaucracies. Sometimes it is due to new developments, with old ones becoming obsolete, and in this sense it is good, since otherwise we would have departments engaged in the care and feeding of bows and arrows. But too often it arises from a simple struggle for power, with one senior man invading another's turf to take over some of his staff and accommodation, and thus to climb higher on the military-executive ladder. Shortly before I got to Wright Field one such internicene war had taken place, and when the smoke cleared it transpired that the section responsible for testing the airborne digital computer had simply been forgotten about. Nobody was given the job at all, and the people who had been working on it were given other jobs, while the computer and its associated star-tracker were left simply to wither on the vine. The Dayton office and the parent company in California were in despair. Although digital computers were the coming thing, they could see that if they did not get their device installed on an aircraft that they would lose a whole generation of development.

That was where I came in. I was accidentally given the task of working with the computer since I was not really on anybody's establishment and nobody else would have to taken off another job to do it. Besides, those in Building 22 had no idea of what I could do, and doubted if I could do anything. The computer project, however, was one of the rare occasions when the job and the man were perfectly matched. It involved development, and I had been working on development under Wing Commander Wrong. The computer needed to be demonstrated, which required a teaching skill; I had been a navigation instructor. Scrounging was required, and I had been a storekeeper sergeant. It was necessary to fill out complicated forms and feed them into the proper channels; I had learned how to do that during my stint at Air Force Headquarters. Intrigue was required. Wing Commander Wrong had given me a post-graduate course in that. Finally it was necessary to make frequent reports, and our clerical staff was slender. I could type.

Meanwhile, my boss at the C and N lab had allotted me a desk and a chair in the section office, where I could sit while I handled a number of odd navigational jobs, like looking after hand-held computers. A few doors down the hall, however, I found an empty laboratory, left over from some completed project, and I asked permission to locate there instead. The boss, willing to humor this new foreigner, agreed, and I set up shop there.

The laboratory was spacious, and it had things like a line with power supplies in aircraft voltages, but it was dirty. I saw one of the building janitors in the hall one day, and asked him to come in and clean it up. Nothing happened. When I checked up, I found that the janitor was not obliged to enter my laboratory at all. The ostensible reason was that janitors could interfere with experiments in progress. The real reason was that the laboratory was a victim of 'grade creep.' The original establishment of the building had called for janitors, but as time went on section heads had found that they could further their careers, and the careers of their subordinates, by altering janitors' positions to make them technicians. They had the same number of men as before, but at a higher grade. Unfortunately it left me with nobody to clean up my laboratory. To sit among squalor offended my ex-sergeant-major's soul. I decided to sweep the floor myself. One thing led to another, and I soon was mopping the floor, waxing it, dusting everything in the room, washing the walls, cleaning the moulding that ran around the room, and even washing the windows. I soon had the cleanest laboratory in Wright Field. It was so clean, indeed, that the section took to holding meetings and briefings in it. If I happened to be in charge of the meeting, I would lay down the law. "I'm the janitor here," I would tell the participants. "Feel free to smoke. But when you do, throw the cigarette butts on the floor where I will find them easy to get it. Don't throw them under the table where I will have to fight to get them out." After that, they even went to the length of putting their butts in the ash-trays.

Without orders, of course, I moved the digital computer and the star-tracker into the laboratory, by driving to the tower and getting the field service engineer to help me load them into the back of my station wagon. Once in the laboratory, the computer was set to work, but bringing in the star-tracker created problems. It had an artificial star it could read, but that was not good enough. When a representative of the star-tracker company visited us, I told him I would like to have the telescope installed on the roof of the building, and connected to the computer in the laboratory. That would involve a bundle of wires, each some fifty feet long. A couple of weeks later a field service engineer from the company appeared and set to work. The wires were led through the window of the building and snake up to the roof. The star-tracker dutifully locked onto the sun and followed it around the sky, while the control box in the lab read out the altitude. I computed the altitude from my astro-navigation books, and they checked very well.

The field service engineer was happy about the set-up, and reported success to his superiors.

Ohio experiences torrential rains, and when they fell water ran along the cable where they came into the laboratory and made puddles on the floor. This caused no particular trouble, since the puddles could be cleaned up quickly with a mop, and I had no trouble getting this done since I wielded the mop myself.

Then one day the star-tracker began to point everywhere in the sky except where the sun was. The engineer checked every lead, to find to his dismay that the electrical signals which should have been coursing up and down the wires were all in the wrong places. Wires which should have been dead carried strong signals, and wires which should have been alive were, but with the wrong voltages. He changed wires, replaced connections, and made measurements.Nothing helped. He spent nights working on his system, appearing the next day haggard and red-eyed. The star-tracker refused to lock onto the sun; the signals were all in the wrong places. One morning he came to me to say, "If I can't get it to work today I'm going to call the company and quit."

I was going about my janitorial duties that morning when I noticed a trickle on the floor. It had not rained recently, and I wondered where the water was coming from. Investigating, I found rainwater had run down the cables leading out the window into a junction-box, where dozen of wires were inter-connected. I called the engineer. He seized the junction box and upended it, leaving a puddle on the floor. Furiously he dried all the connections.Then we turned on the computer and the star-tracker. The tracking head swung toward the sun on the roof like a hungry calf seeking its mother and locked on.

You can keep your job," I told the engineer. "If I hadn't been acting as janitor we never would have found it."

Come on and I'll buy you a beer," he told me at the end of the day. "We deserve one." We headed for a local tavern. After two beers he relaxed a little. "Thanks for your help," he said. Then he leaned toward me. "You know, when I first met you I thought you were the stuffiest guy I had ever met in my life."

"I was," I admitted. "But you've got to admit I'm a pretty good janitor."

With the system working properly in the laboratory, the next step was to install it in a twin-engine C-131 Convair aircraft, the work-horse transport of the USAF. The system had been installed in the aircraft before the reorganization had made it an orphan, and the wiring was still there. The computer company engineer, the star-tracker engineer, and I put the boxes back in the aircraft. We made sure all the gears turned around the right way, and began a series of twenty-two test flights, in which all operated with unexpected accuracy. This was duly reported, with the necessary proof, such as maps with fixes plotted and compared with computer positions, and the errors all analyzed with Standard Deviations worked out, just as I had been taught in the Specialist Navigation Course. Before long I was giving in-flight demonstrations, once or twice to a general. I used the method of demonstration I had used as a navigation instructor, which is to have the student make all the setting himself, which gives him as feeling of accomplishment.

My superiors in Building 22 became supportive of my work, since it always helps an administrator to oversee as project that is going well.   But if they were approving, the people in the Computer Company office in Dayton were ecstatic.   They could see their previously orphaned system working in the laboratory and the air. They got the test results and showed them off. They could see the C-141 with their system on it. Engineers and salesmen began to come from California to gather in my laboratory.

I was elevated in their eyes to the rank of a VIP. I kept telling them not to exaggerate my influence. I reminded them that I was not even a member of the United States Air Force, that I had nobody working for me, that I had no power of command, that I could authorize no expenditures, and that I was not even a qualified engineer, but they gave me the red carpet treatment just the same. Of course I revelled in the attention I was getting. I loved every moment of it.

Meanwhile I kept finding ways to make the tests more productive, almost all of which required expensive equipment like oscilloscopes. Looking round the building, however, I found all sorts of equipment which had been procured for past projects, and left to gather dust when the projects were completed; oscilloscopes, motion picture cameras, vertical cameras, driftmeters, and pen recorders. I acquired it all by scrounging; finding equipment which was not in use and asking for it. In a moment of weakness, finding a need for a mobile aircraft air-conditoning system, I ordered one through the proper channels; my storekeeping training kept breaking through. The request was firmly turned down, on the grounds that the cost was exorbitant and the requirement sketchy.

A few days later while visiting another office I saw a mobile air-conditioning unit outside the window.

"You using that?" I asked casually.

"No," came the answer.

"Mind if I borrow it for a while?"

"Go right ahead."

I had it for the rest of my stay at Wright Field, without benefit of paper work. It made working inside the aircraft when it was parked on the taxi-strip a lot more comfortable. I also received co-operation from such unexpected sources as a printing shop on the base which made special maps for me. After living in the Canadian research and development climate, with the bare minimum of equipment, I was in heaven.

I even scrounged people. My flight test program involved getting fixes from a ground radar station every four minutes and plotting them on a map, at the same time recording the latitude and longitude computed by the airborne computer. Another pair of eyes had to be on an oscilloscope (a device rather like a small round TV screen.) A third pair of eyes had to be on the star-tracker. My staff consisted of me and myself. However, the USAF maintained a technical college at WPAFB, whose student body ran heavily to navigators. The students needed flying time to qualify for flying pay, but their studies kept them in school all day. I did most of my flying at night, because that was when the stars were out. I met some of them when I attended after-hour mathematics classes in their classrooms, and told them of my project. Several of them volunteered to fly with me, and suddenly I had all the capable, energetic trained navigators I needed. They were grateful to me for solving their financial problems, and I was grateful to them for their skilled help. We got along fine.

It even got to the point once when four of them flew with me, and after I showed them what I wanted I did not have to do anything myself at all. The star-tracker engineer, who was flying with me that night, saw me walking up and down the aircraft with my hands clasped behind my back.

"Any orders, Captain Bligh?" he asked.

"None," I answered. "I'd call you Mr. Christian except that I know you're a heathen."

"I'm not a heathen," he said, "I'm a Southern Baptist."

"That's close enough for an Anglican like me," I responded.

"That's what I like about you," he answered. "Not a bigoted bone in your body."

The method of fixing my position during the test flights was to have a ground radar station report the aircraft's range and bearing from it. It was accurate, but I wanted to find out just how accurate. This required a vertical camera to photograph the ground at exactly the same time a radar fix was reported, with an operator.

The operator was a hard-bitten master sergeant, of the breed that looked on officers as natural enemies. I however, with my non-USAF rank badges, my incomprehensible title, and the fact that I was only a foreigner, did not really rank as an officer in his eyes, and he and I came quite friendly, especially when he found out that I had joined the air force as a regular before the war started, the same as he had; he had originally enlisted in the cavalry. He told me that during the war he had flown as a flight engineer in DC3 aircraft, freighting equipment from India to China over the Himalayan mountains, —the 'hump.' On several occasions the cargo was mules, destined for General "Vinegar Joe" Stilwell, a man renowned for his short temper and skill at bawling people out.

The hump was plagued by weather, and the aircraft had reliability problems. Sometimes it was necessary to jettison cargo. The sergeant, who had been brought up on a farm in Tennessee, knew how to jettison mules. He would open the side door of the aircraft, untie the mule, and grasp its testicles. The mule would jump straight up in the air, and when all four hooves were off the floor he would simply push the mule out the door. One day, after they had lost an engine he had to do this four times.

Stilwell was awaiting them once when they arrived in China minus their mules. "He sure give us hell, that old bastard," the sergeant said. "He wanted them mules. He'd 'a' been happier if we'd delivered the mules and thrown out the crew."

The sergeant had abetted me in getting the camera installed. If he flew with it he would draw flying pay. And his flying pay was three times as much as mine was.

During my flights, I became aware that the aircraft was beautifully maintained--much better than I had any right to expect. The ground crew even installed a coil of wire screwed to the navigation table for me to hold my pencils in. I was grateful, but left in wonder. Then one day I was looking through the aircraft logbook, where I saw the following words written: "Project Engineer—Sergeant Emmott." That was the closest the ground crew could get to my foreign, unintelligible rank of Squadron Leader. The ground crews were headed by sergeants, and sergeants looked after their own.

In between flights the Computer Company field service engineer kept the computer going, and made changes to the program as the flight tests demanded them. This required taking out electronic cards which were plugged into 'mother' boards in the various boxes. The cards could then be worked on, with new components soldered into place, and jumpers wired in to make the computer work differently. We invited the engineer and his wife to a party at our house one night. She looked at us as she spoke to my wife. "I don't know what the boys do in that lab at Wright Field," she said. "Every time I call they are playing cards!"

CHAPTER THIRTY-SEVEN

The experimental computer's tests came to an end, and I wrote a report on them. In the meantime the Computer Company had exploited its good reputation to persuade the USAF to embark on the next step in its progress, which was test two "service test" systems, improved developments of the original design. In due course two complete systems were shipped in to my laboratory, the minimum number that can be used in a properly-conducted test, since it always difficult to arrange for the instruments and the aircraft to be available and serviceable at the same time. With two systems, one could be in pieces on the workbench while the other was flying.

We started ground tests on them immediately. It appeared that the systems were running hot, but then a telephone call from the engineers in California assured us that all was well. But our suspicions were confirmed, however, when the power supply burst into flames. Further investigation proved that one of the engineers had misplaced a decimal point.

Another Computer Company engineer arrived, who had flown with the earlier system before I came on the scene, and drafted out the wiring changes necessary to fit the new system into the aircraft. The plane was put into the hangar, all the old wiring was taken out and new wiring was put in. We installed one of the new systems and turned it on. There were a few discrepancies. The airspeed fed to the computer showed 167 knots when the aircraft was standing still, the compass showed a north heading when the aircraft was pointing south, and turned to the right when the aircraft turned left. The TACAN radio-navigation set read 200 miles range when it should have read zero, the bearing was 180 degrees out, and the bearing rotated in the wrong direction! I had expected this; as I had learned when I was doing experimental work under Wing Commander Wrong, everything works backwards the first time it is installed. We sorted things out by swapping leads to gadgets called synchros, and by making changes to the computer program. Sometimes we were lucky. On one flight I found two quite distinct malfunctions, which I decided to cure one at a time. I made the first correction, and it cured the second fault as well. I never found out why.

The aircraft had an older doppler radar navigation set. This is a device which spits radio energy at the ground, listens for the echo coming back, and measures the difference between the frequency of the outgoing and the received signal. This difference is used to determine the aircraft's ground speed, and also the amount it is drifted sideways by the wind. Another division of the Computer Company volunteered to provide its latest doppler radar free of charge to the project, with the object of having it tested. I accepted the offer with alacrity, although of course the decision to install it had to be made by my USAF bosses.

In due course a big crate and two field service engineers arrived at the laboratory. The immediate difficulty was that the radome of the aircraft was held on by some 500 Phillips-head screws, and we had to take it off to install the antenna. The two radar engineers, the star-tracker engineer, and I went down to the flight line to take off the radome. It took us until half-past twelve. The next day we installed the antenna and tested it. That evening we had to spend another four hours putting all the screws back in again. When we finished my friend the star-tracker engineer looked at me and said, "I knew you'd do well, Norm. I've noticed you're real good at screwing things up."

The incident had a fall-out a couple of weeks later. With one of the engineers I went to the flight-line in search of something which would be of help, but for which I had not the slightest right. The foreman I sought looked at us and said, "Oh yes— you're the guys who work till midnight every night on that aircraft." He gave us everything we wanted. The Protestant ethic was alive and well at Wright Field.

Once aboard the aircraft, it soon became apparent that the doppler radar worked well over land, but the question arose—how well would it work over water? A careful analysis of the problem soon established that the only practical way to test it was to fly the aircraft to Bermuda, which happened to be exactly the right distance away for a relevant test. Although on previous occasions I had sometimes had difficulty assembling a crew for night flights over Ohio, I had no trouble at all getting one to go to Bermuda. The operations officer made a few insincere objections, but the flight crew was perfectly happy.

Over the water the doppler worked well, but the star-tracker spasmodically gave highly erroneous results. When we landed at Bermuda, instead of taking off to enjoy the delights of the salubrious island, the Star-Tracker Company engineer and I had to have an auxiliary power unit rolled up to the aircraft which was standing in the broiling sun, while we spent an afternoon taking the star-tracker apart to find what the trouble was. When we returned to Wright Field, however, we found that the despatch officer was saying, "When you guys go to Bermuda, you work. Other people take it as a holiday." Working hard had not been my idea on that afternoon, but I accepted the accolade. I had even less trouble arranging trips to Bermuda thereafter and the students from the air academy were even more willing to fly with me as crew.

I distinguished myself in another way on that flight. I had to leave a message at the Bermuda Operations Room for the aircraft commander, Captain Edwin Hatzenbuehler. When we gathered for the return flight he shook me by the hand. "That's the first time in my air force career. " he told me, "that anybody has ever written me a note and spelled my name right."

Someone asked me why I was so anxious to visit Bermuda. I explained the matter by telling him that my grandfather had served in Bermuda in 1884 as a colour-sergeant in the Royal Irish Rifles. While there he had incurred expenses of three shillings and sixpence for transport, which he had duly claimed through the proper channels. The claim had at last been approved; I wanted to go to Bermuda to collect it. He accepted my explanation, deploring the ravages of inflation. Three and six had been a lot of money in 1884.

We flew the aircraft all over the United States and to Goose Bay, Labrador, demonstrating the equipment to a host of people, including more generals. There was a Canadian detachment at Wright Field, charged with handling the paper work for American equipment being procured for RCAF use, and when we were going somewhere interesting I would arrange for one of the airmen to be taken along. After a few of them had been taken to Los Angeles or Miami, I received excellent co-operation from the staff.

By the time the project was finished we had made 139 flights, totaling 587.2 hours. I also got to make a ground presentation to a German general. I was of mixed emotions, since German generals and myself had not been on the best of terms during the Forties. After the presentation the general came up to me, however, thanked me for my work, and told me I must have gone to a lot of trouble to make a complicated subject sound fairly straightforward. After that, I decided I liked German generals after all. I have always liked German music, German food, German beer and German toy trains, and the only thing I really had against the Germans was that they had tried to kill me.

Wright Field went through the same rain dances as all military bases do. Strict adherence to budget limitations was required of everyone. Two or three times I was called in to the office of the lieutenant colonel in charge of the squadron which did the test flying, to be exhorted to keep my flying to a minimum. I always swore solemnly that I would. As soon as I left the office, however, one of the officers would button-hole me to say, "Keep on flying all you can. If you don't we may lose an aircraft." Similarly, I was told to keep my requests for changes to the aircraft as infrequent as possible, and of course I stated that this would be always foremost in my mind. Then as I walked through the hangar one of the foremen would say to me, "Keep those requests coming in. It's guys like you that make jobs for guys like me."

The base was controlled by the military, with a general in command, and many of the offices were headed by colonels with a coterie of officers on their staffs. But it was the long-time civil servants who really made it run. They encompassed an amazing range of skills; if you wanted a violin made, a lecture on Einstein's theories, the field surveyed or a picture painted, you could find somebody on the field who could do it expertly. I found that one of my most valuable possessions was a telephone directory I'd made myself, with the names of people who were experts in every field in which I was involved. I always got the advice I asked for, and it was always good.

As a Canadian officer, I was not required to appear on any parades or take part in any military duties. I always wore the uniform of the day, which in the summer was just an unadorned khaki shirt and trousers. When fall came, I showed up in my blue uniform complete with my wings, and the secretary in the section office said with surprise, "I didn't know you were rated!" (i.e., that I was aircrew.) As the only Canadian officer in my section, I had the right to determine the order of dress, and since I preferred the non-official RCAF tartan necktie to the regulation black one, I wore that with my blues. Of course, if I had to visit the RCAF detachment I put the black tie back on. On Saint George's Day, as allowed by regulations, I wore a rose in my hat—I had never done so in Canada, but I wanted to impress the foreigners. I could have worn a leek on Saint David's Day, but I did not have the nerve to do it.

I made use of my special status. At times it was desirable to do things for which I had no authority, or to obtain equipment to which I was not entitled. If brought to book (I seldom was!) I would ruefully say that I was only an ignorant foreigner, unfamiliar with USAF rules and regulations, and that I would be more careful in the future. It always worked.

At intervals the Systems Project Office for the C-141 transport would call on me to take part in meetings to discuss equipment to be installed on the aircraft. During these meetings, figuring I was too dumb to lie effectively, I always spoke the plain unvarnished truth. It was later reported to me that several of the highly-placed representatives of the companies competing to put their devices on the C-141 had suffered nervous breakdowns trying to discern what I actually meant by my statements.

At times I was called on to do odd jobs. One of them was going to a base which operated C-130 cargo planes in co-operation with army airborne troops. The aircraft had been fitted with a simpler computer which happened to be built in Canada, and my job was to draw up procedures for using it. One incident involved flying with an army sergeant who was to jump out of the aircraft over a landing zone. As we flew towards it, he looked bored.

Later when I spoke to one of the army officers, the conversation got around to how much an individual man is worth. "I know exactly how much I'm worth," he told me.

"How much?" I asked.

"In 1942 I was in the Philippines, fighting with the guerrillas after the Japanese overran the island. They offered the natives rewards if they turned guerrillas in, and one of them did exactly that to me. The reward was food. I know exactly what I'm worth—a hundred pound bag of rice."

CHAPTER THIRTY-EIGHT

The United States and the United Kingdom are two countries divided by a common language, with Canada somewhere in between. Citizens from one country do not find much of a language barrier dividing them from the others, but when we dig a little deeper the differences grow. For instance, in Summerside one day an Air Force wife, a British war bride, reported that the man next door had knocked her up that morning. Her comment, meant merely that he had awakened her in the morning, drew raucous laughter from those around.

When I arrived at Wright-Patterson Air Force Base I found I fitted in quite well, and shortly after I got there my colleagues ceased to notice anything different about me. My accent sounded American, as does that of all Canadians who speak what is officially termed "Standard Midwestern American with some differences." I pronounced my "R's," as Brits do not, I made "grass" rhyme with "gas" and not "gloss," and if I pronounced "been" to rhyme with "seen" and not "sin," and "again" to rhyme with "pain" and not "men," that passed unnoticed too. The only comment I met was when the engineer from the Star-Tracker Company reproved me for saying I had "paid my jews," instead of saying I had "paid my dyoos." I had to admit he was right.

I had, however, been brought up in an English milieu. Both my parents were British, and so were the parents of most of my playmates where I grew up in British Columbia. I bought English comic papers as a child, read magazines like *Chums*, and read omnivorously of English literature. Then during the war I served in England, and was exposed to English as she is spoke among the common people like Royal Air Force aircrew officers. I became conversant with English catch-phrases and English slang.

So it was that during a conversation with a USAF officer I told him that during my flight test of the computer I had stretched regulations a little, and then had decided to go the whole hog and stretch them a lot. "I might as well be hanged for a sheep as a lamb," I said.

My companion looked at me with surprise. "That's a clever comment," he told me. "It expresses exactly what you wanted to say. I must remember it." I was wise enough to say no more.

Later, when I was sitting in a meeting with some rather senior USAF officers, a question came my ways that I fielded by saying, "Let's do it. Nobody will miss a slice off a cut loaf." A colonel looked at me with appreciation. "That's it exactly! You certainly have a way with the English language."

Driving through one of Dayton's industrial neighbourhoods, another passenger in our automobile remarked on the grimy surroundings. "Where there's muck there's luck," I commented. The man looked at me with profound respect in his eyes, and said, "What a clever way to put it! I've never heard anybody say it so succinctly before." I nodded my head modestly.

One of my friends had a son who looked exactly like him, the same red hair, freckles and blue eyes. I patted the boy on the head and said, "Your dad will never be dead while you're alive."

His father snapped his head round. "My gosh, what a perceptive statement! It says in a nutshell what immortality means when it is expressed through our descendants! You're a real philosopher to put it so clearly!" He shook my hand. "I must report that to my pastor—he'll appreciate it." I heard later that the pastor had indeed used the phrase in his next sermon.

One of our friends was a woman of somewhat flighty disposition according to my straitlaced views, who prided herself on familiarity with the latest fashions and lingo. At that time there was a rock group called "The Crows." We discussed them, since she was enthusiastic over their accomplishments. Being on my best behaviour, I forbore telling her that I considered her to be among those who confused the sounds they made with music. Floundering for words, I said, "Cor stone the crows!"

Her eyes lit up. "What a phrase? Crows do caw, and they're always stoned? It certainly fits!" She went off, repeating the magic words.

At that time the Secretary of Defense in the US government was Robert Macnamara, who enjoyed somewhat less than uncritical acclaim among the serving personnel, who objected to the way he allowed the forces to be run by his 'whiz kids,' and his habits of making rough judgments based on sketchy information. It was no surprise to me when one of my colleagues cornered me and began

240

a tirade against his civilian master. "The trouble is," he said, "that Macnamara runs the Department of Defence as though he owns the whole country. I thought I worked for Uncle Sam, not the Ford Motor Company!" I took a pull at my beer and nodded. "Yes," I said, repeating a common phrase I often had heard in England, "you send a whiz kid to do a man's job, and Bob's your uncle."

"Bob's your uncle! That's the trouble! He thinks he is! He thinks he's Uncle Sam! Say, that's the best statement I've heard all day! You've put your finger on it exactly." He bought me another beer. "You have a real good grasp of the essentials, haven't you? You know, maybe we're too close to the problem. It takes somebody with a detached view to see things so clearly!" I nodded sagely.

The affairs of every military service are periodically sacrificed to political considerations. One of my USAF friends and I were discussing the matter one day when he said, "Sometimes bureaucrats who know nothing about the air force get too far into the act."

I thought back to a remark I had heard on the tarmac in Port Hardy in 1945 and nodded. "That's the biggest understatement," I commented, "since Noah said, 'It looks like rain.'"

He slapped his knee, he slapped my shoulders, he called the attention of his colleagues to this profound and obviously original statement. I nodded solemnly, accepting his encomiums as my due.

I was getting quite a reputation as a wit. I topped it off as I was standing at the bar when one of my blue-suit friends came in. "Having another?" he asked. I thought back to the time I made the same comment to another friend in a bar at Harrogate Yorkshire in 1944, and the answer I had received. "No," I said. "It's just the way my coat is buttoned." He exploded into laughter. Later I heard him pointing me out to a companion. "That's the Canadian exchange officer in Building 22. He's the wittiest man in the world."

CHAPTER THIRTY-NINE

One aspect of life at Wright-Patterson that flattered, embarrassed me, and that I enjoyed and worried about, was the entertainment that was offered to me at every turn. Wright Field was the center for the development of almost everything concerned with manned aircraft, as well as a host of ancillary gear as well, and as such it was always awash with salesmen, engineers and executives from companies all over the United States that developed them, built them, repaired them or sold them. Representatives regularly dropped in at every office on the field, and whenever they did they would invite those they met to have lunch with them. Such hospitality was accepted at the time, and few had any objections to it. It was a salesman's duty to build good relations with anyone who could be useful to him, to smell out everything that was happening at Wright Field, and keep on top of every opportunity to sell his products. A good way was to wine and dine the officers and their civilian counterparts; it was always easier to get the truth over a martini.

To people in strategic positions, hospitality reached far greater heights. Expensive dinners were taken for granted at Dayton. When Wright Field people went to big cities, as they did regularly to visit the plants where equipment for the Air Force was being made, representatives of the companies would appear with tickets to Broadway shows, squire them to night clubs, and provide rooms stocked with scotch and champagne in luxurious hotels, (and ladies of the evening inside them if the salesman knew his client well enough.) Drive-yourself cars at company expense were always available. Trips to hunting lodges came later to special friends in high places.

For the first couple of months I was in Dayton I was invited now and then to the odd lunch mostly as a hanger-on to others who were more important. After I was installed in my laboratory, as the Project Officer for the computer program, however, invitations became frequent. The engineer who looked after the computer, and the one whose charge was the star-tracker, began by inviting me to have a coffee or a beer after work. Then, after the system began to operate properly, and especially after the flights began, my laboratory became a port of call for people from the Dayton office of the Computer Company and the Star-Tracker Company, as well as other company visitors from California or New York. Indeed, I found myself in one of the strategic positions.

The Computer Company knew that the future of their device lay largely in how well it performed, how well I demonstrated it, and what my report said about it. I was sympathetic, and besides that I was intrigued by the challenge of working with the most modern equipment in the world. If the computer malfunctioned, I delighted in finding out why, and making it work better the next time. Regardless of what I did, however, I knew that the company would have showered the same goodies on anybody that happened to be testing their computer.

Whenever we took the system on a trip to such a place as Los Angeles or Atlanta to demonstrate it to potential users, or to show it in action to the people who had designed it, the aircraft crew and myself would always be taken to expensive restaurants and night clubs when we were off duty. We all took that for granted. Back in Dayton, my wife and I were taken to plays and concerts, and of course night clubs. I did find these constant offers a little embarrassing, although I was quite aware that the costs of an evening on the town did not come out of the pockets of whatever salesman or engineer was entertaining me. The company picked up the tab, not my host, and expected to do so. Indeed, the star-tracker engineer on one occasion told me that he had been criticized for not entertaining me enough.

I accepted many of the goodies because everybody was doing it, and I had got used to it on a much smaller scale when I was working for Wing Commander Wrong, who certainly was a key figure in the plans of many aerospace firms in Canada. But I never felt comfortable with the practice, since I knew that there was no such thing as a free lunch, that the host wanted to put me under an obligation, and that a bribe is a bribe is a bribe. A couple of years after I left Wright Field, Secretary of Defence, Robert Macnamara, forbade military personnel or their civilian colleagues to accept so much as a lunch or a cigarette lighter. Personally, I thought the order was overdue.

To salve my conscience, I took to entertaining my business

friends in my home. This sounded more generous than it actually was. We liaison officers were entitled to obtain liquor at embassy prices, without either Canadian or American taxes. Our booze, as a matter of fact, was so cheap that it cost us money to stay sober. We, being exhorted to be ambassadors for our country, were expected to entertain royally. My wife and I did; whenever we had people to the house we played charades, the same as the Queen did. Our guests were always a little uncomfortable at first, but after a few rounds they all were carried away by the game, and put everything into their acting out of some phrase, movie, or book. It was usually the women against the men, and the women usually won, but then a woman's guess is better than a man's certainty. We men did get our own back one time when we asked the women to act out, "I've Got Tears in my Ears from Lying on My Bed Crying Over You." The women said that was unfair, being an obscure song. We had to be unfair if we ever hoped to win.

The most unusual people turned out to be the most talented. One young woman, straight out of the mountains of Tennessee, who had to be coaxed to take part in the game at all, suddenly proved she could act like Sarah Bernhardt. She was the star of the party. We do not know how she made out back in Tennessee, but her husband appreciated her a lot more after that.

It was not only business people we entertained, of course; we had other sets of friends, people we worked with as well as the other Canadians on duty at Wright Field, and our civilian friends, many of whom we had met through the Episcopal church we attended. There were a number of civilians at Wright Field we considered it our duty to entertain. We did so, but since they knew about Embassy-priced liquor, they did not feel it incumbent on them to entertain us back, and they never did.

Our church friends were mostly engineers and professionals, and their very capable wives. In those happy days, before women felt impelled to become astronauts, they all seemed to be wonderful cooks, leaning heavily to German-style meals. A pot-luck supper at the church was something to be marvelled at. We had some wonderful parties with them, and they turned out to be good charade-players also.

Our American friends went to much trouble to help us celebrate our national holidays. One of them was Boxing Day, which they had never heard of, but they listened carefully as we explained it to them. The day after Christmas, as we were relaxing just before lunch, our doorbell rang. Dozens of our friends were there, all carrying cases—shoeboxes, clothes-boxes, wooden boxes, and celluloid boxes. Two men staggered in with an enormous box. With great ceremony they opened it. Inside was a slightly less enormous box. We opened that, to find a third somewhat smaller box, and so on until we came to a match-box. Inside it was their present to us—a toy from a Crackerjack box. But it was the thought that counted. We do not know if we converted our Dayton friends to the Boxing Day principle, but one of them still phones us on Boxing Day every year.

We had to take into account the American holidays also. On one Fourth of July I was able to take advantage of the opportunity to straighten them out on one matter. "Some two hundred years ago," I told them, "a group of colonists abandoned the monarchy, but retained the British system of weights and measures. How much wiser they would have been to retain the monarchy, and abandon the British system of weights and measures." They shared with me my regret at this lost opportunity.

My civilian friends never saw me in uniform; like most regulars, I took off my blue suit when I got home. One day, however, my wife sent me to deliver something to one of our friends from the church. I was in full fig with my air force 5A blue uniform, my gold-plated buttons, my Bates hat from London, copied from the Luftwaffe in the high-crowned style we had admired during the war, my cap-badge with the royal crown above the albatross above the laurel wreath, my embroidered wings and my medal ribbons. I knocked on the door. The lady opened it, and then she stepped back and exclaimed, "Why, you're beautiful!" It made my day.

We visited the homes of our company friends also, of course. One Saturday night we attended a house-warming given by the field service engineer of the star-tracker company. As I drove home the night before, I was turning over in my mind a problem in that had been bothering us for some weeks and at last I came upon a solution.

It was too late by then to confer with my engineer friends about it, and I decided to broach it in a different way. As I helped my wife with the dishes that night, I coached her very carefully on something that she was to say on Saturday.

The star-tracker and the computer communicated by means of a gadget called a two-speed synchro, in which the computer had to make up its mind whether to believe one synchro which turned around once for every full circle, and another which turned around twelve times each circle. These two devices were connected by means of a device called a cross-over network, which never seemed to work right. We were having trouble sorting it out.

On the night my wife waited until she maneuvered five of the engineers into listening to her at once, and then said. "I've been thinking about that problem of yours. If you used only the input from the coarse synchro while the computer is positioning the star-tracker, you'd point the tracker close enough to pick up the star; and then if you used only the input from the fine synchro when you are feeding the altitude back do the computer, you wouldn't need the cross-over network." The engineers nodded politely, and then went on to the buffet table to pick up their suppers. Suddenly one of them, in the most beautiful double-take I have ever seen outside of a Three Stooges movie, whirled toward my wife, dropped his plate, and said, "By God, it'd work!"

There was a quick babble of conversation among the engineers, and then they all agreed that the idea would work, and that it would save all sorts of trouble. Indeed, we adopted the idea the next Monday. One of the men looked at my wife and said, "When did you think of that?"

"Oh, I got to thinking about it yesterday when I was doing the dishes—"

They clustered around her, and three companies offered her a job on the spot. One of them launched a cruel shaft against me, however. He looked at me and said, "Now we know where Emmott gets all his good ideas from."

CHAPTER FORTY

While we were in Dayton, Ohio our four daughters were receiving American educations. We told them that during the pledge to the flag they should hold their hands over their hearts and think of Canada. Officially, they were classed as aliens. My youngest daughter, Mary, came home to me indignantly denying that she was one of them. "Aliens are green and have radio antennas sticking out of their heads," she declared. We decided not to obtain a TV set, preferring that our children learn to read properly, and they accepted our judgment, although they were periodically embarrassed by not knowing anything about as TV program the other children were discussing. My third daughter, Shelagh, had reservations, however. "I know you don't want a TV, Daddy," she said to me, "but couldn't you at least put up an antenna?" My second daughter, Barbara Kirsten, formed the determination at Dayton that she was going to become a doctor. That caused raised eyebrows, but she did achieve her ambition, and went on to become one.

My oldest daughter Elizabeth, who spent her fourteenth to her seventeenth year in Dayton, like her sisters had inherited their mother's looks. When her mother took her to the supermarket bag-boys converged on her from all points of the compass, and she cut quite a swath through high school. I had no sons, but I soon had many sons of other people around the house. My only complaint was that they had an unquenchable thirst for milk, but I considered that was much better than having one for beer.

During the leave periods we would go on camping trips around the eastern United States. During one of them we visited the battlefields of Gettysburg and Antietam. The Civil War was a very interesting war from the standpoint of a professional military man, as I was. I drove along slowly, looking at all the plaques which told which regiment had been stationed where, in a fashion that bored the children out of their minds. I spoke sharply to them about it,

247

and then I noticed with approval that there would be a question from a girl every time I stopped. Later I found that they had made an agreement among themselves that they would take turns in asking a question, always leaving three of the four free to attend to more interesting subjects.

All things must come to an end. My three years at Wright-Patterson Air Force base drew to a close, as did my association with C-131 aircraft serial number 7813. I had to think of the rest of my life.

My compulsory retirement age was coming up in a couple of years. The Air Force likes its people young, to stand the strain of campaigning, not to mention duty-free booze. I was entering my 27th year of service, my family would still require support when the RCAF turfed me out, and I had to consider a second career. My decision was made easier by the fact that four of the companies whose products had passed through my hands offered me a job. One of them was the Computer Company, whose offer was one that I could not refuse.

I submitted my resignation to the RCAF. I was a little miffed by the fact that my beloved RCAF made no effort to keep me, but at that time there was a 'hump' of officers with wartime service, and applications for early retirement were welcome. People leaving the service from Canadian stations were usually honoured by a parade where they took the salute, but I was too far away and in a foreign country. The RCAF did send me a certificate thanking me for my service. My name was misspelled on it, and I asked for another one. It duly came, but this time it was signed not be an Air Vice Marshal, as the first one had been, but by a lowly Air Commodore. The person who had goofed up in preparing the first one had obviously gone to another senior officer to sign it, to avoid embarrassing questions.

My new job called for a move to California, where we lived for eight years before we returned to Canada. The family settled in Escondido, thirty miles north of San Diego, world-famous as the home town of Lawrence Welk. We soon found ourselves with a new set of friends.

The woman across the street was a member of the League of Women Voters, an organization which is viewed by all politicians with the respect ordinarily accorded to a fifty ton tank. Those who have treated it cavalierly have soon found themselves thinking they have been run over by one. She invited my wife to attend their meetings. Soon my wife was pressed into service, and made studies and reports that impressed all the members. One of them was a comprehensive report on the water situation in California, a subject dear to all Californian hearts. She did so well that a year later she was nominated to be Vice-President of the Escondido chapter.

"I'm very flattered," she told the group, "but I'm afraid I'm unable to comply with your request. You see, I feel that to be an officer of the League you should be an American citizen, able to vote in elections. I'm not. I'm a Canadian."

The president of the chapter sprang to her feet. "You shut up!" she shouted angrily. "I'm a Canadian too!"

CHAPTER FORTY-ONE

My introduction to the business world was a shock to me.

Today's industry, the whole world knows, is the most capable, the most productive, the best-managed anywhere; it has submerged friends and foes in consumer goods or military hardware for half a century. If all the countries in the world would only adopt modern business practices, all problems would be solved and all wrongs righted.

So I thought during my years in the Air Force, in the sheltered environment of the service, where there was never a worry about where the next meal was coming from, no bottom line to keep in the black, no fear of the firm going broke. Once in a while the airman was required to demonstrate his skill while being shot at, but these incidents were few and far between, added excitement to life, and were rewarded with medals. The civilian lived in a far more dangerous world. He had to pass a test of competency every day. He could be fired at a moment's notice. Competitors forever prowled about like wolves. It was produce or else. Shape up or ship out was the watchword.

Besides, the equipment the aerospace industry supplied was impressive. It was ingenious, it was effective, it was incredibly modern. Only the cream of the scientific and engineering world could design it and build it, only the best of the business world could manage its production. Whenever I met one of these men I genuflected.

I took the job, in 1963, and set off for the little town in California where the company had built its plant to produce computers. When I got there I would join their cold-eyed, clear-headed organization. I hoped I would measure up.

After a few months on the job, however, I found that the corporation was organized along military lines. The military lines were those of the French Army during the retreat from Moscow, just after the last cavalry horse had been made into soup.

250

The division I worked for, The Computer Company, had been founded by a brilliant engineer just before the second world war to make a device he had invented himself. He had built it into a profitable, creative company which he loved running. Then he made the mistake of falling in love with his secretary. His first wife, who had stuck with him through the hard years when he was making the gadget in his garage and pinching every penny, demanded plenty for divorcing him, and he had to sell his company to raise the money. That was how the multinational, Big Gadgets, Inc., acquired it.

The Computer Company had just obtained a contract to build six pre-production models of the airborne computer. Such a contract was usually followed by a large production contract, to outfit all the aircraft of a certain type in the US Air Force. The sales manager of the company had made sure he got the contract by 'buying in'--bidding artificially low, and risking heavy initial losses to be made up by profits on the production run. The technique was hallowed and illegal and everybody did it.

Once it got the prime contract, the company felt sure enough of its ground to build a new factory to produce the computers. Rumour had it that an influential member of the company had put it there for the noble purpose of locating the work force away from smoggy and crowded Los Angeles, where the division's headquarters and main factories were, bolstered by the fact that he ran a real-estate company in a nearby town, and that he owned the land the factory was built on, and leased the land to the company for a fancy figure. It was true, however, that the neighbouring towns were wonderful places to live.

Unfortunately, the only place to locate a factory in a highly technical business is in a big city. Unusual things are forever being demanded at a moment's notice, such as special oils or industrial diamonds, as well as special skills such as photoprocessing, which are all available in a big city. Whenever something unusual was needed, it had to be sent for from Los Angeles, while operations were held up.

Furthermore, the assembly-line workers tended to be the wives of marines at a nearby base, who left at a moment's notice when their husbands were transferred. In Los Angeles, they could easily be replaced by experienced workers from another plant which had just completed a contract and had to lay them off, but here new workers had to be trained. Engineers were reluctant to take jobs in the boondocks also, regardless of how heavenly the surroundings, because the aerospace industry is notoriously volatile, and they preferred to have alternate sources of employment handy in case this one petered out. Besides these considerations, the big engineering and administrative decisions continued to be made in Los Angeles, which kept engineers and executives shuttling back and forth at considerable expense.

There were other difficulties. The first was that the plant manager was on the skids. He was a brilliant engineer in his early thirties, who had pushed and elbowed his way to the manager's position, only to find himself far out of his depth in this world of Byzantine politics. That he knew it was apparent from his habit of boasting of his accomplishments, and then hugging the agreement of his subordinates to his breast.

His way was not made any smoother by the fact that the Operations Manager, responsible for manufacturing, was patently incompetent. It turned out that he had previously been assistant to the executive who owned the land upon which the factory was built, and had been charged with some rather delicate negotiations. Upon their successful completion, his boss had considered his usefulness over and had summarily fired him. The assistant had, however, foreseen what was about to happen to him, and had closeted himself in the boss's office one Saturday morning with a duplicating machine and keys to the boss's filing cabinets. When he showed the results of his labours to the executive, he was immediately unfired and appointed to the highly-paid post of Operations Manager, a job which he immediately proceeded to screw up.

Meanwhile the Vice-President of Marketing in Los Angeles, who had made the decision to 'buy in,' had a screaming fight with the company president and told him to "stuff his job up his ass." A new VP Marketing was appointed from corporate headquarters in New York, where the top brass considered that the West Coast operation needed to be whipped into shape.

At his first conference with the plant manager, he heard a progress report. 49% of the work had been done, and 99% of the money had been spent. According to the "buy in" decision, this was just about on target. The new man didn't agree. The plant manager got the chop.

He was replaced by a fireball from a sister division in New

Jersey. Tall, eagle-faced, impeccably dressed he seemed just the man to bring order out of chaos. Unfortunately the hatchetman took most of the decisions out of his hands. Over his protests it was decided, in an attempt to save money, to cut the funds allotted for testing the product from $500,000 to $50,000.

Salesmen, when proposing new devices to the military, always promise lighter, stronger, more capable gadgets to do any job. There are always engineers and scientists whose ideas will translate these promises into devices which magically will do everything they should. To achieve this, they insist on constant testing. They put a gear on a shaft, and test it; add a motor, and test that, hook it to a counter and test again. They heat it, freeze it, vibrate it and drop it onto hard surfaces. The process often seems overdone, but if anything has been proved by experience it is that testing is paid for whether it is done or not.

To save more money, shortcuts had been taken in the design of the computers. The indicators were fitted with smaller motors, the shafts the motors drove were mounted in plain holes drilled in the walls of their cases rather than in proper ball-bearing races, and nylon gears were pressed onto metal shafts. The plant manager complained when these assemblies were put together without testing, but he was overruled. After a while he stopped worrying—he had invented a toy which was being produced in Los Angeles, and he took to spending three days a week overseeing its production and two days a week looking after his computer factory.

No tests were carried out on the binary-to-analog converters in the computer either. These were layers of inscribed metal, all intricately glued together. At normal temperatures they worked fine.

Then, in accordance with USAF regulations, the computers were subjected to environmental tests to make sure they could achieve 300 hours Mean Time Between Failures. When the indicators were cooled down below zero, the nylon gears contracted at a slower rate than the metal shafts, and the gears came loose and stayed put while the shafts rotated. When the temperature was raised, the shafts expanded tightly into the holes drilled into the aluminum frames, and the small motors could not turn them at all. Furthermore, when the converters were put on the vibration table to show how well they would last for 300 hours, they disintegrated completely in 58 minutes.

Deliveries to the USAF stopped with a jolt. The USAF, who

wanted the computers to install in aircraft coming off the assembly line, slapped the company with a penalty of $1000 a day for the delay. The company took the obvious way out. The branch manager was fired.

The brass in Los Angeles set about finding a new branch manager. They went about in a scientific way—they closeted themselves with a stack of resumes a foot high for a whole night, and came out with a name. The man was duly installed in the corner office.

Things straightened out. Our new boss was capable enough, and was able to second-guess the Operations Manager enough to keep him from making too many mistakes. The indicators were redesigned, and the boss bootlegged funds to get them tested. They passed the tests and the USAF stopped fining us. Everybody breathed more easily.

After a few months, in celebration of our improved reliability, a meeting was called at Wright Patterson Air Force Base, to be attended by a general, several chicken colonels, a number of civilians of rank equivalent to general, and lots of majors. Our company sent all the Los Angeles brass and several people from the New York corporate office. The president of the corporation was to be the keynote speaker.

He was a tall, impressive man, who wore five-hundred-dollar suits before prices went up, and was on speaking terms with most of the Administration in Washington. Standing up to address the group, he said, "Gentlemen, we know our company has had its problems. We are facing them with no illusions. Deliveries have been late, reliability has been disappointing, performance has been unsatisfactory. There have been design faults. We admit it." He looked around the august gathering. Heads nodded above starred shoulders. It was refreshing to find somebody in industry who would admit shortcomings.

"The problems have been studied as the very highest levels in our company, and we believe we have isolated the cause." He paused for a moment. "Previously," he continued, "The direction of our facility has been under men specializing in development. They have been very skilled in this. Unfortunately their talents have not extended to production, which is what the Air Force needs now. Recognizing this, we have combed the whole United States for a man skilled and experienced in production, and we have selected a man fully equal to the task. He is a graduate of the United States

Naval Academy, who has flown as a carrier pilot, and who has long experience in production width the McSporran Aircraft Company in St. Louis." Heads nodded again. A carrier pilot had to have the Right Stuff, otherwise he would not be alive. McSporran had always made good aircraft.

The corporate president swept a hand grandly toward our branch manager. "Gentlemen— let me introduce John Smith!"

With that our new boss fell across the table and began to snore loudly. He had left something out of his resume At intervals he went on earth-shaking binges, during which he drank anything in a bottle. He had gone out on the town the night before, returning to the motel at four in the morning, and the only way his fellow executives had got him to the meeting was to hold him in a cold shower for half an hour.

The two words he heard when he regained consciousness were, "You're fired!"

The corporate president was fast on his feet, however. He immediately took the whole branch away from the Los Angeles Division and placed it under the New Jersey division, which had gained considerable respect over the years for producing good equipment at a fair price. The general running the meeting said he would give the company a month to shape up. Before the day was out we had a new branch manager, a trusted trouble-shooter from New Jersey, who had pulled hotter chestnuts out of the fire.

He was not left alone to work out the branch's salvation by himself. The president of the New Jersey division determined to give the company the personal attention it needed to make it work. He did it by placing the various departments of the California plant under their individual department heads in New Jersey, with orders to make frequent reports on their progress. These reports were indeed forthcoming. However, the number of times on which a subordinate tells his boss, "I goofed," can be counted on the fingers of an armless man. Everything that went wrong was concealed as long as possible, since those responsible hoped to correct things before the next report. As a result, the New Jersey managers were forever being taken by surprise by disasters which could have been corrected easily if those who created them had not told their superiors that everything was rosy in the garden.

Despite frequent catastrophes, the middle managers, engineers and technicians who were first class ignored stupid orders and did what had to be done. Soon they began to turn out computers that worked. What this proved was that if you have good enough followers you don't need leaders.

The hemorrhages of funds stopped, to be replaced by a steady profit. All of a sudden our plant was the brightest star in corporate heaven. It took time, however, and the stockholders had little patience with pie in the future sky; they wanted dividends right now. The president of the New Jersey division, now with the California branch under his wing, could see himself as the corporate president if he could come out of the next year showing a profit. That wouldn't be easy. The drain on funds during the time of troubles had been severe.

He had to do something drastic. He fired 20% of all groups— sales, administration, research, and development—not directly concerned with production. Personal considerations were ignored. Nobody had a vested pension before he had put in twenty years' service, and someone who lost his job after nineteen years was out in the cold. In the aerospace world a salesman works for three years before he can make a sale, and proving success was difficult. Salesmen with unblemished records, on the verge of making big sales, were let go at a moment's notice; others who had just got big orders followed them, on the grounds that a company with big order backlogs didn't need salesmen. Scientists and engineers got the axe. This, of course, meant eating up the seed corn, since the sales of a company five years ahead depend on the far-out ideas being worked out now, and the contacts salesmen are making far in advance of an immediate sale.

The division president decided to let the future look after itself, and made the cuts. The stockholders congratulated him on his ability to cut costs and maximize profits. He felt the corporate crown descending on his head.

He was not, however, the only piranha in the corporate waters. The threshing of the wounded plant had attracted the attention of a cabal of corporate raiders who specialized in moving in on badly-managed firms and taking over. They prepared a campaign that rivalled one of Napoleon's. First they bought a few shares, to gain access to stockholders' meetings, a drive for proxies followed, and the last step was to have the company's officers dismissed and their own men put in their places.

Building their case was not difficult. The aerospace community

256

was full of bitter, disillusioned men who had been laid off and now hated the company to which they once had been loyal. They were skilled and experienced, and they knew where a thousand bodies had been buried. All the mistakes, failures and dishonesties which had been carefully concealed were brought for the raiders' eyes and ears.

At the next stockholders' meeting they presented the whole damning case. The company president and the corporate president fought hard, but the case against them was too strong and they had to face too many surprises. The raiders went on to get the proxies they needed, and today the corporation no longer exists; it is a division of Bigger Gadgets Inc.

All the executives were fired, from the corporate president down, including the New Jersey division president who had seen the $300,000 job as successor to the corporate president within his grasp. The Operations Manager at the California plant had been swiftly and brutally dejobbed when New Jersey took over, so he had beaten the rush by a few months. All went into outer darkness to the cheers of their erstwhile underlings, who plodded on at their jobs. The corporation was renamed, while the individual divisions, still under their old names but with new managers, kept on much as before.

Shortly afterwards I left the company, to join another company which had a Canadian division. After a couple of years I managed a transfer to it, to return to Toronto, world-famous for the highest tower and the highest taxes. I never did get that computer I had worked on installed in a Canadian aircraft.

Now, when I see a man in uniform, I envy him his life of peace, order and good government. There he is, under the command of men who know how to manage, secure from the attacks of corporate raiders and the ambitions of aggressive vice presidents, contentedly obeying the rules. Compared to the services, the aerospace industry is a nest of vipers, a bottle of scorpions, a darkling battlefield infested by predators each with a dagger poised to strike down his friends.

I still don't know how they managed to send men to the moon.